(Super Power Books Series)

Textbook on

Data Science and Business Intelligence for Corporate Decision-Making

By

Dr. P. S. Aithal

M.Sc.(Physics), M.Sc.(E-Business). M.I.T (I.T.), M.Tech.(I.T.), Ph.D.(Physics), Ph.D.(Business Management), **PostDoc.@PRL**, Ahmedabad, **PostDoc.@CREOL**, UCF, USA, D.Sc.(Technology Management),
Senior Professor, Srinivas University, India
ORCID-ID: : https://orcid.org/0000-0002-4691-8736

ISBN: 9798878887823 (Amazon Kindle)
ISBN: **978-93-94676-44-2**
DOI: **10.5281/zenodo.10614365**
First Edition – 2024.
Price: $10/Rs. 450.

Textbook on

Data Science and Business Intelligence for Corporate Decision-Making

By

Dr. P. S. Aithal

About the Book:

A comprehensive book plan on "Data Science and Business Intelligence for Corporate Decision-Making" with 15 chapters, each with several sections:

Chapter 1: Introduction to Data Science and Business Intelligence

Chapter 2: Foundations of Data Science

Chapter 3: Business Intelligence Tools and Technologies

Chapter 4: Data Visualization for Decision-Making

Chapter 5: Machine Learning for Business Intelligence

Chapter 6: Big Data Analytics

Chapter 7: Data Ethics and Governance

Chapter 8: Data-Driven Decision-Making Process

Chapter 9: Business Intelligence in Marketing

Chapter 10: Financial Analytics and Business Intelligence

Chapter 11: Operational Excellence through Data Analytics

Chapter 12: Human Resources and People Analytics

Chapter 13: Case Studies in Data-Driven Decision-Making

Chapter 14: Future Trends in Data Science and Business Intelligence

Chapter 15: Implementing Data Science Strategies in Corporations

Each chapter dives deep into the concepts, methods, and applications of data science and business intelligence, providing practical insights, real-world examples, and case studies for corporate decision-making processes.

CONTENTS

15.6 Learning Questions

15.6.1 Descriptive Questions

15.6.2 Fill-Up the Blanks with Answers

15.6.3 Multiple Choice Questions with Answers

Each chapter dives deep into the concepts, methods, and applications of data science and business intelligence, providing practical insights and real-world examples for corporate decision-making processes.

****

CHAPTER 1

Introduction to Data Science and Business Intelligence

Objectives of the Chapter:

The objectives of Chapter 1 are to provide a comprehensive overview of Data Science and Business Intelligence (BI) in the context of the rapidly evolving technological landscape. This includes defining Data Science as an interdisciplinary field that employs various techniques to extract insights from structured and unstructured data, combining expertise from statistics, mathematics, computer science, and domain-specific knowledge. The chapter aims to unravel Business Intelligence, delineating it as a set of technologies, processes, and tools facilitating the collection, analysis, and presentation of business information, empowering stakeholders to make informed decisions. Furthermore, the interconnectedness of Data Science and BI is highlighted, emphasizing their shared goal of transforming complex data into actionable intelligence. The second part of the chapter focuses on the importance of Data Science and BI in corporate decision-making, elucidating how these fields drive strategic insights, enhance operational efficiency, and mitigate risks. Lastly, the chapter explores the historical evolution and current trends in Data Science, providing a nuanced understanding of its dynamic nature, including key milestones, methodologies, and technologies. The ultimate goal is to lay the foundation for a deeper exploration of these fields, emphasizing their critical role in corporate decision-making and showcasing the evolving trends in Data Science.

1.1 Overview of Data Science and Business Intelligence:

In the contemporary landscape of rapidly evolving technology and data proliferation, the fusion of Data Science and Business Intelligence (BI) has emerged as a powerful force driving organizational success. This section provides a comprehensive overview of these two interrelated fields, delving into their definitions, core components, and the pivotal role they play in transforming raw data into actionable insights.

1.1.1 Defining Data Science

Data Science is an interdisciplinary field that encompasses a range of techniques, algorithms, processes, and systems to extract valuable insights and knowledge from structured and unstructured data. It combines expertise from statistics, mathematics, computer science, and domain-specific knowledge to discover patterns, trends, and correlations that can inform strategic decision-making.

1.1.2 Unraveling Business Intelligence

Business Intelligence refers to the technologies, processes, and tools that facilitate the collection, analysis, and presentation of business information. BI enables organizations to convert raw data into meaningful and accessible insights, empowering stakeholders at all levels to make informed decisions.

1.1.3 Interconnectedness of Data Science and Business Intelligence

While Data Science focuses on extracting insights from complex data sets, Business Intelligence emphasizes the delivery of these insights to end-users in a comprehensible format. The synergy between these two fields is evident in their shared goal of transforming data into actionable intelligence, bridging the gap between raw information and strategic decision-making.

1.2 Importance in Corporate Decision Making:

This section explores the pivotal role of Data Science and Business Intelligence in shaping corporate decision-making processes. By providing decision-makers with timely and relevant information, organizations can gain a competitive edge and adapt to dynamic market conditions. The significance of data-driven decision-making is underscored, emphasizing how these fields contribute to enhanced operational efficiency, risk mitigation, and overall business performance.

1.2.1 Driving Strategic Insights:

Data Science and Business Intelligence empower organizations to uncover patterns and trends that may go unnoticed through traditional analysis methods. This strategic insight aids in identifying opportunities, optimizing processes, and mitigating risks, thereby fostering a proactive and adaptive decision-making culture.

1.2.2 Enhancing Operational Efficiency:

The integration of data-driven approaches streamlines business operations by providing a real-time understanding of performance metrics and key performance indicators. This efficiency translates into improved resource allocation, streamlined workflows, and an overall more agile and responsive organizational structure.

1.2.3 Mitigating Risks:

By leveraging predictive analytics and data-driven risk assessments, organizations can identify potential threats and vulnerabilities. Data Science and

Business Intelligence contribute to creating a robust risk management framework, enabling proactive measures to safeguard against unforeseen challenges.

1.3 Evolution and Trends in Data Science:

This section delves into the historical evolution of Data Science and explores the current trends shaping the field. From its roots in statistics and computer science to the contemporary era of machine learning and artificial intelligence, this section provides a nuanced understanding of the dynamic nature of Data Science.

1.3.1 Historical Perspective:

Tracing the evolution from statistical analysis and data processing to the emergence of sophisticated machine learning algorithms, this section outlines key milestones that have shaped Data Science into its present form. The evolution of tools, methodologies, and technologies is explored, offering a comprehensive historical backdrop.

1.3.2 Current Trends and Innovations:

Examining the current landscape, this section highlights trends such as deep learning, natural language processing, and the increasing importance of ethical considerations in data usage. The integration of Big Data and the rise of cloud computing are also explored, providing readers with insights into the cutting-edge technologies shaping the future of Data Science.

In conclusion, this chapter lays the foundation for a deeper exploration of Data Science and Business Intelligence by providing an insightful overview, emphasizing their importance in corporate decision-making, and illuminating the evolving trends in the field of Data Science. Understanding these fundamentals is crucial for professionals and enthusiasts alike as they embark on a journey to harness the power of data for informed and strategic decision-making.

1.4 Introductory Case Study on Data Science and Business Intelligence:

Case Study 01: Unleashing the Power of Data Science and Business Intelligence in Retail Optimization

Introduction:

In the competitive landscape of the retail industry, staying ahead requires more than just stocking shelves with popular products. The dynamic nature of consumer behavior, coupled with the vast amounts of data generated daily, presents both challenges and opportunities. This case study explores how a fictional retail giant, "Global Mart," leverages Data Science and Business Intelligence to enhance operational efficiency, optimize inventory management, and elevate the overall customer experience.

Background:

Global Mart, a multinational retail chain, operates in diverse markets with a vast product catalog. Faced with challenges ranging from fluctuating consumer demand to supply chain complexities, the company recognizes the need for a data-driven approach to gain a competitive edge. In response, Global Mart has invested in robust Data Science and Business Intelligence systems.

Objectives:

(1) Optimizing Inventory Management:

- Utilize predictive analytics to anticipate product demand.
- Implement Business Intelligence tools to streamline inventory tracking and management.

(2) Enhancing Customer Experience:

- Leverage data insights to personalize marketing strategies.
- Implement real-time analytics for dynamic pricing and promotions.

(3) Operational Efficiency:

- Integrate Business Intelligence dashboards for quick decision-making.
- Implement Data Science algorithms to optimize supply chain logistics.

Scenario:

The Challenge:

Global Mart is grappling with excess inventory in some locations, leading to increased holding costs and potential losses due to markdowns. At the same time, certain products experience stockouts, resulting in missed sales opportunities and dissatisfied customers. The company recognizes the need for a holistic approach to inventory management and seeks to implement data-driven solutions.

The Solution:

1. Data Collection and Integration:

- Aggregate historical sales data, inventory levels, and external factors (e.g., seasonality, economic indicators).
- Integrate data from various sources, including point-of-sale systems, ERP systems, and external market data.

2. Predictive Analytics for Demand Forecasting:

- Develop predictive models to forecast demand for each product and location.
- Implement machine learning algorithms that consider factors like historical sales, promotions, and external events.

3. Business Intelligence Dashboards:

- Create interactive dashboards that provide real-time insights into inventory levels, sales performance, and key performance indicators.

- Empower decision-makers with user-friendly tools for monitoring and decision-making.

4. Personalized Marketing Strategies:
- Utilize customer segmentation based on purchase history and preferences.
- Implement targeted marketing campaigns through personalized promotions and recommendations.

5. Dynamic Pricing and Promotions:
- Implement dynamic pricing strategies based on real-time demand and inventory levels.
- Integrate promotional offers dynamically to boost sales for specific products or regions.

6. Supply Chain Optimization:
- Apply Data Science algorithms to optimize the supply chain, considering factors like transportation costs, lead times, and supplier reliability.
- Use Business Intelligence tools to monitor and assess the efficiency of supply chain operations.

Discussion Questions:

(1) How can predictive analytics help Global Mart address inventory challenges and optimize stocking levels?

(2) What role do Business Intelligence dashboards play in enhancing decision-making and operational efficiency?

(3) How can personalized marketing strategies improve customer engagement and loyalty?

(4) What challenges might Global Mart face in implementing dynamic pricing and promotions, and how can these be mitigated?

(5) In what ways can Data Science contribute to supply chain optimization, and how might this impact overall business performance?

This case study provides a foundation for exploring the practical applications of Data Science and Business Intelligence in a real-world business scenario. Students and professionals can analyze the challenges faced by Global Mart and propose innovative solutions, fostering a deeper understanding of the strategic integration of data-driven approaches in the retail sector.

1.5 Learning Questions

1.5.1 Descriptive Questions:

(1) What is the driving force behind the organizational success brought about by the fusion of Data Science and Business Intelligence in the contemporary landscape of technology and data proliferation?

(2) How does Data Science leverage interdisciplinary techniques to extract valuable insights from both structured and unstructured data, combining expertise from various fields such as statistics, mathematics, computer science, and domain-specific knowledge?

(3) In what ways does Business Intelligence contribute to shaping corporate decision-making processes by facilitating the collection, analysis, and presentation of business information, and how does it empower stakeholders at all levels to make informed decisions?

(4) How does the interconnectedness of Data Science and Business Intelligence manifest in their shared goal of transforming complex data into actionable intelligence, bridging the gap between raw information and strategic decision-making?

(5) Why is data-driven decision-making emphasized in the exploration of the pivotal role of Data Science and Business Intelligence in corporate decision-making, and how does it contribute to gaining a competitive edge, adapting to dynamic market conditions, and enhancing overall business performance?

(6) How do Data Science and Business Intelligence empower organizations to uncover patterns and trends that may be overlooked through traditional analysis methods, contributing to the identification of opportunities, optimization of processes, and mitigation of risks?

(7) What is the impact of the integration of data-driven approaches on enhancing operational efficiency, providing a real-time understanding of performance metrics and key performance indicators, and creating a more agile and responsive organizational structure?

(8) How do Data Science and Business Intelligence leverage predictive analytics and data-driven risk assessments to identify potential threats and vulnerabilities, contributing to the creation of a robust risk management framework for proactive measures against unforeseen challenges?

(9) What is the historical perspective of Data Science, tracing its evolution from statistical analysis and data processing to the emergence of sophisticated machine learning algorithms, and what key milestones have shaped it into its present form?

(10) In the examination of current trends and innovations in Data Science, what technologies, methodologies, and advancements are highlighted, including trends such as deep learning, natural language processing, ethical considerations, the integration of Big Data, and the rise of cloud computing?

1.5.2 Fill-up the Blanks Questions:

(1) Data Science is an interdisciplinary field that combines expertise from _____, _____, _____, and _____ to extract valuable insights from structured and unstructured data.
Answer: statistics, mathematics, computer science, domain-specific knowledge

(2) Business Intelligence refers to the technologies, processes, and tools that facilitate the collection, analysis, and presentation of _____ information.
Answer: business

(3) The interconnectedness of Data Science and Business Intelligence is evident in their shared goal of transforming data into _____ intelligence.
Answer: actionable

(4) By providing decision-makers with timely and relevant information, organizations using Data Science and Business Intelligence can gain a _____ edge and adapt to dynamic market conditions.
Answer: competitive

(5) Data Science and Business Intelligence empower organizations to uncover patterns and trends that may go unnoticed through _____ analysis methods.
Answer: traditional

(6) The integration of data-driven approaches streamlines business operations by providing a real-time understanding of _____ and key performance indicators.
Answer: performance metrics

(7) By leveraging predictive analytics and data-driven risk assessments, organizations can identify potential _____ and vulnerabilities.
Answer: threats

(8) Tracing the evolution of Data Science from statistical analysis and data processing to the emergence of sophisticated _____ outlines key milestones.
Answer: machine learning algorithms

(9) Examining the current landscape highlights trends such as deep learning, natural language processing, and the increasing importance of ethical considerations in _____.
Answer: data usage

(10) The chapter lays the foundation for a deeper exploration of Data Science and Business Intelligence, emphasizing their importance in corporate decision-making and illuminating the evolving trends in the field of _____.
Answer: Data Science and BI.

1.5.3 Multiple Choice Questions:

(1) What is the driving force behind organizational success in the contemporary landscape?
   A. Business Operations
   B. Evolutionary Algorithms
   C. Fusion of Data Science and Business Intelligence (BI)
   D. Traditional Analysis Methods
   Answer: C. Fusion of Data Science and Business Intelligence (BI)

(2) What does Data Science encompass in its interdisciplinary approach?
   A. Techniques from Literature
   B. Range of Algorithms in Biology
   C. Techniques, Algorithms, Processes, and Systems
   D. Processes in Physics
   Answer: C. Techniques, Algorithms, Processes, and Systems

(3) What does Business Intelligence refer to?
   A. Business Opportunities
   B. Collection of Business Cards
   C. Technologies, Processes, and Tools for Business Information
   D. Business Operations Manual
   Answer: C. Technologies, Processes, and Tools for Business Information

(4) How does the interconnectedness of Data Science and Business Intelligence manifest?
   A. Focus on Transforming Data
   B. Emphasis on Unstructured Data
   C. Synergy in Transforming Data into Actionable Intelligence
   D. Bridging the Gap between Information and Communication
   Answer: C. Synergy in Transforming Data into Actionable Intelligence

(5) What is underscored in the importance of Data Science and Business Intelligence in corporate decision-making processes?
   A. Traditional Decision-Making
   B. Data-Driven Decision-Making
   C. Operational Inefficiency
   D. Historical Decision-Making
   Answer: B. Data-Driven Decision-Making

(6) What aids in fostering a proactive and adaptive decision-making culture?
   A. Traditional Analysis Methods
   B. Strategic Insights
   C. Operational Inefficiency

D. Manual Workflows

Answer: B. Strategic Insights

(7) What does the integration of data-driven approaches streamline in business operations?

A. Resource Allocation

B. Creative Processes

C. Historical Workflows

D. Traditional Workflows

Answer: A. Resource Allocation

(8) What do Data Science and Business Intelligence contribute to creating for safeguarding against unforeseen challenges?

A. Predictive Analytics Framework

B. Operational Efficiency Framework

C. Risk Management Framework

D. Resource Allocation Framework

Answer: C. Risk Management Framework

(9) What does the section on Evolution and Trends in Data Science explore?

A. Evolution of Machine Learning Algorithms

B. Evolution of Statistical Analysis

C. Evolution of Natural Language Processing

D. Evolution of Deep Learning

Answer: B. Evolution of Statistical Analysis

(10) What does the current trends and innovations section highlight?

A. Rise of Traditional Computing

B. Rise of Cloudy Weather

C. Rise of Ethical Considerations

D. Rise of Historical Analysis

Answer: C. Rise of Ethical Considerations

****

CHAPTER 2

Foundations of Data Science

Objectives of the Chapter:

The objectives of the provided information are to comprehensively understand data types and sources, outlining the significance of each, and to grasp the techniques involved in data collection, cleaning, and preprocessing. The first objective focuses on elucidating various data types, including categorical, numerical, and time series data, and detailing internal and external data sources such as sensor data, social media data, and web scraping. Understanding the importance of these data types and sources in decision-making, acknowledging challenges, and adapting to evolving data landscapes is emphasized. The second objective delves into the concepts of data collection, cleaning, and preprocessing, emphasizing the sources and methods involved in data collection, the identification and techniques for cleaning, and the transformation and handling of imbalances in the data preprocessing phase. The analysis explores the impact of data quality on decision-making, the computational efficiency gained through preprocessing, and the role in enhancing model performance. The third objective revolves around exploratory data analysis (EDA) techniques, elucidating the overview and importance of EDA, and detailing techniques such as descriptive statistics, data distribution visualization, correlation analysis, categorical data exploration, outlier detection, and data transformation and scaling. The analysis highlights the role of EDA in identifying data patterns, detecting outliers, aiding feature selection and engineering, supporting data-driven decision-making, and communicating findings effectively. Overall, the objectives aim to equip individuals and organizations with the knowledge and skills to extract meaningful insights from data, make informed decisions, and adapt to the evolving data landscape.

2.1 Understanding Data Types and Sources:

1. Data Types:

1.1 Categorical Data:

Categorical data represents categories or labels and is often used to group data into discrete classes. Examples include gender, color, or product type. Categorical data can be nominal (unordered categories) or ordinal (ordered categories).

1.2 Numerical Data:

Numerical data consists of measurable quantities and can be further classified into two types:

- Continuous Data: Represents measurements that can take any value within a given range, such as temperature or height.
- Discrete Data: Represents distinct and separate values, usually counting numbers, like the number of products sold.

1.3 Time Series Data:

Time series data is collected over a sequence of equally spaced time intervals. It is crucial for analyzing trends and patterns over time, making it applicable in various domains like finance, weather forecasting, and sales.

2. Data Sources:

2.1 Internal Data Sources:

Internal data originates from within an organization and includes:

- Transactional Data: Captures day-to-day operations, such as sales transactions or customer interactions.
- Operational Data: Reflects the ongoing activities and processes within the organization.

2.2 External Data Sources:

External data comes from outside the organization and can include:

- Publicly Available Data: Information accessible to anyone, like government data or open datasets.
- Third-Party Data: Data purchased or obtained from external sources, such as market research reports or data vendors.

2.3 Sensor Data:

Sensor data is generated by various sensors and IoT devices, capturing real-time information from the physical world. Examples include temperature sensors, GPS devices, and motion detectors.

2.4 Social Media Data:

Data sourced from social media platforms provides insights into customer sentiments, preferences, and trends. It includes text, images, and user interactions.

2.5 Web Scraping:

Web scraping involves extracting data from websites. It enables the collection of information such as product prices, reviews, or news articles from the internet.

3. Analysis:

1. Significance of Understanding Data Types:

1.1 Data Analysis and Interpretation:

Different data types require distinct analytical approaches. For instance, numerical data allows for statistical analysis, while categorical data may involve frequency distributions and cross-tabulations.

1.2 Data Visualization:

Understanding data types is essential for effective data visualization. Visual representations, such as bar charts for categorical data or line graphs for time series data, aid in conveying insights.

2. Impact of Data Sources on Decision-Making:
2.1 Data Quality and Reliability:
The reliability and quality of internal and external data sources influence the accuracy of decision-making. Assessing the credibility of sources is crucial for making informed choices.
2.2 Diversity of Data Sources:
Leveraging a variety of data sources provides a comprehensive view of business operations and external factors. Integrating internal and external data enriches analysis and strategic planning.

3. Challenges in Handling Different Data Types:
3.1 Integration Challenges:
Integrating diverse data types can be complex, requiring careful consideration of compatibility and standardization to ensure meaningful analysis.
3.2 Privacy and Ethical Concerns:
Handling sensitive data, especially from external sources, raises privacy and ethical concerns. Organizations must implement robust practices to ensure compliance with regulations.

4. Adaptability to Evolving Data Landscapes:
4.1 Technological Advances:
Advancements in technology, including machine learning and artificial intelligence, enable the analysis of diverse data types at scale, fostering innovation in decision-making processes.
4.2 Continuous Learning:
Given the evolving nature of data types and sources, individuals and organizations must engage in continuous learning to stay abreast of emerging trends and technologies.

Understanding data types and sources is foundational to extracting meaningful insights from the vast array of information available. As organizations navigate the data landscape, a nuanced comprehension of data types and sources empowers them to make informed decisions, enhance operations, and stay competitive in an ever-changing business environment.

2.2 Data Collection, Cleaning, and Preprocessing:

Concepts:
1. Data Collection:

1.1 Sources of Data:

- Primary Data: Collected directly from original sources through methods like surveys, interviews, or experiments.
- Secondary Data: Obtained from existing sources such as databases, reports, or public datasets.

1.2 Methods of Data Collection:

- Surveys: Gathering information through structured questionnaires.
- Observations: Collecting data by directly observing phenomena.
- Sensor Data: Capturing real-time information through sensors and IoT devices.
- Web Scraping: Extracting data from websites.

2. Data Cleaning:

2.1 Identification of Errors and Inconsistencies:

- Outliers: Data points significantly deviating from the norm.
- Missing Values: Entries with no recorded information.
- Inconsistent Formats: Variations in data presentation.

2.2 Techniques for Data Cleaning:

- Imputation: Filling in missing values using statistical methods.
- Outlier Detection and Handling: Identifying and addressing outliers to prevent distortion.
- Standardization: Ensuring consistent formats for variables.

2.3 Importance of Data Cleaning:

- Ensures data accuracy and reliability.
- Mitigates the risk of biased analyses caused by errors.
- Facilitates meaningful insights during subsequent analysis.

3. Data Preprocessing:

3.1 Data Transformation:

- Normalization: Scaling numerical features to a standard range.
- Encoding: Converting categorical variables into numerical representations.

3.2 Feature Engineering:

- Creating New Variables: Generating additional features for better model performance.
- Dimensionality Reduction: Reducing the number of features while preserving relevant information.

3.3 Handling Imbalanced Data:

- Resampling Techniques: Balancing the distribution of classes.
- Synthetic Data Generation: Creating artificial data to balance minority classes.

3.4 Text and Image Data Preprocessing:

- Tokenization: Breaking down text into individual words or tokens.

- Image Normalization: Standardizing pixel values for consistency.

Analysis:

1. Data Quality and Decision-Making:

1.1 Impact of Unclean Data:
- Inaccurate or incomplete data can lead to flawed analyses and misguided decision-making.
- Decision-makers may base strategies on unreliable information, resulting in suboptimal outcomes.

1.2 Role of Data Cleaning:
- Ensures the reliability and trustworthiness of the data used for decision-making.
- Supports the generation of accurate insights, contributing to informed strategic choices.

2. Computational Efficiency:

2.1 Efficiency in Analysis:
- Clean and preprocessed data accelerates the analysis process, reducing computation time.
- Streamlined datasets facilitate faster model training and evaluation.

3. Enhancing Model Performance:

3.1 Importance of Preprocessing:
- Well-preprocessed data improves the performance of machine learning models.
- Feature engineering and normalization contribute to model generalization and predictive accuracy.

3.2 Addressing Class Imbalances:
- Handling imbalanced data enhances model fairness and the ability to generalize to underrepresented classes.
- Prevents biased predictions that favour the majority class.

4. Challenges and Considerations:

4.1 Ethical Considerations:
- Balancing the need for data cleaning with ethical considerations regarding privacy and bias.
- Ensuring fairness in data preprocessing to avoid perpetuating societal inequalities.

4.2 Continuous Monitoring:
- Data cleaning and preprocessing are iterative processes requiring continuous monitoring.

- As data evolves, adjustments to cleaning and preprocessing techniques may be necessary.

Data collection, cleaning, and preprocessing form the foundational steps in the data analysis pipeline. The quality of insights derived from data is inherently linked to the rigor applied during these stages. Organizations that prioritize thorough data management practices are better positioned to harness the full potential of their data, fostering more informed decision-making and driving innovation.

2.3 Exploratory Data Analysis Techniques:

1. Overview of Exploratory Data Analysis (EDA):
Exploratory Data Analysis is a critical phase in the data analysis process that involves summarizing and visualizing the main characteristics of a dataset. EDA helps analysts and data scientists understand the underlying patterns, relationships, and potential outliers within the data before formal statistical modeling.

2. Exploratory Data Analysis Techniques:

2.1 Descriptive Statistics:
- Mean, Median, Mode: Measures of central tendency that provide insights into the average or most representative values in the dataset.
- Standard Deviation, Variance: Measures of dispersion indicating the spread of the data points.

2.2 Data Distribution Visualization:
- Histograms: Display the frequency distribution of a continuous variable.
- Box Plots: Illustrate the distribution of a dataset, highlighting central tendency and spread.
- Kernel Density Plots: Estimate the probability density function of a continuous variable.

2.3 Pair Plots and Scatter Plots:
- Pair Plots: Display pairwise relationships between variables in a dataset, useful for identifying patterns and correlations.
- Scatter Plots: Visualize the relationship between two continuous variables, showcasing trends and potential outliers.

2.4 Correlation Analysis:
- Correlation Coefficients (e.g., Pearson, Spearman): Quantify the strength and direction of linear relationships between variables.
- Heatmaps: Visual representations of correlation matrices, providing an overview of variable relationships.

2.5 Categorical Data Exploration:
- Bar Charts: Display the distribution of categorical variables.

- Pie Charts: Illustrate the proportion of different categories within a variable.

2.6 Outlier Detection:
- Z-Score Analysis: Identifies data points that deviate significantly from the mean.
- Box Plots and Scatter Plots: Visual tools for detecting observations that fall outside the norm.

2.7 Data Transformation and Scaling:
- Log Transformation: Alters the scale of data to handle skewed distributions.
- Min-Max Scaling: Normalizes variables to a specific range, enhancing comparability.

2.8 Time Series Analysis:
- Line Plots: Visualize changes in a variable over time.
- Seasonal Decomposition: Separates time series data into components like trend, seasonality, and residual.

Examples:

Example 1: Descriptive Statistics
Consider a dataset of monthly sales for a retail business. Calculating the mean, median, and standard deviation provides insights into the average sales, the midpoint, and the variability in the sales data.

Example 2: Box Plot
Using a box plot, you can visualize the distribution of employee salaries across different departments in a company, highlighting potential outliers and differences in salary ranges.

Example 3: Scatter Plot and Correlation Analysis
Examining the relationship between the number of hours studied and exam scores for students can be achieved through scatter plots and correlation coefficients, revealing the strength and direction of the relationship.

Analysis:

1. Data Pattern Identification:
- EDA techniques allow analysts to identify patterns, trends, and relationships within the dataset, providing a foundation for further analysis.

2. Outlier Detection and Data Quality:
- Outliers, identified through EDA, can impact the quality of statistical models. Addressing outliers enhances the accuracy of subsequent analyses.

3. Feature Selection and Engineering:
- EDA aids in the identification of influential features, guiding the selection and creation of variables for predictive modeling.

4. Data-Driven Decision-Making:

- By understanding the characteristics of the data through EDA, stakeholders can make informed decisions, whether in business, research, or policy development.

5. Communication of Findings:

- Visualizations generated during EDA serve as powerful tools for communicating insights to diverse audiences, fostering a shared understanding of the data.

Exploratory Data Analysis is a dynamic and iterative process, where the choice of techniques depends on the nature of the data and the goals of analysis. Employing a combination of statistical measures and visualizations enhances the depth of understanding, facilitating more robust and meaningful conclusions.

2.4 Case Study on Foundations of Data Science:

Case Study 2: Foundations of Data Science

Introduction:

In this case study, we delve into the development and implementation of an academic initiative titled "Foundations of Data Science" at TechU University. This program aims to provide students with a comprehensive understanding of fundamental concepts, methodologies, and tools in the field of data science.

Context:

TechU University recognizes the increasing importance of data science in various industries and endeavours to equip its students with the skills needed to thrive in a data-driven world. The "Foundations of Data Science" program is designed to cater to students from diverse academic backgrounds, fostering an interdisciplinary approach to data science education.

Objectives:

(1) Introduce Key Concepts:
- Provide a solid understanding of foundational concepts such as statistics, probability, and linear algebra as they relate to data science.

(2) Develop Programming Skills:
- Integrate hands-on programming exercises using languages like Python or R to enhance students' coding proficiency.

(3) Explore Data Collection and Cleaning:
- Emphasize the importance of data quality through practical examples of data collection, cleaning, and preprocessing.

(4) Teach Exploratory Data Analysis (EDA):
- Instruct students on EDA techniques, including visualization and statistical analysis, to extract meaningful insights from data.

(5) Introduce Machine Learning Fundamentals:
- Cover basic machine learning algorithms and their applications, highlighting both supervised and unsupervised learning.

(6) Encourage Critical Thinking and Problem-Solving:
- Develop students' ability to approach real-world problems analytically, fostering critical thinking skills.

Implementation:

1. Curriculum Design:

(1) Foundational Courses:
- Introduction to Statistics and Probability
- Linear Algebra for Data Science
- Programming for Data Science

(2) Core Modules:
- Data Collection and Cleaning Techniques
- Exploratory Data Analysis
- Introduction to Machine Learning

(3) Application Projects:
- Integration of hands-on projects to apply learned concepts in real-world scenarios.

2. Interactive Learning Platforms:
- Utilize interactive online platforms for coding exercises and simulations, providing a dynamic learning environment.

3. Guest Lectures and Industry Insights:
- Invite guest speakers from industry experts to share practical insights and case studies, connecting theoretical concepts with real-world applications.

4. Collaborative Projects:
- Foster collaboration among students from different disciplines through team projects, encouraging diverse perspectives in problem-solving.

Impact and Evaluation:

1. Assessment Methods:
- Continuous Evaluation: Regular quizzes and assignments to assess understanding of theoretical concepts.
- Project Assessments: Evaluation of hands-on projects to gauge practical application of learned skills.
- Peer Reviews: Incorporate peer assessment components for collaborative projects, promoting teamwork and accountability.

2. Student Feedback:
- Conduct regular feedback sessions to gather insights on the effectiveness of the curriculum, teaching methods, and overall learning experience.

3. Post-Course Surveys:
- Administer surveys to assess students' confidence levels in applying data science techniques and their perception of the course's relevance to their career goals.

4. Industry Placement Rates:
- Track the placement rates of students who have completed the "Foundations of Data Science" program to measure its impact on career opportunities.

Challenges and Adaptations:

1. Diverse Student Backgrounds:
- Address the challenge of varying levels of prior knowledge by incorporating optional introductory modules for students with less exposure to certain foundational concepts.

2. Technological Infrastructure:
- Ensure access to necessary technology and software, offering support for students who may face challenges with technology adoption.

3. Changing Industry Trends:

- Regularly update the curriculum to align with emerging trends and industry demands, ensuring the program remains relevant.

Conclusion:

The "Foundations of Data Science" program at TechU University serves as a model for institutions seeking to provide students with a solid grounding in data science. By integrating theoretical knowledge with practical applications, fostering collaboration, and adapting to the evolving needs of the industry, this program aims to empower students with the skills necessary to navigate and contribute to the dynamic field of data science.

Case Study Questions:

(1) What are the key objectives of the "Foundations of Data Science" program at TechU University? How do these objectives align with the current needs of the industry?

(2) Examine the curriculum design of the program. How do the foundational courses and core modules contribute to achieving the program's objectives?

(3) Evaluate the impact of interactive learning platforms and hands-on projects in enhancing students' understanding and practical application of data science concepts.

(4) Explore the significance of guest lectures and industry insights in connecting theoretical concepts with real-world applications. How does this approach contribute to a well-rounded data science education?

(5) Assess the methods used for continuous evaluation, project assessments, and peer reviews. How do these assessment strategies ensure a comprehensive evaluation of students' knowledge and skills?

(6) Examine the role of collaborative projects in fostering teamwork and diversity in problem-solving. How might this approach prepare students for collaborative work environments in the industry?

(7) Investigate the strategies employed for addressing the diverse backgrounds of students. How do optional introductory modules contribute to creating an inclusive learning environment?

(8) Evaluate the effectiveness of post-course surveys in gauging students' confidence levels and perceptions of the program's relevance to their career goals. How can this feedback be used for continuous improvement?

(9) Analyze the tracking of industry placement rates. How might this metric reflect the success of the program in preparing students for careers in data science?

(10) Discuss the adaptations made to address challenges such as diverse student backgrounds, technological infrastructure, and changing industry trends. How have these adaptations contributed to the overall success of the program?

2.5 Learning Questions:

2.5.1 Descriptive Questions:

(1) What are the two main classifications of categorical data, and how do they differ?

(2) Provide examples of three types of numerical data, specifying whether they fall under continuous or discrete categories.

(3) Explain the significance of time series data and its application in various domains.

(4) Enumerate two types of internal data sources and describe their respective roles in an organization.

(5) Differentiate between publicly available data and third-party data as external data sources, providing examples for each.

(6) How does sensor data contribute to decision-making, and what are some examples of sensors generating real-time information?

(7) In what ways can web scraping be utilized for data collection, and what types of information can be extracted using this technique?

(8) Elaborate on the distinct analytical approaches required for numerical and categorical data during the data analysis and interpretation phase.

(9) How do the reliability and diversity of data sources impact decision-making processes, and why is assessing source credibility crucial?

(10) Explain the challenges associated with integrating diverse data types, and what measures must organizations take to address privacy and ethical concerns when handling external data.

(11) In the context of data cleaning, why is the identification of outliers, missing values, and inconsistent formats crucial for ensuring data accuracy and reliability?

(12) Describe the significance of data preprocessing, specifically focusing on how it accelerates the analysis process and contributes to computational efficiency.

(13) How does well-preprocessed data enhance the performance of machine learning models, and what role does handling class imbalances play in model fairness?

(14) Enumerate and explain two ethical considerations related to data cleaning and preprocessing, emphasizing the need for fairness and privacy.

(15) Highlight the iterative nature of data cleaning and preprocessing, emphasizing the importance of continuous monitoring as data evolves.

(16) In exploratory data analysis (EDA), discuss the role of descriptive statistics in providing insights into the main characteristics of a dataset.

(17) Explain the purpose of data distribution visualization techniques such as histograms, box plots, and kernel density plots in EDA.

(18) How do scatter plots and correlation analysis contribute to understanding relationships between two continuous variables during EDA?

(19) Provide examples of categorical data exploration techniques and their applications, such as bar charts and pie charts.

(20) In the context of EDA, explain the significance of outlier detection, data transformation, and scaling techniques in understanding and communicating data patterns.

2.5.2 Fill-up the Blanks Questions:

(1) Categorical data represents _____ or labels and is often used to group data into discrete classes.
  - Answer: categories

(2) Numerical data can be classified into two types: Continuous Data represents measurements that can take any value within a given range, such as _____ or height.
  - Answer: temperature

(3) Time series data is crucial for analyzing trends and patterns over _____, making it applicable in various domains.
  - Answer: time

(4) Internal data sources originate from within an organization and include Transactional Data, which captures day-to-day operations, such as sales transactions or _____.
  - Answer: customer interactions

(5) External data sources come from outside the organization and can include Publicly Available Data, which is information accessible to anyone, like government data or _____ datasets.
  - Answer: open

(6) Sensor data is generated by various sensors and IoT devices, capturing real-time information from the _____ world.
  - Answer: physical

(7) Data sourced from social media platforms provides insights into customer sentiments, preferences, and trends, including text, images, and _____ interactions.
  - Answer: user

(8) Web scraping involves extracting data from websites, enabling the collection of information such as product prices, reviews, or _____ articles from the internet.
  - Answer: news

(9) Understanding data types is essential for effective data visualization. Visual representations, such as bar charts for categorical data or _____ for time series data, aid in conveying insights.
  - Answer: line graphs

(10) Advancements in technology, including machine learning and artificial intelligence, enable the analysis of diverse data types at scale, fostering innovation in _____ processes.
  - Answer: decision-making

2.5.3 Multiple Choice Questions:

(1) What is an example of categorical data?
  A. Temperature

B. Height
C. Color
D. Discrete Data
- Answer: c. Color

(2) Which type of numerical data represents distinct and separate values, usually counting numbers?
A. Continuous Data
B. Discrete Data
C. Categorical Data
D. Time Series Data
- Answer: b. Discrete Data

(3) Time series data is essential for analyzing trends and patterns over:
A. Space
B. Time
C. Categories
D. Frequency
- Answer: b. Time

(4) What does internal data include?
A. Sensor Data
B. Web Scraping Data
C. Transactional Data
D. Publicly Available Data
- Answer: c. Transactional Data

(5) Where does external data come from?
A. Within the organization
B. Government data
C. Sales transactions
D. Customer interactions
- Answer: b. Government data

(6) Sensor data is generated by various sensors and IoT devices, capturing real-time information from the:
A. Virtual world
B. Financial world
C. Physical world
D. Social media world
- Answer: c. Physical world

(7) What type of data provides insights into customer sentiments, preferences, and trends from social media platforms?
A. Transactional Data
B. Categorical Data
C. Sensor Data
D. Social Media Data
- Answer: d. Social Media Data

(8) Web scraping involves extracting data from:
   A. Internal databases
   B. Social media platforms
   C. IoT devices
   D. Websites
   • Answer: d. Websites

(9) Which of the following is a challenge in handling different data types?
   A. Integration Challenges
   B. Technological Advances
   C. Continuous Learning
   D. Diversity of Data Sources
   • Answer: a. Integration Challenges

(10) How do advancements in technology, including machine learning and artificial intelligence, contribute to decision-making processes?
   A. By creating challenges
   B. By reducing computational efficiency
   C. By hindering data analysis
   D. By enabling the analysis of diverse data types at scale
   • Answer: d. By enabling the analysis of diverse data types at scale

****

CHAPTER 3

Business Intelligence Tools and Technologies

Objectives of the Chapter:

To provide a conceptual overview of Business Intelligence (BI) tools and platforms, emphasizing their significance in the modern business landscape. The chapter aims to elucidate the key components of BI tools, such as data integration, warehousing, modeling, visualization, reporting, querying, analysis, collaboration, and mobile BI. Additionally, the chapter introduces examples of popular BI tools, highlighting their features and strengths. The significance of BI tools is outlined, emphasizing their role in informed decision-making, operational efficiency, competitive advantage, improved visibility, and enhanced collaboration within organizations. In summary, the chapter seeks to underscore the pivotal role of BI tools in transforming raw data into actionable insights, fostering a data-driven culture, and enabling organizations to thrive in today's dynamic business environment.

3.1 Introduction to BI Tools and Platforms

Conceptual Overview:

Business Intelligence (BI) tools and platforms are essential components in the modern business landscape, facilitating data-driven decision-making and providing valuable insights for organizations. BI encompasses a set of technologies, processes, and applications that transform raw data into meaningful and actionable information. These tools empower users to analyze, visualize, and share business data, enabling informed decision-making across various levels of an organization.

Key Components of BI Tools and Platforms:

(1) Data Integration:
- BI tools integrate data from various sources, including databases, spreadsheets, and cloud-based storage systems.
- Data integration ensures a unified view, allowing users to analyze comprehensive datasets seamlessly.

(2) Data Warehousing:
- BI platforms often leverage data warehouses to store and manage large volumes of structured and unstructured data.
- Data warehouses enable efficient querying and reporting, providing a centralized repository for business data.

(3) Data Modeling and Transformation:
- BI tools offer capabilities for modeling and transforming raw data into a structured format suitable for analysis.

- Transformation processes may involve cleaning, filtering, and aggregating data to derive meaningful insights.

(4) Visualization and Reporting:
- Visualization features allow users to create interactive charts, graphs, and dashboards.
- Reporting functionalities enable the generation of customized reports, supporting data-driven storytelling.

(5) Querying and Analysis:
- BI tools provide intuitive interfaces for querying databases and conducting ad-hoc analysis.
- Users can explore data, apply filters, and derive insights without the need for extensive technical expertise.

(6) Collaboration and Sharing:
- BI platforms promote collaboration by allowing users to share reports and dashboards with colleagues.
- Collaborative features enhance knowledge sharing and foster a data-driven culture within organizations.

(7) Mobile BI:
- Many BI tools offer mobile compatibility, enabling users to access and interact with data on smartphones and tablets.
- Mobile BI facilitates real-time decision-making, especially for professionals on the go.

Examples of BI Tools and Platforms:

(1) Tableau:
- Renowned for its powerful visualization capabilities, Tableau allows users to create interactive dashboards and reports.

(2) Power BI (Microsoft):
- A widely used BI tool, Power BI integrates seamlessly with Microsoft products and offers robust data modeling and visualization features.

(3) QlikView/Qlik Sense:
- Qlik's associative data modeling approach allows users to explore and analyze data relationships dynamically.

(4) Looker:
- Looker focuses on collaborative exploration of data, providing a platform for creating and sharing insights.

(5) MicroStrategy:
- Known for its enterprise-level BI solutions, MicroStrategy offers comprehensive features for data discovery, reporting, and mobile BI.

(6) Google Data Studio:

- Google's BI tool allows users to create customizable and shareable reports with data visualizations, integrating seamlessly with other Google products.

(7) Sisense:
- Sisense is recognized for its ability to handle large and complex datasets, providing an end-to-end BI solution.

Significance of BI Tools and Platforms:
- Informed Decision-Making: BI tools empower organizations to make informed decisions based on accurate and timely data.
- Operational Efficiency: By providing a consolidated view of business data, BI tools streamline operations and enhance overall efficiency.
- Competitive Advantage: Organizations leveraging BI gain a competitive advantage by responding quickly to market trends and making data-driven strategic decisions.
- Improved Visibility: BI tools offer improved visibility into key performance indicators, helping organizations monitor and measure their success against goals.
- Enhanced Collaboration: BI platforms promote collaboration by providing a centralized hub for data sharing and analysis, fostering a collaborative and data-driven culture.

In summary, BI tools and platforms play a pivotal role in transforming raw data into actionable insights, fostering a data-driven culture, and enabling organizations to thrive in today's dynamic business environment.

3.2 Comparative Analysis of BI Software

Business Intelligence Software: Introduction
Business Intelligence (BI) software is a suite of tools, applications, and technologies that empower organizations to collect, analyze, and visualize data, aiding in informed decision-making and strategic planning. BI software plays a crucial role in transforming raw data into actionable insights, providing executives, analysts, and other stakeholders with the tools needed to gain a comprehensive understanding of their business landscape.

Key Features of BI Software:
(1) Data Integration:
- BI tools allow organizations to integrate data from diverse sources, providing a unified view of information.

(2) Data Modeling and Transformation:
- Capabilities for modeling and transforming data, ensuring that it is structured and ready for analysis.

(3) Visualization and Reporting:

- Intuitive visualization features for creating interactive dashboards, reports, and charts, facilitating data-driven storytelling.

(4) Ad-Hoc Querying and Analysis:
- User-friendly interfaces for ad-hoc querying and analysis, enabling users to explore data without extensive technical knowledge.

(5) Collaboration and Sharing:
- Tools that facilitate collaboration by allowing users to share insights, reports, and dashboards with colleagues.

(6) Mobile BI:
- Compatibility with mobile devices, ensuring that users can access and interact with data on-the-go.

(7) Data Security and Governance:
Robust security features to protect sensitive business data and ensure compliance with regulations.

Comparative Analysis of BI Software:

Let's compare several popular BI software options to understand their strengths, weaknesses, and unique features:

1. Tableau:
Strengths:
- Powerful visualization capabilities.
- User-friendly interface.
- Large community and extensive support.

Weaknesses:
- Cost may be a barrier for smaller organizations.

2. Power BI (Microsoft):
Strengths:
- Seamless integration with Microsoft products.
- Robust data modeling features.
- Affordable pricing options.

Weaknesses:
- Steeper learning curve for complex features.

3. QlikView/Qlik Sense:
Strengths:
- Associative data modeling approach for dynamic exploration.
- Excellent data visualization capabilities.

Weaknesses:
- Cost may be a factor for some organizations.

4. Looker:
Strengths:
- Focus on collaborative exploration.
- Modern architecture for scalable solutions.

Weaknesses:

- Learning curve for some advanced features.

5. MicroStrategy:
Strengths:
- Enterprise-level BI solutions.
- Comprehensive features for data discovery and reporting.

Weaknesses:
- May be perceived as complex for smaller organizations.

6. Google Data Studio:
Strengths:
- Integration with other Google products.
- Free version available with limited features.

Weaknesses:
- Less feature-rich compared to some enterprise-level solutions.

7. Sisense:
Strengths:
- Ability to handle large and complex datasets.
- End-to-end BI solution.

Weaknesses:
- Cost may be a consideration.

Considerations for Choosing BI Software:

(1) Scalability:
- Assess the scalability of the BI software to accommodate growing data and user needs.

(2) Ease of Use:
- Consider the user-friendliness of the software and the learning curve for your team.

(3) Integration Capabilities:
- Evaluate how well the BI software integrates with your existing data sources and systems.

(4) Cost:
- Understand the total cost of ownership, including licensing, implementation, and maintenance costs.

(5) Customization:
- Assess the level of customization the software offers to meet your organization's specific requirements.

(6) Support and Community:
- Consider the availability of support services and the size and activity of the user community.

(7) Security and Compliance:
- Ensure that the BI software meets your organization's security and compliance standards.

Conclusion:

Business Intelligence software is a critical asset for organizations seeking to harness the power of data for strategic decision-making. The choice of BI software depends on various factors, including the organization's size, industry, and specific requirements. A thorough comparative analysis, considering strengths, weaknesses, and unique features, is essential for selecting the most suitable BI solution that aligns with an organization's goals and objectives.

3.3 Implementing BI Solutions in Corporate Settings:

Implementing Business Intelligence (BI) solutions in corporate settings involves the strategic integration of tools, processes, and technologies to transform raw data into actionable insights. This process empowers organizations to make informed decisions, optimize operations, and gain a competitive edge in the business landscape. Let's explore the key steps and considerations involved in implementing BI solutions, illustrated with examples.

Key Steps in Implementing BI Solutions:

1. Define Business Objectives:
- Clearly articulate the business objectives and goals that BI solutions aim to address. This ensures alignment with organizational priorities.

Example:
- Objective: Improve sales performance.
- BI Solution: Implement dashboards that provide real-time insights into sales metrics, customer behavior, and market trends.

2. Assess Data Sources:
- Identify and assess relevant data sources, both internal and external, that contribute to achieving business objectives.

Example:
- Data Sources: CRM systems, ERP databases, external market reports.
- BI Solution: Integrate data from these sources to create a comprehensive view of customer interactions and market dynamics.

3. Data Modeling and Transformation:
- Design a data model that structures and transforms raw data into a format suitable for analysis, ensuring consistency and accuracy.

Example:
- Transformation: Cleanse and standardize customer data to create a unified customer profile.
- BI Solution: Use ETL (Extract, Transform, Load) tools to automate the data transformation process.

4. Select BI Tools:
- Choose BI tools that align with business requirements, considering factors such as visualization capabilities, scalability, and ease of use.

Example:

- Tool Selection: Select Tableau for its robust visualization features and ability to create interactive dashboards.

5. Develop Dashboards and Reports:

- Create customized dashboards and reports that provide relevant insights, making data accessible to users at various levels within the organization.

Example:

- Dashboard Elements: Visualize sales performance, customer demographics, and product trends in a comprehensive sales dashboard.

6. Training and Change Management:

- Provide comprehensive training to users to ensure effective utilization of BI tools. Implement change management strategies to facilitate a smooth transition.

Example:

- Training: Conduct workshops on using BI tools and interpreting key performance indicators (KPIs).
- Change Management: Communicate the benefits of BI implementation and address any concerns through continuous communication.

7. Implement Data Security Measures:

- Establish robust data security measures to protect sensitive information and ensure compliance with regulations.

Example:

- Security Measures: Implement role-based access controls to restrict data access based on user roles and responsibilities.

8. Iterative Testing and Optimization:

- Conduct iterative testing to identify and address any issues. Continuously optimize BI solutions based on user feedback and changing business needs.

Example:

- Testing: Validate data accuracy and dashboard functionality through user testing.
- Optimization: Incorporate feedback to enhance visualizations or add new data sources.

9. Monitor and Evaluate Performance:

- Establish key performance indicators (KPIs) to monitor the effectiveness of BI solutions and evaluate their impact on business outcomes.

Example:

- KPIs: Track improvements in sales conversion rates, customer satisfaction scores, and operational efficiency.

Considerations for Successful BI Implementation:

(1) User Adoption:

- Ensure user buy-in by demonstrating the value of BI solutions in addressing specific business challenges.

(2) Scalability:
- Choose scalable BI solutions that can grow with the organization's data and analytical needs.

(3) Data Governance:
- Implement data governance policies to maintain data quality, integrity, and compliance.

(4) Collaboration:
- Foster a collaborative culture where departments can share insights and collaborate on data-driven initiatives.

(5) Continuous Improvement:
- Embrace a culture of continuous improvement, regularly updating BI solutions to address changing business requirements.

Case Example:

Company X's BI Implementation:
- Objective: Improve supply chain efficiency.
- Data Sources: ERP system, logistics databases, supplier information.
- BI Solution: Implemented a BI platform integrating real-time data on inventory levels, supplier performance, and demand forecasts.
- Results: Reduced stockouts by 20%, improved supplier relationships, and optimized inventory management.

Conclusion:

Implementing BI solutions in corporate settings is a strategic process that requires careful planning, alignment with business objectives, and a focus on user adoption. By selecting the right tools, transforming and modeling data effectively, and fostering a data-driven culture, organizations can unlock the full potential of BI to gain insights, make informed decisions, and drive success in a competitive business environment.

3.4 Teaching Case Study on Business Intelligence Tools and Technologies

Teaching Case Study: Business Intelligence Tools and Technologies:

Introduction:

TechEdu University recognizes the growing importance of Business Intelligence (BI) in shaping organizational strategies and decision-making processes. To address this, a course on "Business Intelligence Tools and Technologies" has been designed. The case study follows the journey of TechEdu University in implementing this course, highlighting key components, challenges, and the impact on students' learning experiences.

Context:

TechEdu University aims to equip students with practical knowledge of BI tools and technologies, preparing them for the evolving demands of the business landscape. The course covers a range of BI tools, data visualization techniques, and hands-on exercises to provide students with a comprehensive understanding of how to harness data for strategic decision-making.

Objectives:

(1) Introduce BI Tools:
- Familiarize students with a diverse range of BI tools and technologies available in the market.

(2) Hands-on Application:
- Provide hands-on experience with popular BI tools to develop practical skills in data analysis and visualization.

(3) Real-world Case Studies:
- Present real-world case studies demonstrating the impact of BI in different industries and business scenarios.

(4) Collaborative Learning:
- Foster collaboration among students through group projects and interactive sessions.

Implementation:

(1) Course Structure:
- Foundational Concepts: Introduction to BI, data warehousing, and data modeling.
- BI Tools Exploration: Hands-on sessions with tools such as Tableau, Power BI, and QlikView.
- Advanced Techniques: Advanced visualization techniques, predictive analytics, and machine learning in BI.
- Real-world Applications: Analyzing case studies from industries like retail, healthcare, and finance.

(2) Practical Exercises:
- Hands-on Workshops: Conduct workshops where students work on projects using BI tools to analyze provided datasets.
- Industry Projects: Collaborate with industry partners to provide real datasets for students to analyze, addressing practical challenges.

(3) Guest Lectures:
- Industry Experts: Invite BI professionals to share insights on industry trends, challenges, and the practical application of BI tools.

(4) Tool-specific Experts:
- Guest lectures from experts specializing in specific BI tools to provide in-depth knowledge.

(5) Collaborative Learning:
- Group Projects: Assign group projects requiring students to collectively analyze a business problem using BI tools.

(6) Peer Learning Sessions:
- Organize peer-led sessions where students share tips and tricks they've discovered while using BI tools.

Impact and Evaluation:

(1) Assessment Methods:
Project Evaluation: Assess group projects based on the effectiveness of BI tool usage, insights generated, and presentation quality.

Hands-on Exam: Conduct a hands-on exam where students use BI tools to analyze a given dataset within a specified timeframe.

(2) Student Feedback:
- Mid-course Feedback: Collect mid-course feedback to make adjustments and address any challenges faced by students.
- End-of-course Survey: Administer a comprehensive survey at the end of the course to gauge overall satisfaction and perceived learning outcomes.

(3) Performance Metrics:
- Tool Proficiency: Evaluate students' proficiency in using BI tools through practical assessments and quizzes.
- Problem-solving Skills: Assess students' ability to apply BI tools to solve complex business problems presented in case studies.

(4) Post-course Success:
- Internship Placements: Track the success of students in securing internships or entry-level positions where they can apply BI skills.
- Continued Learning: Monitor students' engagement with BI communities, webinars, and additional certifications post-course completion.

Challenges and Adaptations:

(1) Technology Accessibility:
- Challenge: Varied technology accessibility among students.
- Adaptation: Ensure access to BI tools on campus computers and facilitate remote access for students with limited resources.

(2) Diverse Backgrounds:
- Challenge: Students with diverse academic backgrounds entering the course.
- Adaptation: Conduct pre-course workshops to provide foundational knowledge for students with limited prior exposure to BI concepts.

Case Study Questions:

(1) How does the course structure ensure a balance between foundational BI concepts, hands-on tool exploration, and advanced techniques?

(2) Evaluate the effectiveness of hands-on workshops and industry projects in developing practical skills among students. Provide specific examples.

(3) Assess the impact of guest lectures from industry professionals on students' understanding of BI trends and practical applications.

(4) Discuss the role of collaborative learning in the course, specifically in group projects and peer-led sessions. How does this approach enhance the overall learning experience?

(5) Analyze the assessment methods employed, including project evaluation, hands-on exams, and metrics for tool proficiency. How do these assessments measure students' competence in BI tools and technologies?

(6) Evaluate the mid-course feedback and end-of-course survey results. What adjustments were made based on the feedback, and how did it contribute to the course's overall effectiveness?

(7) Assess the impact of the course on students' problem-solving skills, particularly in their ability to apply BI tools to real-world business challenges presented in case studies. Provide examples.

(8) Track the success of students in securing internships or entry-level positions post-course completion. How does the course contribute to students' readiness for practical applications in the industry?

(9) Explore students' continued engagement with BI communities, webinars, and additional certifications after completing the course. How does the course inspire ongoing learning and professional development?

(10) Discuss the adaptations made to address challenges related to technology accessibility and diverse academic backgrounds. How did these adaptations contribute to the overall success of the course?

3.5 Learning Questions:

3.5.1 Descriptive Questions:

(1) How do Business Intelligence (BI) tools contribute to informed decision-making in organizations?

(2) What are the key components of BI tools and platforms that facilitate the seamless analysis of comprehensive datasets?

(3) In what ways do BI tools transform raw data into actionable information suitable for analysis?

(4) How does the integration of data warehouses contribute to efficient querying and reporting in BI platforms?

(5) What role do visualization features play in enabling users to share business data and support data-driven storytelling?

(6) How does mobile compatibility in BI tools facilitate real-time decision-making, especially for professionals on the go?

(7) What are the strengths and weaknesses of Tableau as a BI tool based on the comparative analysis provided?

(8) How do BI tools enhance collaboration within organizations by providing a centralized hub for data sharing and analysis?

(9) What considerations are essential when choosing BI software, particularly in terms of scalability and integration capabilities?

(10) Can you provide an example of a successful BI implementation, such as Company X's case, and the specific results achieved in terms of supply chain efficiency?

3.5.2 Fill-up the Blanks Questions:

(1) BI tools integrate data from various sources, including databases, spreadsheets, and cloud-based storage systems, ensuring a _____ view for users to analyze datasets seamlessly.
- Answer: Unified

(2) BI platforms often leverage data warehouses to store and manage large volumes of structured and unstructured data, enabling efficient _____ and reporting.
- Answer: Querying

(3) BI tools offer capabilities for modeling and transforming raw data into a structured format suitable for analysis, involving processes such as cleaning, filtering, and aggregating data to derive _____ insights.
- Answer: Meaningful

(4) Visualization features in BI tools allow users to create interactive charts, graphs, and dashboards, facilitating _____ storytelling through customized reports.

- Answer: Data-driven

(5) BI tools provide intuitive interfaces for querying databases and conducting ad-hoc analysis, allowing users to explore data, apply filters, and derive insights without the need for extensive _____.
- Answer: Technical expertise

(6) BI platforms promote collaboration by allowing users to share reports and dashboards with colleagues, fostering a collaborative and _____ culture within organizations.
- Answer: Data-driven

(7) Many BI tools offer mobile compatibility, enabling users to access and interact with data on smartphones and tablets, facilitating _____ decision-making.
- Answer: Real-time

(8) Tableau is renowned for its powerful visualization capabilities, user-friendly interface, and support from a large _____.
- Answer: Community

(9) Power BI from Microsoft seamlessly integrates with Microsoft products, offers robust data modeling features, and provides affordable _____ options.
- Answer: Pricing

(10) Sisense is recognized for its ability to handle large and complex datasets, providing an end-to-end BI solution that addresses _____ considerations.
- Answer: Cost

3.5.3 Multiple Choice Questions:

(1) What is the primary purpose of Business Intelligence (BI) tools and platforms in the modern business landscape?
- A. Facilitating data integration
- B. Enabling data visualization
- C. Transforming raw data into actionable insights
- D. Managing cloud-based storage systems
- Answer: c. Transforming raw data into actionable insights

(2) Which component of BI tools ensures a unified view by integrating data from various sources such as databases and spreadsheets?
- A. Data Modeling and Transformation
- B. Data Warehousing
- C. Visualization and Reporting
- D. Querying and Analysis
- Answer: b. Data Warehousing

(3) What is the role of BI tools in data modeling and transformation?
- A. Creating interactive dashboards
- B. Storing and managing large volumes of data
- C. Transforming raw data into a structured format suitable for analysis
- D. Allowing users to explore and analyze data relationships
- Answer: c. Transforming raw data into a structured format suitable for analysis

(4) Which feature of BI tools allows users to create interactive charts, graphs, and dashboards?
- A. Data Warehousing
- B. Data Integration
- C. Visualization and Reporting
- D. Mobile BI
- Answer: c. Visualization and Reporting

(5) What is the significance of Mobile BI in BI platforms?

    A. It facilitates real-time decision-making for professionals on the go.

    B. It focuses on collaborative exploration of data.

    C. It ensures a unified view of information.

    D. It enables efficient querying and reporting.

- Answer: a. It facilitates real-time decision-making for professionals on the go.

(6) Which BI tool is known for its powerful visualization capabilities and allows users to create interactive dashboards and reports?

    A. Power BI (Microsoft)

    B. QlikView/Qlik Sense

    C. Tableau

    D. Google Data Studio

- Answer: c. Tableau

(7) What is a potential weakness of Tableau as a BI tool?

    A. Cost may be a barrier for smaller organizations.

    B. Steeper learning curve for complex features.

    C. Limited support and community.

    D. Lack of mobile compatibility.

- Answer: a. Cost may be a barrier for smaller organizations.

(8) Which step in implementing BI solutions involves defining clear business objectives and goals?

    A. Data Modeling and Transformation

    B. Selecting BI Tools

    C. Developing Dashboards and Reports

    D. Defining Business Objectives

- Answer: d. Defining Business Objectives

(9) What is an essential consideration for successful BI implementation regarding user adoption?

    A. Cost-effectiveness

    B. Scalability

    C. Demonstrating the value of BI solutions

    D. Data security measures

- Answer: c. Demonstrating the value of BI solutions

(10) In the case example of Company X's BI implementation, what was the specific objective addressed by the BI solution?

    A. Enhancing customer satisfaction

    B. Improving sales performance

    C. Optimizing marketing strategies

    D. Streamlining human resources processes

- Answer: b. Improving sales performance

****

CHAPTER 4

Data Visualization for Decision Making

Objectives of the Chapter:

To provide a comprehensive understanding of key principles that enhance clarity, engagement, and overall effectiveness in communicating insights through data visualization. The chapter aims to elucidate principles such as clarity and simplicity, relevance to the audience, appropriate chart types, effective use of color and contrast, consistency, interactivity for exploration, data integrity and accuracy, storytelling narrative, whitespace and layout, and accessibility. Each principle is accompanied by illustrations and examples, emphasizing the practical application of these principles in creating impactful visualizations. The chapter also emphasizes the idea that effective data visualization is a blend of art and science, with the goal of not just presenting data but telling a compelling and actionable story. By adhering to these principles, the chapter aims to guide readers in creating visualizations that convey complex information in a comprehensible manner, engage the audience, and empower them to make informed decisions based on the presented data.

4.1 Principles of Effective Data Visualization:

Data visualization is a powerful tool for transforming complex information into clear and understandable insights. To create impactful visualizations, it is essential to follow principles that enhance clarity, engagement, and the overall effectiveness of the communicated message. Here, we'll discuss key principles of effective data visualization with illustrations and examples:

(1) Clarity and Simplicity:

Principle: Keep visualizations simple and clear to facilitate quick and accurate interpretation.

Illustration:

Example: A bar chart displaying monthly sales figures should have a clean design with easily distinguishable bars and clear axis labels.

(2) Relevance to the Audience:

Principle: Tailor visualizations to the specific needs and knowledge level of the target audience.

Illustration:

Example: For executives, a high-level dashboard with key performance indicators may be more relevant, while analysts may require detailed, interactive visualizations.

(3) Use of Appropriate Chart Types:

Principle: Choose chart types that effectively represent the data and support the intended message.

Illustration:

Example: Use a line chart for showing trends over time, a bar chart for comparisons, and a pie chart for illustrating part-to-whole relationships.

(4) Color and Contrast:

Principle: Employ color strategically to highlight key elements and create a visual hierarchy.

Illustration:

Example: Use a contrasting color for important data points or trends in a line chart to draw attention to specific information.

(5) Consistency:

Principle: Maintain consistency in design elements, labels, and scales across multiple visualizations.

Illustration:

Example: If using a specific color scheme for a series of charts, ensure that the same colors represent similar categories or data points consistently.

(6) Interactivity for Exploration:

Principle: Provide interactive elements for users to explore and gain deeper insights.

Illustration:

Example: In a dashboard, allow users to hover over data points to view additional information or filter the data based on specific criteria.

(7) Data Integrity and Accuracy:

Principle: Ensure data accuracy and integrity to build trust in the visualization.

Illustration:

Example: Clearly label axes, provide context for data units, and verify that the visualization accurately represents the underlying data.

(8) Storytelling Narrative:

Principle: Create a narrative flow in the visualization to guide the audience through a logical sequence.

Illustration:

Example: In a series of visualizations, arrange them in a sequence that tells a story, guiding the viewer from introduction to conclusion.

(9) Whitespace and Layout:

Principle: Use whitespace effectively to reduce clutter and improve overall visual appeal.

Illustration:

Example: Adequate spacing between elements in a dashboard or chart enhances readability and prevents visual overload.

(10) Accessibility:

Principle: Design visualizations that are accessible to a diverse audience, considering color-blindness and other accessibility requirements.

Illustration:

Example: Use patterns or textures in addition to color to differentiate elements for users with color vision deficiencies.

Conclusion:

Effective data visualization is a blend of art and science. By adhering to these principles, you can create visualizations that not only convey complex information in a comprehensible manner but also engage and empower your audience to make informed decisions based on the presented data. Remember that the goal is not just to present data but to tell a compelling and actionable story through visualization.

4.2 Tools and Techniques for Data Visualization:

Tools and Techniques for Data Visualization:

Data visualization tools and techniques play a crucial role in transforming complex datasets into meaningful and actionable insights. Here, we'll explore some popular tools and techniques, providing explanations and examples for each:

Data Visualization Tools:

1. Tableau:

Description: Tableau is a powerful and widely-used business intelligence and data visualization tool. It allows users to create interactive and shareable dashboards and reports.

Example: A sales manager can use Tableau to visualize regional sales performance over time, compare product categories, and identify trends.

2. Power BI (Microsoft):

Description: Power BI is a business analytics tool by Microsoft that enables users to visualize and share insights across an organization, or embed them in an app or website.

Example: A financial analyst can use Power BI to create a dynamic dashboard illustrating budget versus actual spending, forecasting trends, and highlighting variances.

3. QlikView/Qlik Sense:

Description: QlikView and Qlik Sense use associative data modeling to allow users to explore and visualize data dynamically, making it easy to discover insights.

Example: An HR manager can use Qlik Sense to analyze employee data, explore relationships between variables like performance and training, and identify patterns.

4. D3.js:

Description: D3.js is a JavaScript library for producing dynamic, interactive data visualizations in web browsers. It gives developers the flexibility to create custom visualizations.

Example: A web developer can use D3.js to build a customized interactive map showing global population density with color-coded regions.

5. Google Data Studio:

Description: Google Data Studio is a free and easy-to-use tool for creating interactive reports and dashboards. It integrates seamlessly with other Google products.

Example: A marketing team can use Google Data Studio to visualize website traffic, conversion rates, and the performance of online marketing campaigns.

Data Visualization Techniques:

1. Bar Charts:

Description: Bar charts represent data using rectangular bars, where the length of each bar corresponds to the value it represents.

Example: A bar chart can display monthly sales figures for different products, making it easy to compare performance.

2. Line Charts:

Description: Line charts show data points connected by straight lines, useful for displaying trends over time.

Example: A line chart can illustrate stock prices over the course of a year, helping to identify patterns and trends.

3. Pie Charts:

Description: Pie charts represent data in a circular graph, with each slice of the pie representing a proportion of the whole.

Example: A pie chart can display the distribution of expenses in a budget, highlighting the percentage allocated to different categories.

4. Scatter Plots:

Description: Scatter plots use points to represent individual data points, making them useful for visualizing relationships between two variables.

Example: A scatter plot can depict the correlation between the number of hours studied and exam scores for a group of students.

5. Heatmaps:

Description: Heatmaps use color gradients to represent the intensity of values in a matrix, making it easy to identify patterns.

Example: A heatmap can visualize website traffic, with colors indicating the level of activity on different pages over a specified time period.

6. Treemaps:

Description: Treemaps visualize hierarchical data using nested rectangles, with each branch represented by a rectangle subdivided into smaller ones.

Example: A treemap can display the hierarchical structure of organizational departments, with each rectangle representing a department and its subdivisions.

7. Bubble Charts:

Description: Bubble charts extend scatter plots by adding a third dimension, using varying sizes of bubbles to represent a third variable.

Example: A bubble chart can represent population density in different cities, with the size of each bubble indicating the population size.

8. Choropleth Maps:

Description: Choropleth maps use color variations to represent data by region, making them effective for visualizing geographical patterns.

Example: A choropleth map can illustrate unemployment rates across different states or countries, using color gradients to show the level of unemployment.

9. Sankey Diagrams:

Description: Sankey diagrams visualize the flow of data or resources between multiple entities, using connected arrows to represent the direction and quantity.

Example: A Sankey diagram can illustrate the flow of energy in a manufacturing process, showing how energy is distributed and utilized.

10. Word Clouds:

Description: Word clouds visualize the frequency of words in a text by varying the size of each word based on its occurrence.

Example: A word cloud can display the most frequently used words in customer reviews, providing insights into common themes or sentiments.

Conclusion:

Effective data visualization involves the strategic use of tools and techniques to communicate insights clearly and engagingly. The choice of tools depends on factors such as ease of use, scalability, and integration capabilities, while the selection of techniques depends on the type of data and the story you want to tell. Whether creating dashboards, reports, or interactive web visualizations, combining the right tools with suitable techniques enhances the impact of data visualizations in conveying meaningful insights.

4.3 Communicating Insights Through Visualizations:

Communicating Insights Through Visualizations

Effective data visualization is a powerful means of conveying complex information in a clear and compelling manner. When done well, visualizations can facilitate understanding, drive decision-making, and tell a story that resonates with the audience. In this detailed note, we will explore key principles and strategies for communicating insights through visualizations, illustrated with examples.

Principles of Communicating Insights Through Visualizations:

1. Clarity and Simplicity:

Principle: Keep visualizations simple to avoid cognitive overload and ensure clarity of the message.

Example: A bar chart showing quarterly sales figures with clear labels and minimal design elements.

2. Contextualization:

Principle: Provide context to help viewers understand the significance of the data points in relation to the broader picture.

Example: A line chart depicting website traffic should include annotations explaining events like marketing campaigns or website redesigns.

3. Storytelling Narrative:

Principle: Structure visualizations to tell a compelling story, guiding the audience through a sequence of insights.

Example: A series of visualizations that starts with an overview, delves into specific trends, and concludes with actionable insights.

4. Interactivity for Exploration:

Principle: Incorporate interactive elements that allow users to explore the data, uncover patterns, and gain deeper insights.

Example: A dashboard with filters and tooltips, enabling users to interactively explore regional sales performance.

5. Visual Hierarchy:

Principle: Use visual cues such as color, size, and placement to establish a hierarchy and emphasize key elements.

Example: A heatmap where darker shades represent higher values, immediately drawing attention to areas with significant activity.

6. Consistency:

Principle: Maintain consistency in design elements, color schemes, and labeling across multiple visualizations for coherence.

Example: Ensuring that the same color represents the same category in different charts within a report.

7. Annotations and Callouts:

Principle: Use annotations and callouts to highlight specific data points or events, providing additional context.

Example: Adding a callout to a data point in a line chart to explain a sudden spike or drop in performance.

8. Use of Appropriate Visualizations:

Principle: Select visualization types that effectively represent the data and support the intended message.

Example: Choosing a bar chart for comparing sales across different regions and a line chart for showing trends over time.

Strategies for Effective Communication:

1. Understand Your Audience:

Strategy: Tailor visualizations to the knowledge level and needs of the audience to ensure relevance.

2. Provide Actionable Insights:

Strategy: Clearly articulate actionable insights derived from the visualizations to drive decision-making.

3. Iterative Design and Testing:

Strategy: Engage in iterative design, testing, and feedback loops to refine visualizations for maximum impact.

4. Accessibility Considerations:

Strategy: Design visualizations with accessibility in mind, ensuring they are comprehensible to diverse audiences.

5. Align with Key Messages:

Strategy: Ensure that visualizations align with the key messages and objectives of the communication.

Examples:

Example 1: Sales Performance Dashboard

(1) Visualization Elements:

Bar chart for monthly sales comparisons.

Line chart for tracking sales trends over time.

Map showing regional sales performance.

Callouts highlighting key achievements and challenges.

(2) Communication Strategy:

The dashboard provides a comprehensive view of sales performance, allowing executives to quickly grasp the overall picture and identify areas for improvement.

Example 2: Website Analytics Report

(1) Visualization Elements:

- Line chart illustrating website traffic trends.
- Pie chart depicting the distribution of traffic sources.
- Heatmap showcasing user engagement on different webpages.
- Annotations explaining significant changes in traffic.

(2) Communication Strategy:

The report communicates insights into website performance, including traffic sources, popular pages, and user engagement patterns. Interactive elements allow users to explore further.

Example 3: Financial Performance Infographic

(1) Visualization Elements: Doughnut chart representing budget allocation, Bar chart illustrating revenue and expenditure, Icons and symbols to visually convey key financial metrics.

(2) Communication Strategy: The infographic communicates financial performance in a visually engaging and easily digestible format, making it accessible to a broad audience.

Conclusion:

Effectively communicating insights through visualizations is a multidimensional process that requires a thoughtful combination of principles and strategies. By embracing clarity, context, storytelling, and user interaction, visualizations become powerful tools for conveying complex information. The provided examples demonstrate the application of these principles and strategies in real-world scenarios, emphasizing the importance of aligning visualizations with key messages and understanding the needs of the audience for impactful communication.

4.4 Teaching Case Study:

Teaching Case Study: Enhancing Decision-Making through Data Visualization:

Introduction:

TechEdu University recognizes the importance of data visualization in improving decision-making processes across various industries. This case study focuses on the implementation of a course titled "Data Visualization for Decision Making" at TechEdu. The course aims to equip students with the skills to create meaningful visualizations that support effective decision-making.

Context:

TechEdu University is launching a new program to address the increasing demand for professionals skilled in data visualization. The "Data Visualization for Decision Making" course is designed to provide students with hands-on experience using various tools and techniques to communicate insights and support decision-making processes.

Objectives:

Develop Visualization Skills:
- Enable students to use data visualization tools to represent complex data sets clearly and effectively.

Understand Decision-Making Context:
- Familiarize students with the context of decision-making and how visualizations can aid in the process.

Explore Diverse Tools:
Introduce students to a range of data visualization tools and techniques, emphasizing their application in decision support.

Case-Based Learning:
Engage students in real-world cases where data visualization contributes to decision-making.

Implementation:

1. Course Structure:
- Foundational Concepts: Introduction to data visualization principles and their role in decision-making.
- Tool Exploration: Hands-on sessions with tools like Tableau, Power BI, and Excel for creating different types of visualizations.
- Decision-Making Frameworks: Understanding decision-making processes and how visualizations can enhance them.
- Industry Applications: Analyzing case studies from various industries where data visualization played a crucial role in decision support.

2. Practical Exercises:
- Scenario Analysis: Students analyze business scenarios and create visualizations to support decision-making, considering factors like risk and uncertainty.

- Dashboard Development: Designing interactive dashboards that provide a comprehensive overview for decision-makers.

3. Guest Speakers:

- Industry Experts: Inviting professionals who have successfully utilized data visualization in decision-making to share their experiences.
- Tool-specific Experts: Guest sessions from experts specializing in specific visualization tools.

4. Collaborative Projects:

- **Team-Based Projects:** Assigning projects that require collaboration in creating visualizations for complex datasets.
- **Peer Review Sessions:** Conducting peer review sessions where students provide constructive feedback on each other's visualizations.

Impact and Evaluation:

1. Assessment Methods:

- Project Evaluation: Assessing individual and group projects based on the effectiveness of visualizations in supporting decision-making.
- Class Participation: Evaluating students based on their engagement in discussions and contribution to case analysis.

2. Student Feedback:

- Mid-course Feedback: Collecting feedback to make adjustments and address any challenges faced by students.
- End-of-course Survey: Administering a comprehensive survey to gauge overall satisfaction and perceived learning outcomes.

3. Performance Metrics:

- Visualization Competency: Evaluating students' proficiency in using visualization tools through practical assessments.
- Decision Impact: Assessing the impact of visualizations on decision-making scenarios presented in class.

4. Post-course Success:

- Portfolio Development: Encouraging students to develop a portfolio showcasing their best visualization projects.
- Industry Engagement: Tracking students' engagement with industry professionals and events post-course completion.

Case Study Questions:

(1) How does the course structure ensure a balance between foundational concepts, hands-on tool exploration, and real-world applications in decision-making scenarios?

(2) Evaluate the impact of practical exercises, such as scenario analysis and dashboard development, in enhancing students' ability to apply data visualization in decision support. Provide specific examples.

(3) Assess the contribution of guest speakers, especially industry experts, in providing insights into the real-world applications of data visualization in decision-making.

(4) Discuss the role of collaborative projects in fostering teamwork and encouraging students to create effective visualizations for complex datasets. How does peer review contribute to the learning process?

(5) Examine the effectiveness of assessment methods, including project evaluation and class participation, in measuring students' competency in data visualization and its impact on decision scenarios.

(6) Analyze the mid-course feedback and end-of-course survey results. What adjustments were made based on the feedback, and how did it contribute to the course's overall effectiveness?

(7) Evaluate the performance metrics used, such as visualization competency and decision impact. How do these metrics provide insights into students' proficiency and the practical application of data visualization skills?

(8) Track the success of students in developing a portfolio showcasing their best visualization projects. How does this contribute to their post-course professional development?

(9) Explore the ongoing engagement of students with industry professionals and events after completing the course. How does the course inspire continued learning and networking in the field of data visualization?

(10) Discuss the strategies employed to ensure that the course aligns with key messages and objectives, providing students with a comprehensive understanding of data visualization for decision-making.

4.5 Learning Questions:

4.5.1 Descriptive Questions:

(1) How does the principle of "Clarity and Simplicity" contribute to the effectiveness of data visualizations, and what are some key elements of a well-designed bar chart according to the given example?

(2) Explain the principle of "Relevance to the Audience" in the context of data visualization. Provide an example illustrating how tailoring visualizations to different audience needs can enhance communication.

(3) Discuss the importance of using appropriate chart types in data visualization, citing examples of when a line chart, bar chart, and pie chart would be most effective in representing different types of data.

(4) How does the strategic use of "Color and Contrast" contribute to effective data visualization, and provide an example of how contrasting colors can be employed to highlight specific information in a visual representation?

(5) Explain the significance of "Consistency" in design elements, labels, and scales across multiple visualizations. How can maintaining consistency enhance the coherence of a series of visualizations?

(6) Describe the role of "Interactivity for Exploration" in data visualization. Provide an example of how interactive elements in a dashboard can empower users to gain deeper insights from the presented data.

(7) What are the key principles behind ensuring "Data Integrity and Accuracy" in visualizations? Provide examples of how accurate labeling, context, and representation contribute to building trust in the visualization.

(8) How does the principle of "Storytelling Narrative" enhance the effectiveness of a sequence of visualizations? Provide an example of arranging visualizations in a narrative flow to guide the viewer through a logical sequence.

(9) Discuss the importance of "Whitespace and Layout" in data visualizations. How does effective use of whitespace contribute to reducing clutter and improving overall visual appeal?

(10) Explain the principle of "Accessibility" in the design of visualizations. Provide examples of how incorporating patterns or textures, in addition to colour, can enhance accessibility for users with colour vision deficiencies.

4.5.2 Fill-up the Blanks Questions:

(1) The principle of Clarity and Simplicity suggests keeping visualizations simple and clear to facilitate _____ and _____ interpretation.
- Answer: quick and accurate

(2) Fill in the Blank: Customizing visualizations based on the target audience's needs and _____ level ensures relevance.
- Answer: knowledge

(3) Fill in the Blank: The key principle is to select chart types that align with the data's nature and enhance the intended _____.
- Answer: message.

(4) Fill in the Blank: Strategic use of color helps highlight key elements and establishes a _____ in visual hierarchy.
- Answer: visual hierarchy.

(5) Fill in the Blank: Consistency across visualizations ensures uniformity in design elements, _____, and scales.
- Answer: labels

(6) Fill in the Blank: Interactivity in visualizations enables users to explore and gain _____ insights.
- Answer: deeper

(7) Fill in the Blank: Building trust in visualizations involves ensuring accuracy and _____ of the data.
- Answer: integrity.

(8) Fill in the Blank: A narrative flow in visualizations guides the audience through a _____ sequence, enhancing engagement.
- Answer: logical.

(9) Fill in the Blank: Effective use of whitespace contributes to reducing _____ and improving visual appeal.
- Answer: clutter

(10) Fill in the Blank: Designing accessible visualizations involves considering the needs of a _____ audience, including those with color vision deficiencies.
- Answer: diverse Top of Form

4.5.3 Multiple Choice Questions:

(1) What is the primary goal of effective data visualization?
A. Increase complexity
B. Enhance confusion
C. Transform complex information into clear insights

D. Hide information
Answer: C. Transform complex information into clear insights

(2) Which principle emphasizes tailoring visualizations to the specific needs and knowledge level of the target audience?
   A. Clarity and Simplicity
   B. Relevance to the Audience
   C. Storytelling Narrative
   D. Data Integrity and Accuracy
   Answer: B. Relevance to the Audience

(3) What is the recommended approach for choosing chart types in data visualization?
   A. Random selection
   B. Choose the most complex chart type
   C. Use chart types that align with the data and support the intended message
   D. Always use pie charts
   Answer: C. Use chart types that align with the data and support the intended message

(4) How does the principle of Color and Contrast contribute to effective data visualization?
   A. By using random colors
   B. By minimizing the use of colors
   C. By employing color strategically to highlight key elements and create a visual hierarchy
   D. By avoiding contrast to maintain a monochromatic palette
   Answer: C. By employing color strategically to highlight key elements and create a visual hierarchy

(5) What does the principle of Consistency in data visualization emphasize?
   A. Changing design elements frequently
   B. Maintaining inconsistency in labels
   C. Consistency in design elements, labels, and scales across multiple visualizations
   D. Ignoring color schemes
   Answer: C. Consistency in design elements, labels, and scales across multiple visualizations

(6) What does the principle of Interactivity for Exploration suggest?
   A. Avoid any form of interactivity
   B. Provide interactive elements for users to explore and gain deeper insights
   C. Use only static visualizations
   D. Limit user engagement with the data
   Answer: B. Provide interactive elements for users to explore and gain deeper insights

(7) How can the principle of Data Integrity and Accuracy be achieved in data visualization?
   A. Hide the data source
   B. Provide misleading labels
   C. Ensure data accuracy and integrity, label axes, and provide context
   D. Use random data points
   Answer: C. Ensure data accuracy and integrity, label axes, and provide context

(8) What is the purpose of the Storytelling Narrative principle in data visualization?

A. Create confusion
B. Add unnecessary details
C. Guide the audience through a logical sequence in visualizations
D. Avoid creating a narrative flow
Answer: C. Guide the audience through a logical sequence in visualizations

(9) How does the principle of Whitespace and Layout contribute to effective data visualization?
A. Increase clutter
B. Improve overall visual appeal
C. Use whitespace inefficiently
D. Avoid spacing between elements
Answer: B. Improve overall visual appeal

(10) What does the Accessibility principle in data visualization focus on?
A. Ignoring diverse audiences
B. Designing visualizations for a specific audience only
C. Designing visualizations that are accessible to a diverse audience
D. Exclusively considering color vision deficiencies
Answer: C. Designing visualizations that are accessible to a diverse audience

(11) Which tool is described as a powerful business intelligence and data visualization tool widely used for creating interactive dashboards and reports?
A. D3.js
B. Tableau
C. Power BI
D. Google Data Studio
Answer: B. Tableau

(12) What is the main purpose of Power BI by Microsoft?
A. Website development
B. Business analytics and data visualization
C. JavaScript library
D. Interactive mapping
Answer: B. Business analytics and data visualization

(13) Which tool uses associative data modeling and is known for allowing users to explore and visualize data dynamically?
A. Google Data Studio
B. QlikView/Qlik Sense
C. D3.js
D. Power BI
Answer: B. QlikView/Qlik Sense

(14) What is the primary purpose of D3.js?
A. Business analytics
B. Interactive reports
C. Dynamic and interactive data visualizations in web browsers
D. Geographical mapping
Answer: C. Dynamic and interactive data visualizations in web browsers

(15) Which tool is described as a free and easy-to-use tool for creating interactive reports and dashboards that integrates seamlessly with other Google products?
   A. Tableau
   B. Power BI
   C. Google Data Studio
   D. QlikView/Qlik Sense
      Answer: C. Google Data Studio

(16) What type of chart represents data using rectangular bars, where the length of each bar corresponds to the value it represents?
   A. Line chart
   B. Pie chart
   C. Bar chart
   D. Scatter plot
      Answer: C. Bar chart

(17) Which visualization type is useful for displaying trends over time by connecting data points with straight lines?
   A. Bubble chart
   B. Treemap
   C. Line chart
   D. Sankey diagram
      Answer: C. Line chart

(18) What type of chart represents data in a circular graph, with each slice of the pie representing a proportion of the whole?
   A. Scatter plot
   B. Bubble chart
   C. Pie chart
   D. Heatmap
      Answer: C. Pie chart

(19) Which visualization type uses color gradients to represent the intensity of values in a matrix?
   A. Treemap
   B. Scatter plot
   C. Word cloud
   D. Heatmap
      Answer: D. Heatmap

(20) What visualization type is effective for illustrating the flow of data or resources between multiple entities using connected arrows?
   A. Choropleth map
   B. Sankey diagram
   C. Word cloud
   D. Bubble chart
      Answer: B. Sankey diagram

****

58

CHAPTER 5

Machine Learning for Business Intelligence

Objectives of the Chapter:

To establish a foundational comprehension of Machine Learning (ML) and its pivotal role in artificial intelligence. It introduces readers to ML as a subset of AI, underscoring its capacity to enable computers to learn autonomously from data without explicit programming. The chapter focuses on elucidating various types of ML algorithms, encompassing supervised, unsupervised, and reinforcement learning, providing lucid explanations and practical examples for each category. Noteworthy algorithms such as Linear Regression, Decision Trees, Random Forest, Support Vector Machines, K-Nearest Neighbors, K-Means Clustering, Neural Networks, Naive Bayes, and Principal Component Analysis are explored, aiming to furnish readers with a conceptual and descriptive overview. This knowledge serves as a bedrock for subsequent part on "Predictive Modeling and Forecasting" and "ML Applications in Corporate Decision Making," which delve into the practical applications of ML in predicting future outcomes and making informed decisions within corporate environments. This showcase how ML techniques contribute to efficiency, provide valuable insights, and play a transformative role in diverse business scenarios. Further to provide a comprehensive understanding of ML algorithms, lays the essential groundwork for readers to navigate the subsequent applications and implications of ML in corporate decision-making contexts.

5.1 Introduction to Machine Learning Algorithms:

Introduction to Machine Learning Algorithms

Machine Learning (ML) is a subset of artificial intelligence that empowers computers to learn from data and improve their performance over time without explicit programming. Machine Learning algorithms play a pivotal role in extracting meaningful patterns, making predictions, and aiding decision-making processes. This introduction provides a conceptual and descriptive overview of various types of Machine Learning algorithms with illustrative examples.

Types of Machine Learning Algorithms:

1. Supervised Learning:

In supervised learning, the algorithm is trained on a labeled dataset, where the input data is paired with corresponding output labels. The goal is to learn a mapping function from input to output.

Examples:

- Linear Regression: Predicting house prices based on features like square footage and number of bedrooms.

- Classification (e.g., Logistic Regression): Classifying emails as spam or non-spam.

2. Unsupervised Learning:

Unsupervised learning involves training the algorithm on an unlabeled dataset, and it must find patterns and relationships within the data on its own.

Examples:

- Clustering (e.g., K-Means): Grouping customers based on purchasing behavior without predefined categories.
- Dimensionality Reduction (e.g., Principal Component Analysis): Simplifying complex datasets while preserving essential information.

3. Reinforcement Learning:

Reinforcement learning involves training an algorithm to make sequences of decisions by rewarding or penalizing based on the outcomes of its actions.

Example:

- Game Playing (e.g., AlphaGo): Learning optimal strategies by playing games and receiving rewards or penalties.

Common Machine Learning Algorithms:

1. Linear Regression:

Linear regression models the relationship between a dependent variable and one or more independent variables by fitting a linear equation.

Example:

- Predicting the price of a house based on its square footage.

2. Decision Trees:

Decision trees recursively split the dataset based on features to make decisions. They are used for both classification and regression tasks.

Example:

- Classifying whether an email is spam or non-spam based on features like sender and content.

3. Random Forest:

Random Forest is an ensemble learning method that builds multiple decision trees and merges their predictions.

Example:

- Predicting customer churn by combining predictions from multiple decision trees.

4. Support Vector Machines (SVM):

SVMs classify data points by finding the hyperplane that best separates classes in a high-dimensional space.

Example:

- Classifying handwritten digits based on their pixel values.

5. K-Nearest Neighbors (KNN):

KNN classifies data points based on the majority class among their k nearest neighbors in feature space.
Example:
- Predicting whether a patient has a particular disease based on the features of similar patients.

6. K-Means Clustering:
K-Means partitions data into k clusters by minimizing the sum of squared distances from data points to the cluster centers.
Example:
- Grouping customers based on purchasing behavior.

7. Neural Networks:
Neural networks simulate the human brain by using interconnected nodes (neurons) arranged in layers. They are effective for complex tasks and deep learning.
Example:
- Image classification tasks, such as recognizing objects in photos.

8. Naive Bayes:
Naive Bayes is a probabilistic algorithm based on Bayes' theorem. It is commonly used for text classification tasks.
Example:
- Classifying emails as spam or non-spam based on word frequencies.

9. Principal Component Analysis (PCA):
PCA reduces the dimensionality of data while preserving its essential features by identifying orthogonal axes with maximum variance.
Example:
- Simplifying facial recognition datasets while retaining key facial features.

Conclusion:

Machine Learning algorithms form the foundation of data-driven decision-making in various domains. Understanding the principles and applications of these algorithms is crucial for harnessing the power of ML in solving real-world problems. Whether predicting outcomes, grouping data points, or uncovering hidden patterns, machine learning algorithms continue to revolutionize the way we analyze and leverage data for enhanced decision support.

5.2 Predictive Modeling and Forecasting:

Predictive Modeling and Forecasting: Concepts and Examples
Predictive modeling and forecasting are integral components of data analytics, aiming to predict future outcomes based on historical data patterns. These techniques find applications across various industries, assisting in decision-making, risk assessment, and strategic planning. In this detailed description, we

will explore the concepts of predictive modeling and forecasting, along with illustrative examples.

Predictive Modeling:

Concept:

Predictive modeling involves building mathematical models that predict future outcomes based on patterns and relationships identified in historical data. These models can be applied to a wide range of scenarios, from sales forecasts to disease spread predictions.

Example:

Consider a retail business that wants to predict future sales for better inventory management. A predictive model could analyze historical sales data, taking into account factors such as seasonality, promotions, and economic indicators. The model may use techniques like linear regression, decision trees, or neural networks to generate predictions. By leveraging this model, the business can anticipate sales trends and adjust inventory levels accordingly.

Forecasting:

Concept:

Forecasting is the process of estimating future values or trends based on historical data and patterns. It involves making informed predictions about future outcomes, helping organizations plan and allocate resources effectively.

Example:

Imagine a utility company seeking to forecast electricity demand to optimize power generation and distribution. Using historical data on factors like weather patterns, time of day, and economic activity, a forecasting model can be developed. Time series analysis or methods like exponential smoothing may be employed to predict future electricity demand accurately. This enables the utility company to plan for peak demand periods, avoid shortages, and optimize energy production.

Time Series Forecasting:

Concept:

Time series forecasting specifically deals with predicting future values based on the temporal order of data points. This is crucial for understanding trends, seasonality, and cyclic patterns in time-ordered datasets.

Example:

In finance, time series forecasting can be applied to predict stock prices. By analyzing historical stock prices, trading volumes, and relevant economic indicators, a time series forecasting model can predict future stock prices. Techniques such as ARIMA (AutoRegressive Integrated Moving Average) or LSTM (Long Short-Term Memory) neural networks can be employed for accurate predictions. Investors and financial analysts use these forecasts to make informed decisions on buying or selling stocks.

Machine Learning for Predictive Modeling and Forecasting:
Concept:

Machine learning algorithms play a significant role in predictive modeling and forecasting. These algorithms can automatically learn patterns from data, adapt to changing conditions, and improve accuracy over time.

Example:

In healthcare, machine learning can be applied to predict disease outbreaks. By analyzing historical health data, environmental factors, and demographic information, a machine learning model can forecast the likelihood of disease outbreaks in specific regions. This information aids healthcare organizations and policymakers in allocating resources for preventive measures and timely responses.

Challenges and Considerations:
Concept:

Predictive modeling and forecasting come with challenges, including the need for high-quality data, model interpretability, and the potential impact of unforeseen events.

Example:

During the COVID-19 pandemic, traditional forecasting models faced challenges due to the unprecedented nature of the crisis. The rapid spread of the virus and the global impact required constant adjustments to forecasting models. Machine learning models, adaptable to changing conditions, played a role in predicting the trajectory of the pandemic and guiding public health responses.

Conclusion:

Predictive modeling and forecasting are invaluable tools for organizations seeking to anticipate future trends, make informed decisions, and stay ahead in dynamic environments. Whether predicting sales, optimizing resource allocation, or anticipating disease outbreaks, these techniques provide a data-driven approach to planning and decision-making. As technology advances, the integration of machine learning enhances the accuracy and adaptability of predictive models, making them indispensable in a data-driven world.

5.3 ML Applications in Corporate Decision Making:

Machine Learning Applications in Corporate Decision Making

Machine Learning (ML) has emerged as a transformative technology, offering powerful tools for data analysis and decision support in corporate environments. Leveraging ML applications in corporate decision-making processes can lead to enhanced efficiency, improved insights, and more informed strategic choices. This detailed description explores the various ways ML is applied in corporate decision making, supported by illustrative examples.

1. Demand Forecasting:
Concept:

ML algorithms can analyze historical sales data, market trends, and other relevant factors to predict future demand for products or services. This aids in optimizing inventory levels, production planning, and resource allocation.

Example:

A retail company uses ML models to forecast demand for different products based on factors like seasonal trends, promotions, and economic indicators. By accurately predicting demand, the company can optimize stock levels, reduce overstock or stockouts, and improve overall supply chain efficiency.

2. Customer Segmentation and Personalization:
Concept:

ML algorithms analyze customer data to identify patterns and preferences, enabling businesses to segment their customer base and tailor products, services, and marketing strategies to specific customer segments.

Example:

An e-commerce platform uses ML to analyze customer behavior, purchasing history, and demographics. The platform then segments customers into groups with similar characteristics. This segmentation allows for personalized marketing campaigns, product recommendations, and a more tailored customer experience.

3. Fraud Detection and Risk Management:
Concept:

ML algorithms can analyze vast amounts of transaction data to detect patterns indicative of fraudulent activities. This is crucial for financial institutions and other businesses to mitigate risks and enhance security.

Example:

A credit card company employs ML models to detect unusual spending patterns or anomalies in transaction data. If the system identifies a transaction that deviates from a customer's typical behavior, it may trigger an alert for potential fraud, prompting further investigation and preventive actions.

4. Employee Recruitment and HR Analytics:
Concept:

ML applications support the recruitment process by analyzing resumes, predicting candidate suitability, and identifying the best talent. HR analytics

using ML can also provide insights into employee retention, performance, and engagement.
Example:
A human resources department utilizes ML algorithms to screen resumes and identify candidates with the highest likelihood of success based on historical hiring data. Additionally, predictive analytics may assess factors contributing to employee turnover, enabling proactive measures to improve retention.

5. Dynamic Pricing Optimization:
Concept:
ML algorithms analyze market conditions, competitor pricing, and customer behavior to optimize pricing strategies dynamically. This ensures businesses can adjust prices in real-time to maximize revenue.
Example:
An e-commerce platform uses ML to analyze competitor prices, demand fluctuations, and customer purchasing behavior. The platform adjusts product prices dynamically, optimizing for maximum revenue based on real-time market conditions.

6. Supply Chain Management:
Concept:
ML models optimize supply chain processes by predicting demand, identifying potential disruptions, and improving overall efficiency. This leads to better inventory management, reduced costs, and enhanced responsiveness.
Example:
A manufacturing company employs ML algorithms to predict demand variations, assess supplier reliability, and optimize production schedules. By anticipating demand fluctuations and potential supply chain disruptions, the company can ensure a steady supply of materials and minimize production delays.

7. Credit Scoring and Loan Approval:
Concept:
ML algorithms assess various factors, including credit history, income, and financial behavior, to predict creditworthiness. This facilitates more accurate loan approval processes and risk assessment.
Example:
A financial institution uses ML to analyze applicants' financial histories and predict their likelihood of repaying loans. The system assigns credit scores based on comprehensive data analysis, assisting in making informed decisions regarding loan approvals and interest rates.

8. Market Research and Competitive Analysis:

Concept:

ML applications analyze market trends, customer feedback, and competitor activities to provide comprehensive market research. This helps businesses make informed decisions and stay competitive.

Example:

A marketing department uses ML algorithms to analyze social media, customer reviews, and competitor activities. The insights gained from sentiment analysis and competitive intelligence inform marketing strategies, product development, and overall corporate positioning.

Conclusion:

Machine Learning applications have become indispensable tools for corporate decision-makers seeking to navigate an increasingly complex and data-driven business environment. From forecasting demand and optimizing pricing to enhancing HR analytics and mitigating risks, ML contributes significantly to making informed, data-driven decisions. As businesses continue to embrace the power of ML, the impact on corporate decision-making processes is poised to grow, fostering innovation, efficiency, and strategic agility.

5.4 Teaching Case Study:

Teaching Case Study: Machine Learning for Business Intelligence

Introduction:

In the evolving landscape of business intelligence, organizations are increasingly leveraging Machine Learning (ML) to extract meaningful insights from vast datasets. This case study explores the integration of ML into business intelligence processes, examining its applications, challenges, and the transformative impact on decision-making.

Objectives:

(1) Understand ML Integration in Business Intelligence:
- Explore how Machine Learning is integrated into traditional Business Intelligence processes to enhance analytical capabilities.

(2) Identify ML Applications in Business Intelligence:
- Analyze specific use cases where Machine Learning algorithms contribute to improved data analysis, reporting, and decision support.

(3) Evaluate Challenges and Considerations:
- Examine challenges and considerations associated with integrating Machine Learning into Business Intelligence systems, including data quality, model interpretability, and scalability.

(4) Assess Impact on Decision-Making:
- Evaluate the impact of ML-driven Business Intelligence on strategic decision-making, resource allocation, and overall business performance.

Case Study:

Company Profile: XYZ Retailers

XYZ Retailers, a global retail giant, is known for its diverse product range and extensive customer base. To stay competitive, the company has embraced advanced technologies, including Machine Learning, to enhance its Business Intelligence capabilities.

Scenario: Enhancing Customer Segmentation

XYZ Retailers aims to improve customer segmentation to tailor marketing strategies and promotions more effectively. Traditional Business Intelligence methods have been effective, but the company is eager to explore the potential of Machine Learning in refining customer segmentation.

Implementation Steps:

(1) Data Collection:
- XYZ Retailers gathers extensive customer data, including purchase history, online behavior, demographics, and feedback.

(2) Feature Engineering:
- The data team explores feature engineering techniques to enhance the dataset, identifying relevant variables for customer segmentation.

(3) Algorithm Selection:
- Machine Learning experts decide on an algorithm for customer segmentation. Clustering algorithms like K-Means or hierarchical clustering are considered for their ability to group customers based on similarities.

(4) Model Training:
- The chosen algorithm is trained on historical data, allowing it to identify patterns and group customers into segments.

(5) Validation and Fine-Tuning:
- The model is validated using a subset of data not used in training. Fine-tuning is performed to optimize segmentation accuracy.

(6) Integration with BI Tools:
- The ML-driven customer segmentation model is integrated into the existing Business Intelligence system, ensuring seamless incorporation into decision-making processes.

Questions for Discussion:

(1) How does integrating Machine Learning into Business Intelligence differ from traditional BI approaches? Discuss the key distinctions.

(2) What are the specific advantages of employing Machine Learning for customer segmentation in the retail industry? How can it enhance marketing strategies and customer engagement?

(3) Identify potential challenges XYZ Retailers might face in implementing Machine Learning for customer segmentation. How can these challenges be mitigated?

(4) Evaluate the impact of accurate customer segmentation on XYZ Retailers' decision-making processes, marketing effectiveness, and overall business performance.

(5) Discuss the role of feature engineering in enhancing the effectiveness of Machine Learning algorithms for customer segmentation. Provide examples of relevant features for this scenario.

(6) How can XYZ Retailers ensure the interpretability of the Machine Learning model results in the context of customer segmentation? Why is interpretability crucial in business decision-making?

(7) Explore scalability considerations when integrating ML into Business Intelligence. How can XYZ Retailers ensure that the system can handle the increasing volume of customer data over time?

(8) Examine ethical considerations associated with using Machine Learning in customer segmentation. How can XYZ Retailers ensure fair and unbiased outcomes in the segmentation process?

(9) Discuss the potential resistance or concerns from employees in adapting to ML-driven Business Intelligence. How can XYZ Retailers manage change and promote a culture of data-driven decision-making?

(10) Considering the success of ML-driven customer segmentation, identify other areas within XYZ Retailers where Machine Learning could be applied to enhance Business Intelligence. Provide examples and potential benefits.

Conclusion:

Machine Learning has the potential to revolutionize Business Intelligence, providing organizations with advanced analytical capabilities to extract insights and drive strategic decision-making. Through the exploration of customer segmentation at XYZ Retailers, this case study encourages participants to critically assess the impact, challenges, and ethical considerations associated with integrating ML into BI processes.

5.5 Learning Questions:

5.5.1 Descriptive Questions:

(1) What is the fundamental concept behind supervised learning in machine learning, and how does it differ from unsupervised learning? Provide examples of each type.

(2) Can you explain the role of reinforcement learning in machine learning, and provide an example of its application in a real-world scenario?

(3) How do decision trees work in machine learning, and what tasks can they be used for? Provide an example of a decision tree application.

(4) Explain the concept of K-Nearest Neighbors (KNN) in machine learning and provide an illustrative example of its application.

(5) What is the purpose of Principal Component Analysis (PCA) in machine learning, and how does it contribute to simplifying complex datasets? Provide a practical example.

(6) In the context of machine learning, how do Random Forests differ from individual decision trees, and what advantages do they offer? Provide an example of a situation where Random Forests could be beneficial.

(7) Describe the role of Neural Networks in machine learning and provide an example of a task where they are particularly effective.

(8) What is the primary objective of Naive Bayes in machine learning, and how is it commonly applied, especially in text classification tasks? Offer a practical example.

(9) How does time series forecasting differ from general forecasting, and what techniques are commonly used in time series analysis? Provide an example of a scenario where time series forecasting is crucial.

(10) How do machine learning algorithms contribute to predictive modeling and forecasting in healthcare, particularly in predicting disease outbreaks? Provide an example of how historical data is utilized in this context.

5.5.2 Fill-up the Blanks Questions:

(1) _____ involves training an algorithm on a labeled dataset, where the input data is paired with corresponding output labels, aiming to learn a mapping function from input to output.
- Answer: Supervised Learning

(2) Unsupervised learning requires training an algorithm on _____ dataset, where the algorithm must find patterns and relationships within the data on its own.
- Answer: Unlabeled

(3) Reinforcement learning involves training an algorithm through sequences of decisions, rewarding or penalizing based on the outcomes of its actions, such as in the case of playing games like _____.
- Answer: AlphaGo

(4) Linear regression models the relationship between a dependent variable and one or more independent variables by fitting a _____.
- Answer: Linear Equation

(5) Decision trees are used for both classification and regression tasks, recursively splitting the dataset based on features to make decisions. For example, they can classify emails as spam or non-spam based on features like _____.
- Answer: Sender and Content

(6) Random Forest, as an ensemble learning method, builds multiple decision trees and merges their predictions to enhance accuracy, as seen in predicting customer churn by combining predictions from _____.
- Answer: Multiple Decision Trees

(7) SVMs classify data points by finding the hyperplane that best separates classes in a high-dimensional space, as seen in classifying handwritten digits based on their _____.
- Answer: Pixel Values

(8) KNN classifies data points based on the majority class among their k nearest neighbors in feature space, as demonstrated in predicting whether a patient has a particular disease based on the features of _____.
- Answer: Similar Patients

(9) PCA reduces the dimensionality of data while preserving essential features by identifying orthogonal axes with maximum _____.
- Answer: Variance

(10) Machine learning can be applied in healthcare to predict disease outbreaks by analyzing historical health data, environmental factors, and demographic information, enabling the forecast of the likelihood of disease outbreaks in specific _____.

- Answer: Regions

5.5.3 Multiple Choice Questions:

(1) What is Machine Learning (ML)?
    A. A subset of natural language processing
    B. A subset of artificial intelligence
    C. A type of programming language
    D. A form of data encryption
    - Answer: B. A subset of artificial intelligence

(2) In which type of learning is the algorithm trained on a labeled dataset with corresponding output labels?
    A. Unsupervised Learning
    B. Reinforcement Learning
    C. Supervised Learning
    D. Neural Network Learning
    - Answer: C. Supervised Learning

(3) Which algorithm is used for grouping customers based on purchasing behavior without predefined categories?
    A. Linear Regression
    B. K-Nearest Neighbors (KNN)
    C. K-Means Clustering
    D. Random Forest
    - Answer: C. K-Means Clustering

(4) What does Principal Component Analysis (PCA) aim to achieve?
    A. Increase dataset complexity
    B. Preserve essential features while reducing dimensionality
    C. Enhance model interpretability
    D. Optimize clustering performance
    - Answer: B. Preserve essential features while reducing dimensionality

(5) Which type of algorithm simulates the human brain using interconnected nodes (neurons) arranged in layers?
    A. Naive Bayes
    B. Decision Trees
    C. Neural Networks
    D. Support Vector Machines (SVM)
    - Answer: C. Neural Networks

(6) In which scenario might a predictive model be applied?
    A. Identifying clusters in a dataset
    B. Forecasting future outcomes based on historical data
    C. Training an algorithm for game playing
    D. Grouping customers based on purchasing behavior
    - Answer: B. Forecasting future outcomes based on historical data

(7) What does time series forecasting specifically deal with?
    A. Predicting future values based on the temporal order of data points
    B. Analyzing image classification tasks
    C. Clustering customers based on purchasing behavior

D. Detecting fraudulent activities in transactions
  - Answer: A. Predicting future values based on the temporal order of data points

(8) Which machine learning application is crucial for detecting unusual spending patterns or anomalies in transaction data?
  A. Demand Forecasting
  B. Employee Recruitment and HR Analytics
  C. Fraud Detection and Risk Management
  D. Dynamic Pricing Optimization
  - Answer: C. Fraud Detection and Risk Management

(9) What role does machine learning play in predicting disease outbreaks in healthcare?
  A. Identifying clusters in a dataset
  B. Forecasting future sales for inventory management
  C. Analyzing social media for market research
  D. Analyzing historical health data to forecast outbreak likelihood
  - Answer: D. Analyzing historical health data to forecast outbreak likelihood

(10) Which ML application is used to analyze competitor prices, demand fluctuations, and customer purchasing behavior for real-time pricing adjustments?
  A. Market Research and Competitive Analysis
  B. Credit Scoring and Loan Approval
  C. Supply Chain Management
  D. Dynamic Pricing Optimization
  - Answer: D. Dynamic Pricing Optimization

(11) What is the primary goal of ML algorithms in the context of credit scoring and loan approval?
  A. Analyzing market trends
  B. Predicting disease outbreaks
  C. Forecasting electricity demand
  D. Assessing creditworthiness based on various factors
  - Answer: D. Assessing creditworthiness based on various factors

(12) In which application does ML help businesses segment their customer base and tailor products, services, and marketing strategies?
  A. Employee Recruitment and HR Analytics
  B. Customer Segmentation and Personalization
  C. Market Research and Competitive Analysis
  D. Fraud Detection and Risk Management
  - Answer: B. Customer Segmentation and Personalization

(13) Which algorithm is commonly used for text classification tasks, such as classifying emails as spam or non-spam based on word frequencies?
  A. Decision Trees
  B. Naive Bayes
  C. Support Vector Machines (SVM)
  D. Random Forest
  - Answer: B. Naive Bayes

(14) What is the primary concept of predictive modeling?
  A. Building mathematical models for clustering
  B. Estimating future values based on historical data patterns
  C. Analyzing social media for market research
  D. Analyzing competitor prices for pricing adjustments
  - Answer: B. Estimating future values based on historical data patterns

(15) Which method is employed for predicting future electricity demand accurately in the utility company example?
   A. Time Series Forecasting
   B. K-Means Clustering
   C. Neural Networks
   D. Linear Regression
   • Answer: A. Time Series Forecasting

(16) What is a significant challenge in predictive modeling and forecasting mentioned during the COVID-19 pandemic?
   A. Lack of historical data
   B. Overemphasis on model interpretability
   C. Unprecedented events impacting forecasting models
   D. Inability to adapt to changing conditions
   • Answer: C. Unprecedented events impacting forecasting models

(17) What does ML contribute to in the context of supply chain management?
   A. Analyzing social media for market research
   B. Detecting fraudulent activities in transactions
   C. Optimizing supply chain processes by predicting demand
   D. Forecasting electricity demand for power generation
   • Answer: C. Optimizing supply chain processes by predicting demand

(18) Which application helps businesses make informed decisions and stay competitive by analyzing market trends and competitor activities?
   A. Credit Scoring and Loan Approval
   B. Demand Forecasting
   C. Market Research and Competitive Analysis
   D. Employee Recruitment and HR Analytics
   • Answer: C. Market Research and Competitive Analysis

(19) In which scenario might a company use ML to adjust product prices dynamically based on real-time market conditions?
   A. Customer Segmentation and Personalization
   B. Fraud Detection and Risk Management
   C. Dynamic Pricing Optimization
   D. Supply Chain Management
   • Answer: C. Dynamic Pricing Optimization

(20) What is the overarching impact of ML applications in corporate decision-making processes according to the conclusion?
   A. Limited impact on strategic choices
   B. Decreased efficiency in decision-making
   C. Fostering innovation, efficiency, and strategic agility
   D. Insignificant role in improving insights
   • Answer: C. Fostering innovation, efficiency, and strategic agility

****

CHAPTER 6

Big Data Analytics

Objectives of the Chapter:

The objectives encompassed in the comprehensive chapter on "Understanding Big Data and its Challenges," "Technologies for Handling Big Data," and "Leveraging Big Data for Business Insights" converge on providing a holistic understanding of the concept, challenges, and strategic utilization of Big Data in the contemporary business landscape. The initial part of the chapter aims to elucidate the characteristics and challenges associated with Big Data, emphasizing its volume, velocity, variety, and complexity. The subsequent part of the chapter on technologies delves into key frameworks such as Hadoop, Apache Spark, NoSQL databases, Apache Flink, Apache Kafka, and others, elucidating their features and applications in addressing Big Data challenges. The final part of the chapter leveraging Big Data for business insights focuses on the practical implementation of Big Data technologies in collecting, storing, processing, and analyzing data to derive actionable intelligence. The overarching goal is to equip organizations with the knowledge required to navigate the complexities of Big Data, adopt suitable technologies, and leverage data-driven insights for informed decision-making and strategic advantages in the evolving business landscape.

6.1 Understanding Big Data and its Challenges:

Understanding Big Data and its Challenges

Introduction: Big Data refers to the massive volume of structured and unstructured data that is generated at an unprecedented rate. This data comes from various sources such as social media, sensors, devices, and business transactions. The term "Big Data" is characterized by its volume, velocity, variety, and complexity. As organizations increasingly rely on data-driven decision-making, understanding Big Data and the challenges associated with it becomes crucial.

Characteristics of Big Data:

(1) Volume:
Big Data is massive in scale, often measured in petabytes or even exabytes. This sheer volume challenges traditional data processing methods.

(2) Velocity:
Data is generated and collected at an unprecedented speed. Real-time or near-real-time processing is essential for many applications, such as financial trading and monitoring social media trends.

(3) Variety:

Big Data encompasses a wide range of data types, including structured data (e.g., databases), unstructured data (e.g., text, images), and semi-structured data (e.g., JSON, XML). Managing this variety poses a significant challenge.

(4) Complexity:

The complexity of Big Data arises from its varied sources, formats, and the need for advanced analytics. Integrating and analyzing diverse data sets can be intricate.

Challenges in Managing Big Data:

(1) Storage:

Storing massive volumes of data requires scalable and cost-effective solutions. Traditional relational databases may struggle with the sheer size of Big Data, leading to the adoption of distributed file systems like Hadoop Distributed File System (HDFS).

(2) Processing:

Traditional data processing tools are often not equipped to handle the velocity and variety of Big Data. Technologies like Apache Spark and Hadoop MapReduce have emerged to enable distributed processing across clusters.

(3) Analysis:

Extracting meaningful insights from Big Data requires advanced analytics tools. Machine learning and data mining techniques are crucial for identifying patterns, trends, and correlations within vast datasets.

(4) Privacy and Security:

As the volume of data grows, so does the risk of privacy breaches and security threats. Protecting sensitive information becomes a paramount concern, and compliance with data protection regulations is essential.

(5) Integration:

Combining and integrating data from various sources can be challenging due to differences in formats, structures, and semantics. Data integration tools and approaches are required to ensure a unified view of the information.

(6) Scalability:

Big Data solutions must scale horizontally to accommodate growing data volumes. Scalability challenges can arise in terms of both hardware infrastructure and software architecture.

(7) Quality:

Ensuring the quality of Big Data is a complex task. Inaccurate or incomplete data can lead to flawed analyses and decision-making. Data cleansing and validation processes are critical to maintaining data quality.

(8) Cost Management:

Managing the infrastructure, storage, and processing resources for Big Data can be expensive. Organizations need to balance the benefits of insights gained from Big Data with the associated costs.

Conclusion:

Understanding and effectively managing Big Data is essential for organizations seeking to harness the power of data-driven insights. Overcoming the challenges associated with Big Data involves adopting appropriate technologies, implementing robust security measures, and ensuring that data processes align with organizational goals. As technology continues to evolve, addressing these challenges will become increasingly vital for organizations looking to gain a competitive edge in today's data-driven world.

6.2 Technologies for Handling Big Data:

Technologies for Handling Big Data

The effective handling of Big Data requires a suite of technologies that can manage the volume, velocity, variety, and complexity of large datasets. Several technologies have emerged to address the challenges associated with Big Data processing, storage, and analysis. Here, we will explore some key technologies along with examples of their implementation:

(1) Hadoop:

Overview: Apache Hadoop is an open-source framework designed for distributed storage and processing of large datasets across clusters of computers.

Key Features:

- Hadoop Distributed File System (HDFS): Provides scalable and distributed storage for Big Data.
- MapReduce: A programming model for processing and generating large datasets in parallel.

Example: Many organizations, including Yahoo, Facebook, and eBay, use Hadoop for processing and analyzing vast amounts of data.

(2) Apache Spark:

Overview: Apache Spark is an open-source, in-memory data processing engine that supports both batch and real-time processing.

Key Features:

- In-memory processing: Enables faster data processing by caching intermediate results in memory.
- Spark SQL, MLlib, GraphX: Additional libraries for SQL-based querying, machine learning, and graph processing.

Example: Spark is widely used in various industries for tasks like data analytics, machine learning, and graph processing. Companies like Netflix and IBM leverage Spark for large-scale data processing.

(3) NoSQL Databases:

Overview: NoSQL databases are a class of databases that provide flexible and scalable storage options for unstructured and semi-structured data.

Key Types:

- Document-oriented (e.g., MongoDB)

- Key-value stores (e.g., Cassandra)
- Column-family stores (e.g., HBase)
- Graph databases (e.g., Neo4j)

Example: MongoDB is commonly used for storing and retrieving large volumes of unstructured data, while Cassandra is favored for its distributed and highly scalable nature.

(4) Apache Flink:

Overview: Apache Flink is an open-source stream processing framework designed for real-time analytics and event-driven applications.

Key Features:

- Event time processing: Supports accurate processing of events based on their timestamps.
- Stateful processing: Enables the retention of state across events for complex analysis.

Example: Flink is used in applications where real-time processing is crucial, such as fraud detection, monitoring IoT devices, and analyzing social media streams.

(5) Apache Kafka:

Overview: Apache Kafka is a distributed streaming platform that facilitates the building of real-time data pipelines and streaming applications.

Key Features:

- Publish-subscribe model: Allows multiple producers and consumers to exchange data.
- Fault tolerance and scalability: Ensures data availability and scalability across clusters.

Example: Kafka is widely used for log aggregation, event streaming, and building data pipelines. Companies like LinkedIn and Airbnb use Kafka for handling large volumes of streaming data.

(6) Apache Storm:

Overview: Apache Storm is an open-source, real-time stream processing system for processing large volumes of data in a distributed and fault-tolerant manner.

Key Features:

- Spout and Bolt architecture: Facilitates the creation of data processing topologies.
- Scalability: Can scale horizontally to handle increasing data loads.

Example: Storm is employed in scenarios requiring low-latency data processing, such as real-time analytics and monitoring in industries like finance and telecommunications.

(7) Data Warehousing Solutions:

Overview: Data warehousing solutions provide a centralized repository for storing and managing large volumes of structured data.

Example: Amazon Redshift, Google BigQuery, and Snowflake are cloud-based data warehousing solutions that enable organizations to run complex queries on large datasets. They are suitable for business intelligence and analytics applications.

(8) Machine Learning Frameworks:

Overview: Machine learning frameworks enable the development and deployment of machine learning models on large datasets.

Example: TensorFlow and Apache Mahout are popular frameworks used for machine learning on Big Data. These frameworks facilitate the creation of predictive models, recommendation systems, and other advanced analytics.

Conclusion: The technologies mentioned above represent a subset of the rich ecosystem developed to handle Big Data efficiently. As the field continues to evolve, new technologies and enhancements to existing ones will play a crucial role in meeting the growing demands of organizations dealing with large and complex datasets. Depending on the specific requirements, organizations can choose and integrate these technologies to build robust and scalable Big Data solutions tailored to their needs.

6.3 Leveraging Big Data for Business Insights:

Leveraging Big Data for Business Insights:

In the modern business landscape, data has become a valuable asset, and the ability to extract meaningful insights from large datasets, often referred to as Big Data, is a key competitive advantage. Leveraging Big Data for business insights involves collecting, processing, and analyzing vast amounts of structured and unstructured data to derive actionable intelligence. Here is a detailed exploration of how organizations can harness Big Data for valuable business insights:

(1) Data Collection and Integration:

Sources of Big Data: Organizations collect data from various sources, including customer interactions, social media, sensors, logs, and transactions. The challenge is to integrate these diverse datasets into a cohesive and unified view.

Example: Retail companies combine customer purchase data with social media sentiment analysis to understand consumer behavior and preferences.

(2) Data Storage and Management:

Data Warehousing and Big Data Platforms: Storing and managing large volumes of data requires scalable solutions. Data warehouses and Big Data platforms like Hadoop, Apache Spark, and NoSQL databases provide the infrastructure for storage and processing.

Example: Cloud-based data warehouses like Amazon Redshift and Google BigQuery allow organizations to scale their storage and processing capabilities dynamically.

(3) Data Processing and Analysis:

Advanced Analytics: Organizations employ various analytics techniques, including descriptive, diagnostic, predictive, and prescriptive analytics, to extract insights from data.

Example: Predictive analytics can help financial institutions forecast customer churn or identify potential fraudulent activities based on historical transaction data.

(4) Real-time Analytics:

Stream Processing: Real-time analytics enable organizations to respond swiftly to changing conditions. Stream processing technologies like Apache Flink and Apache Kafka process data as it is generated.

Example: E-commerce companies use real-time analytics to personalize product recommendations for online shoppers based on their browsing and purchasing behavior.

(5) Customer Insights:

Customer Segmentation: Big Data allows organizations to segment their customer base effectively, enabling targeted marketing and personalized customer experiences.

Example: Online streaming services analyze user preferences to recommend content and create personalized playlists, enhancing user satisfaction and retention.

(6) Operational Efficiency:

Supply Chain Optimization: Big Data analytics can optimize supply chain processes by analyzing data related to inventory levels, production schedules, and distribution patterns.

Example: Manufacturing companies use predictive analytics to anticipate equipment failures, reducing downtime and maintenance costs.

(7) Fraud Detection and Security:

Anomaly Detection: Big Data analytics can identify unusual patterns or behaviors that may indicate fraudulent activities or security threats.

Example: Financial institutions use machine learning algorithms to detect unusual spending patterns and flag potentially fraudulent transactions in real-time.

(8) Market and Competitive Analysis:

Sentiment Analysis: Organizations analyze social media and customer feedback to gauge market sentiment and understand how their brand is perceived.

Example: Retailers monitor social media platforms to assess customer opinions on new product releases and make data-driven decisions on marketing strategies.

(9) Business Intelligence Platforms:

Data Visualization: Business Intelligence (BI) platforms help visualize complex data sets, making it easier for decision-makers to understand trends and patterns.

Example: Tableau and Power BI enable organizations to create interactive dashboards and reports for better decision-making.

(10) Continuous Improvement:
Feedback Loops: Establishing feedback loops based on analytics results allows organizations to continuously improve their processes and strategies.
Example: Online retailers use A/B testing and customer feedback to refine website designs, product offerings, and marketing campaigns.

Conclusion: Leveraging Big Data for business insights is not just about collecting and processing data; it's about transforming raw information into actionable intelligence that drives strategic decision-making. As technology advances and organizations continue to refine their data analytics strategies, the potential for deriving valuable insights from Big Data will only grow, enabling businesses to stay competitive and innovative in their respective industries.

6.4 Teaching Case Study:

6.4.1 Case Study:

Teaching Case Study: Understanding Big Data and its Challenges
Introduction: The case study revolves around a fictional company, TechSolutions Inc., a medium-sized technology firm that has recently recognized the importance of leveraging Big Data for business growth. The company is keen on understanding Big Data and its challenges to make informed decisions and stay competitive in the industry.
Case Background: TechSolutions Inc. operates in the software development sector, providing custom solutions to a diverse range of clients. The company's leadership has decided to invest in Big Data analytics to enhance its decision-making processes, improve customer experiences, and gain a competitive edge in the market.
Objectives:
(1) To understand the concept of Big Data and its relevance to business operations.
(2) To identify the key characteristics of Big Data and their impact on data management.
(3) To recognize the challenges associated with handling and processing Big Data.
(4) To explore potential solutions and strategies for overcoming Big Data challenges.
Detailed Description:

(1) To understand the concept of Big Data and its relevance to business operations.
Concept of Big Data and Its Relevance to Business Operations
Definition of Big Data: Big Data refers to extremely large and complex datasets that cannot be easily managed, processed, or analyzed using traditional data processing tools. This data comes from a myriad of sources, including but not limited to, business transactions, social media interactions, sensors, devices, and other digital sources. The term "Big Data" is characterized by its three Vs: Volume, Velocity, and Variety.
(1) Volume:
Significance: Big Data involves massive amounts of data. This could be terabytes, petabytes, or even exabytes of information generated by organizations, individuals, and machines.
Relevance to Business Operations: The volume of data enables businesses to gain insights from a vast pool of information, helping in more accurate decision-making and trend analysis.

(2) Velocity:

Significance: Velocity refers to the speed at which data is generated, collected, and processed. In many cases, real-time or near-real-time processing is required.

Relevance to Business Operations: Swift data processing allows businesses to respond quickly to changing conditions, making timely decisions that can impact operational efficiency and customer satisfaction.

(3) Variety:

Significance: Variety reflects the diverse types of data – structured, unstructured, and semi-structured – that Big Data encompasses.

Relevance to Business Operations: Handling various data types allows businesses to gain a more comprehensive understanding of their operations, customers, and market trends.

(2) Relevance to Business Operations:

(1) Data-Driven Decision Making:

How it Works: Big Data analytics enables organizations to analyze large datasets to identify patterns, trends, and correlations.

Business Impact: Informed decision-making based on data insights leads to improved strategies, enhanced operational efficiency, and better overall performance.

(2) Customer Insights:

How it Works: Big Data allows businesses to analyze customer behavior, preferences, and feedback.

Business Impact: Companies can tailor their products, services, and marketing strategies to meet customer expectations, leading to increased customer satisfaction and loyalty.

(3) Operational Efficiency:

How it Works: Big Data analytics optimizes internal processes by identifying inefficiencies and areas for improvement.

Business Impact: Streamlined operations result in cost savings, improved resource allocation, and increased productivity.

(4) Competitive Advantage:

How it Works: Businesses leveraging Big Data gain a competitive edge by staying agile, innovative, and responsive to market changes.

Business Impact: The ability to adapt quickly to market trends and customer needs allows companies to outperform competitors and maintain a strong market position.

(5) Innovation and Product Development:

How it Works: Big Data facilitates research and development by providing insights into market demands and emerging trends.

Business Impact: Companies can innovate and develop new products/services that align with market demands, ensuring sustained growth and relevance.

(6) Risk Management:

How it Works: Big Data analytics can identify potential risks and threats to the business, including fraud detection and cybersecurity.

Business Impact: Proactive risk management minimizes losses, protects the brand reputation, and enhances overall resilience.

(7) Supply Chain Optimization:

How it Works: Big Data enables better visibility and optimization of the supply chain by analyzing data related to inventory, logistics, and demand forecasting.

Business Impact: Enhanced supply chain management leads to cost reductions, faster deliveries, and improved customer satisfaction.

In conclusion, the concept of Big Data is instrumental in transforming business operations across industries. By leveraging the vast amount of data available, organizations can make informed decisions, gain a competitive advantage, and achieve higher levels of efficiency and innovation in their operations. As technology continues to advance, the relevance of Big Data in business operations will only continue to grow.

(3) To identify the key characteristics of Big Data and their impact on data management:

Key Characteristics of Big Data and Their Impact on Data Management:

(1) Volume:

Characteristics: Refers to the sheer size of the data generated, often in petabytes or exabytes.

Impact on Data Management: Traditional databases may struggle with the scale, necessitating scalable storage solutions like distributed file systems (e.g., Hadoop Distributed File System) and NoSQL databases.

(2) Velocity:

Characteristics: Describes the speed at which data is generated, collected, and processed, often in real-time or near-real-time.

Impact on Data Management: Requires fast and efficient processing tools, such as stream processing frameworks (e.g., Apache Kafka and Apache Flink), to handle and analyze data as it's generated.

(3) Variety:

Characteristics: Encompasses diverse data types, including structured, unstructured, and semi-structured data.

Impact on Data Management: Challenges traditional relational databases; organizations adopt flexible NoSQL databases (e.g., MongoDB, Cassandra) and data lakes to accommodate various data formats.

(4) Veracity:

Characteristics: Refers to the reliability and trustworthiness of the data.

Impact on Data Management: Organizations need robust data quality and cleansing processes to ensure accurate analysis and decision-making. Implementing data governance frameworks is crucial for maintaining data integrity.

(5) Variability:

Characteristics: Describes the inconsistency in the data flow, which can be irregular or unpredictable.

Impact on Data Management: Requires adaptive data processing techniques to handle fluctuations in data volume and ensure consistent data quality. Real-time analytics tools are essential for handling variable data streams.

(6) Value:

Characteristics: The usefulness and relevance of the data for making informed decisions.

Impact on Data Management: Emphasizes the need for organizations to identify and prioritize valuable data. Implementing advanced analytics and machine learning models helps extract meaningful insights, turning raw data into actionable intelligence.

(7) Complexity:

Characteristics: Reflects the intricacy of data due to its diverse sources, formats, and structures.

Impact on Data Management: Organizations need sophisticated data integration tools and approaches to handle the complexity of Big Data. Data cataloging and metadata management become essential for understanding and organizing complex datasets.

(8) Accessibility:

Characteristics: Describes the ease with which data can be accessed and utilized by different stakeholders.

Impact on Data Management: Requires implementing secure and efficient data access controls to ensure that authorized users can access the necessary data while maintaining data privacy and security.

(9) Agility:

Characteristics: Reflects the ability to adapt quickly to changes in data requirements and business needs.

Impact on Data Management: Organizations must adopt agile data management practices, enabling them to respond swiftly to evolving business conditions and incorporate new data sources or analytics tools.

(10) Security:

Characteristics: Involves protecting data from unauthorized access, breaches, and ensuring compliance with data protection regulations.

Impact on Data Management: Organizations must prioritize data security measures, including encryption, access controls, and regular security audits, to safeguard sensitive information in Big Data environments.

In conclusion, the key characteristics of Big Data pose both challenges and opportunities for data management. Organizations that effectively manage these characteristics can harness the power of Big Data to make informed decisions, drive innovation, and gain a competitive edge in today's data-driven business landscape.

(4) To recognize the challenges associated with handling and processing Big Data.

Handling and processing Big Data pose numerous challenges due to the unique characteristics of large and complex datasets. These challenges can impact various aspects of data management and analytics. Here are some key challenges associated with handling and processing Big Data:

(1) Volume Overload:

Challenge: Managing and storing massive amounts of data generated at unprecedented scales.

Impact: Traditional databases may struggle with the sheer volume, requiring the adoption of scalable storage solutions like distributed file systems (e.g., Hadoop Distributed File System) and cloud-based storage.

(2) Velocity of Data Streams:

Challenge: Processing data in real-time or near-real-time as it is generated.

Impact: Requires specialized stream processing frameworks (e.g., Apache Kafka, Apache Flink) to handle continuous data streams, ensuring timely analysis and decision-making.

(3) Variety of Data Types:

Challenge: Handling diverse data types, including structured, unstructured, and semi-structured data.

Impact: Traditional relational databases may not accommodate the variety of data, leading to the adoption of flexible NoSQL databases, data lakes, and advanced data integration techniques.

(4) Veracity and Data Quality:

Challenge: Ensuring the accuracy, reliability, and trustworthiness of the data.

Impact: Organizations need robust data quality assurance processes, including data cleansing, validation, and governance, to maintain the integrity of the data used for analysis.

(5) Variability in Data Flows:

Challenge: Managing fluctuations and inconsistencies in the volume and format of data.

Impact: Requires adaptive data processing techniques and real-time analytics tools to handle variable data flows effectively and maintain consistent data quality.

(6) Complexity of Data Integration:

Challenge: Integrating data from diverse sources with different formats, structures, and semantics.

Impact: Organizations need sophisticated data integration tools, data cataloging, and metadata management to create a unified view of data for analysis.

(7) Cost Management:

Challenge: Balancing the costs associated with storing, processing, and analyzing large volumes of data.

Impact: Organizations must optimize infrastructure costs, considering factors like storage, processing power, and data transfer, to ensure cost-effective Big Data solutions.

(8) Security and Privacy Concerns:

Challenge: Protecting sensitive data from unauthorized access, breaches, and ensuring compliance with data protection regulations.

Impact: Organizations need robust security measures, including encryption, access controls, and regular security audits, to mitigate the risks associated with handling and processing sensitive information.

(9) Lack of Skilled Personnel:

Challenge: Shortage of skilled professionals with expertise in Big Data technologies and analytics.

Impact: Organizations may face challenges in implementing and maintaining Big Data solutions due to a lack of qualified personnel. Training programs and recruitment efforts may be required to address this gap.

(10) Interoperability and Standardization:

Challenge: Ensuring interoperability between different Big Data tools and platforms and establishing industry-wide standards.

Impact: Lack of standardization can lead to compatibility issues and hinder seamless integration between different components of a Big Data ecosystem.

(11) Ethical and Legal Considerations:

Challenge: Addressing ethical concerns related to data collection, usage, and ensuring compliance with privacy regulations.

Impact: Organizations must navigate complex legal landscapes and establish ethical guidelines to build trust with users and avoid legal repercussions.

Effectively addressing these challenges requires a comprehensive strategy that involves a combination of technological solutions, organizational policies, and skilled personnel. As the field of Big Data continues to evolve, ongoing efforts are crucial to overcome these challenges and unlock the full potential of large-scale data analytics.

(5) To explore potential solutions and strategies for overcoming Big Data challenges.

Overcoming Big Data challenges requires a holistic approach that involves a combination of technological solutions, strategic planning, and organizational readiness. Here are potential solutions and strategies for addressing key challenges associated with handling and processing Big Data:

(1) Scalable Infrastructure:

Solution: Adopt scalable and distributed storage and processing solutions.

Strategy: Utilize cloud-based platforms such as Amazon Web Services (AWS), Microsoft Azure, or Google Cloud to dynamically scale infrastructure based on data requirements.

(2) Real-time Processing:

Solution: Implement stream processing frameworks.

Strategy: Use technologies like Apache Kafka and Apache Flink to process and analyze data in real-time, ensuring timely insights and decision-making.

(3) Flexible Data Storage:

Solution: Embrace NoSQL databases and data lakes.

Strategy: Use databases like MongoDB, Cassandra, or HBase for handling diverse data types and store unstructured data in data lakes for flexible analysis.

(4) Data Quality Assurance:

Solution: Implement robust data quality processes.

Strategy: Conduct regular data cleansing, validation, and governance activities to ensure accurate, reliable, and trustworthy data.

(5) Adaptive Data Processing:

Solution: Utilize adaptive data processing techniques.

Strategy: Implement solutions that can dynamically adjust to changes in data flows, ensuring consistency and reliability even in the face of variable data volumes.

(6) Advanced Data Integration:

Solution: Use sophisticated data integration tools.

Strategy: Deploy tools like Apache NiFi or Talend to integrate data seamlessly from various sources, creating a unified and coherent view for analysis.

(7) Cost Optimization:

Solution: Optimize infrastructure costs.

Strategy: Leverage serverless computing, pay-as-you-go cloud services, and resource optimization techniques to manage costs effectively while ensuring performance.

(8) Security Measures:

Solution: Implement comprehensive security protocols.

Strategy: Employ encryption, access controls, and regular security audits to safeguard data. Ensure compliance with data protection regulations such as GDPR or HIPAA.

(9) Skills Development:

Solution: Invest in training programs and recruitment efforts.

Strategy: Provide training for existing staff or hire professionals with expertise in Big Data technologies and analytics to bridge the skills gap within the organization.

(10) Interoperability and Standardization:

Solution: Promote interoperability and standardization.

Strategy: Encourage the adoption of industry-wide standards and use tools that support open-source and widely accepted protocols to enhance interoperability between different components of the Big Data ecosystem.

(11) Ethical and Legal Frameworks:

Solution: Develop ethical guidelines and adhere to legal standards.

Strategy: Establish clear policies for ethical data collection and usage. Stay informed about and comply with privacy regulations, and ensure transparency with users regarding data practices.

(12) Collaboration and Knowledge Sharing:

Solution: Foster collaboration within the organization and industry.

Strategy: Encourage cross-functional collaboration among data scientists, analysts, and IT professionals. Participate in industry forums and share best practices to stay updated on emerging solutions.

(13) Continuous Monitoring and Improvement:

Solution: Establish a monitoring and improvement framework.

Strategy: Implement tools for continuous monitoring of data processes and performance. Regularly review and refine strategies based on evolving business needs and technological advancements.

By adopting a comprehensive approach that incorporates these solutions and strategies, organizations can navigate the challenges posed by Big Data effectively. It's essential to align these efforts with specific business goals, foster a data-driven culture, and remain agile in response to evolving technological landscapes.

Case Analysis Questions:

(1) How can the adoption of Big Data benefit Tech Innovations Ltd. in terms of operational efficiency and customer satisfaction?

(2) Assess the potential risks associated with integrating Big Data solutions into Tech Innovations Ltd.'s existing infrastructure.

(3) Prioritize the challenges identified in the case, providing reasons for your prioritization.

(4) What strategies would you recommend for Tech Innovations Ltd. to overcome the challenges associated with handling Big Data?

(5) How can the company ensure ethical practices in collecting, processing, and analyzing Big Data?

(6) Discuss the role of real-time analytics in enhancing decision-making for Tech Innovations Ltd.

(7) Evaluate the long-term impact of leveraging Big Data on Tech Innovations Ltd.'s market position and innovation capabilities.

6.5 Learning Questions:

6.5.1 Descriptive Questions:

(1) What are the four characteristics that define Big Data, according to the provided information?

(2) How does the velocity of data in Big Data pose challenges, and why is real-time processing essential for certain applications?

(3) Explain the challenge associated with the variety of Big Data. How does it impact data management?

(4) In the context of managing Big Data, why might traditional relational databases struggle with storage, and what alternative solution is mentioned?

(5) Why is privacy and security highlighted as a significant challenge in managing Big Data? How can organizations address these concerns?

(6) Describe the importance of scalability in Big Data solutions. What challenges may arise in terms of hardware infrastructure and software architecture?

(7) What role does advanced analytics play in overcoming the challenge of analysis in Big Data? Provide examples of techniques mentioned.

(8) How does the quality of Big Data impact decision-making? What processes are critical for maintaining data quality?

(9) Elaborate on the cost management challenge associated with Big Data. How can organizations balance the benefits with the associated costs?

(10) In the section on Technologies for Handling Big Data, provide an overview of Apache Hadoop and its key features. Offer an example of its implementation by organizations.

6.5.2 Fill-up the Blanks Questions:

(1) Big Data is characterized by its volume, velocity, variety, and _____.
Answer: Complexity

(2) Traditional relational databases may struggle with the sheer size of Big Data, leading to the adoption of distributed file systems like _____.
Answer: Hadoop Distributed File System (HDFS)

(3) Apache Spark is an open-source, in-memory data processing engine that supports both batch and _____ processing.
Answer: Real-time

(4) NoSQL databases provide flexible and scalable storage options for unstructured and semi-structured data, including types like document-oriented (e.g., _____).
Answer: MongoDB

(5) Apache Flink is an open-source stream processing framework designed for real-time analytics and event-driven applications, supporting accurate processing of events based on their _____.
Answer: Timestamps

(6) Apache Kafka is a distributed streaming platform that facilitates the building of real-time data pipelines and streaming applications using a publish-subscribe model for exchanging data and ensuring fault tolerance and scalability across _____.
Answer: Clusters

(7) Data warehousing solutions provide a centralized repository for storing and managing large volumes of structured data, and examples include Amazon Redshift, Google BigQuery, and _____.
Answer: Snowflake

(8) Machine learning frameworks like TensorFlow and Apache Mahout facilitate the creation of predictive models, recommendation systems, and other advanced analytics on large _____.
Answer: Datasets

(9) Retail companies combine customer purchase data with social media sentiment analysis to understand consumer behaviour and preferences through effective _____.
Answer: Integration

(10) Establishing feedback loops based on analytics results allows organizations to continuously improve their processes and strategies, as seen in practices like A/B testing and customer feedback in online _____.
Answer: Retail

6.5.3 Multiple Choice Questions:

(1) What term is used to describe the massive volume of structured and unstructured data generated at an unprecedented rate?
   A. Big Information
   B. Huge Data

C. Massive Data
D. Big Data
- Answer: D) Big Data

(2) Which characteristic of Big Data refers to the speed at which data is generated and collected, requiring real-time or near-real-time processing for applications like financial trading?
  A. Volume
  B. Velocity
  C. Variety
  D. Complexity
  - Answer: B) Velocity

(3) What poses a significant challenge in Big Data management due to the wide range of data types, including structured, unstructured, and semi-structured data?
  A. Volume
  B. Variety
  C. Velocity
  D. Complexity
  - Answer: B) Variety

(4) The complexity of Big Data arises from its varied sources, formats, and the need for advanced analytics. What is crucial for integrating and analyzing diverse data sets?
  A. Scalability
  B. Quality
  C. Processing
  D. Integration
  - Answer: D) Integration

(5) What technology provides scalable and distributed storage for Big Data in a distributed framework like Hadoop?
  A. Apache Spark
  B. NoSQL Databases
  C. Hadoop Distributed File System (HDFS)
  D. Apache Kafka
  - Answer: C) Hadoop Distributed File System (HDFS)

(6) Which open-source, in-memory data processing engine supports both batch and real-time processing, with additional libraries for SQL-based querying, machine learning, and graph processing?
  A. Apache Flink
  B. Apache Kafka
  C. Apache Spark
  D. Apache Storm
  - Answer: C) Apache Spark

(7) What type of databases provide flexible and scalable storage options for unstructured and semi-structured data, with examples like MongoDB and Cassandra?
  A. Relational Databases

B. NoSQL Databases
C. Column-family Stores
D. Graph Databases
- Answer: B) NoSQL Databases

(8) Which technology is designed for real-time analytics and event-driven applications, supporting accurate processing of events based on their timestamps?
A. Apache Kafka
B. Apache Flink
C. Apache Storm
D. Apache Spark
- Answer: B) Apache Flink

(9) What distributed streaming platform facilitates the building of real-time data pipelines and streaming applications, ensuring fault tolerance and scalability across clusters?
A. Apache Kafka
B. Apache Storm
C. Apache Flink
D. Hadoop Distributed File System (HDFS)
- Answer: A) Apache Kafka

(10) Which cloud-based data warehousing solutions enable organizations to run complex queries on large datasets and are suitable for business intelligence and analytics applications?
A. Amazon Redshift
B. Google BigQuery
C. Snowflake
D. All of the above
- Answer: D) All of the above

(11) What popular machine learning framework is used for machine learning on Big Data, facilitating the creation of predictive models and recommendation systems?
A. TensorFlow
B. Apache Mahout
C. Spark SQL
D. Hadoop MapReduce
- Answer: A) TensorFlow

(12) What involves the collection and integration of data from various sources, including customer interactions, social media, sensors, logs, and transactions?
A. Advanced Analytics
B. Customer Insights
C. Data Processing
D. Data Collection and Integration
- Answer: D) Data Collection and Integration

(13) What type of analytics enables organizations to respond swiftly to changing conditions by processing data as it is generated?
A. Predictive Analytics
B. Real-time Analytics

C. Descriptive Analytics
D. Diagnostic Analytics
- Answer: B) Real-time Analytics

(14) How do organizations use Big Data to optimize supply chain processes by analyzing data related to inventory levels, production schedules, and distribution patterns?
   A. Customer Segmentation
   B. Fraud Detection
   C. Supply Chain Optimization
   D. Sentiment Analysis
   - Answer: C) Supply Chain Optimization

(15) What can identify unusual patterns or behaviors in data that may indicate fraudulent activities or security threats?
   A. Anomaly Detection
   B. Customer Segmentation
   C. Sentiment Analysis
   D. Stream Processing
   - Answer: A) Anomaly Detection

(16) Which business intelligence platforms help visualize complex data sets, making it easier for decision-makers to understand trends and patterns?
   A. Apache Kafka
   B. Tableau
   C. Apache Flink
   D. Power BI
   - Answer: D) Power BI

(17) What allows organizations to continuously improve their processes and strategies based on analytics results?
   A. A/B Testing
   B. Customer Segmentation
   C. Feedback Loops
   D. Supply Chain Optimization
   - Answer: C) Feedback Loops

(18) In which industry might real-time analytics be crucial, such as in fraud detection, monitoring IoT devices, and analyzing social media streams?
   A. Healthcare
   B. Finance
   C. Manufacturing
   D. Retail
   - Answer: B) Finance

(19) What enables organizations to personalize product recommendations for online shoppers based on their browsing and purchasing behavior?
   A. Market and Competitive Analysis
   B. Customer Insights
   C. Operational Efficiency

D. Continuous Improvement
- Answer: B) Customer Insights

(20) What is a key competitive advantage in the modern business landscape, involving the extraction of meaningful insights from large datasets?
A. Real-time Analytics
B. Big Data
C. Feedback Loops
D. Anomaly Detection
- Answer: B) Big Data

****

Data Ethics and Governance

Objectives of the Chapter:

To underscore the critical significance of ethical considerations and robust governance in the realm of Big Data analytics. The section on ethical data handling delineates various concerns, including privacy protection, bias mitigation, and trust-building, and emphasizes the need for organizations to navigate these ethical challenges responsibly. The segment on regulatory frameworks provides a comprehensive overview of key global regulations governing data handling, outlining their focuses and implications for organizations engaged in Big Data analytics. Lastly, the exploration of data governance in corporations outlines key considerations, from leadership and framework establishment to data stewardship, security, and compliance, with the ultimate goal of guiding organizations in implementing structured approaches to manage data as a valuable asset. Collectively, these objectives converge on fostering a culture of responsible and ethical data practices, ensuring compliance with regulations, and establishing robust data governance frameworks to support informed decision-making and sustainable business success.

7.1 Importance of Ethical Data Handling:

In the era of Big Data analytics, where vast amounts of data are collected, processed, and analyzed to extract insights, ethical considerations play a crucial role in ensuring responsible and fair use of information. Here are several reasons highlighting the importance of ethical data handling in the context of Big Data analytics:

(1) Privacy Protection:

Concern: Big Data often involves the collection of personal and sensitive information. Ethical data handling safeguards individuals' privacy rights.

Importance: Respecting privacy builds trust with users and customers. Organizations must ensure that data is collected and used transparently, with clear consent, and in compliance with privacy regulations.

(2) Avoiding Discrimination and Bias:

Concern: Biases in data collection and analysis can lead to discriminatory outcomes, reinforcing existing prejudices.

Importance: Ethical data handling involves recognizing and mitigating biases. It ensures fairness in decision-making, promoting inclusivity and preventing discrimination based on gender, race, or other protected characteristics.

(3) Maintaining Trust and Reputation:

Concern: Unethical data practices, such as data breaches or misuse, can severely damage an organization's reputation.

Importance: Ethical handling of data builds trust with stakeholders. Organizations that prioritize ethical considerations are more likely to retain customer loyalty and safeguard their brand reputation.

(4) Legal Compliance:

Concern: Data privacy laws and regulations, such as GDPR or HIPAA, impose legal obligations on organizations regarding the handling of personal information.

Importance: Adhering to ethical data practices ensures legal compliance, protecting organizations from legal consequences and financial penalties associated with non-compliance.

(5) Ensuring Informed Consent:

Concern: Lack of transparency in data collection practices can result in individuals unknowingly providing personal information.

Importance: Ethical data handling involves obtaining informed consent from individuals before collecting their data. This empowers individuals to make informed decisions about how their information is used.

(6) Data Security:

Concern: Inadequate data security measures can lead to data breaches, exposing sensitive information to unauthorized access.

Importance: Ethical data handling includes implementing robust security measures to protect data from unauthorized access, ensuring the confidentiality and integrity of the information.

(7) Responsible Data Use:

Concern: The potential for data misuse, such as selling or sharing data without proper consent, raises ethical concerns.

Importance: Ethical data handling involves using data responsibly and ensuring that it is used only for the purposes for which it was collected. Organizations should be transparent about how data is used and shared.

(8) Building Customer Trust:

Concern: Customers are increasingly concerned about how their data is handled and used.

Importance: Organizations that prioritize ethical data handling build trust with their customers. Trust is essential for customer retention and positive relationships, which are critical for the success of businesses.

(9) Mitigating Unintended Consequences:

Concern: Unintended consequences, such as unforeseen biases in algorithms, can arise from inadequate ethical considerations.

Importance: Ethical data handling involves continuous monitoring and evaluation to identify and address unintended consequences. It mitigates the risks of negative impacts on individuals or communities.

(10) Corporate Social Responsibility (CSR):

Concern: Organizations are increasingly expected to demonstrate corporate social responsibility.

Importance: Ethical data handling is a key aspect of CSR. Organizations that prioritize ethical considerations contribute to the well-being of society by ensuring fair and responsible use of data.

In conclusion, the importance of ethical data handling in Big Data analytics cannot be overstated. It is integral to protecting individuals' rights, ensuring fairness, building trust, and maintaining legal compliance. Ethical considerations should be an integral part of the entire data lifecycle, from collection to analysis and sharing of insights. Organizations that embrace ethical data practices not only comply with legal requirements but also contribute to a positive and responsible data-driven culture.

7.2 Regulatory Frameworks and Compliance:

The handling of Big Data comes with significant responsibilities, particularly in safeguarding privacy, ensuring data security, and adhering to ethical practices. Various regulatory frameworks and compliance standards have been established globally to govern the collection, processing, and usage of data, including Big Data. Here are some key regulatory frameworks and compliance standards that organizations need to consider in the context of Big Data handling:

(1) General Data Protection Regulation (GDPR):

Region: European Union (EU) and European Economic Area (EEA)

Focus: GDPR is one of the most comprehensive data protection regulations globally. It emphasizes the protection of individuals' privacy rights, including the right to be forgotten, data portability, and explicit consent for data processing. Organizations handling data of EU citizens must comply with GDPR.

(2) Health Insurance Portability and Accountability Act (HIPAA):

Region: United States

Focus: HIPAA is specific to the healthcare industry and regulates the handling of protected health information (PHI). It sets standards for the security and privacy of PHI and mandates safeguards to protect the confidentiality and integrity of healthcare data.

(3) California Consumer Privacy Act (CCPA):

Region: California, United States

Focus: CCPA is aimed at protecting the privacy rights of California residents. It grants individuals the right to know what personal information is being collected and how it is used, the right to opt-out of the sale of personal information, and the right to request the deletion of their data.

(4) Personal Data Protection Act (PDPA):

Region: Singapore

Focus: PDPA in Singapore governs the collection, use, and disclosure of personal data. It outlines the obligations of organizations in ensuring transparency, obtaining consent, and protecting individuals' rights regarding their personal information.

(5) Information Security Management System (ISMS) - ISO/IEC 27001:

Region: Globally recognized

Focus: ISO/IEC 27001 is an international standard for information security management. While it does not specifically target Big Data, its principles are applicable to the secure handling of information, including data protection, access controls, and risk management.

(6) Family Educational Rights and Privacy Act (FERPA):

Region: United States

Focus: FERPA protects the privacy of student education records. Educational institutions that receive federal funds must comply with FERPA, which regulates the disclosure and access to student records, ensuring the confidentiality of educational data.

(7) Payment Card Industry Data Security Standard (PCI DSS):

Region: Globally recognized, particularly in the payment industry

Focus: PCI DSS is designed to secure payment card transactions. While not specific to Big Data, its principles are relevant to organizations handling financial data and emphasize secure processing, storage, and transmission of payment card information.

(8) Gramm-Leach-Bliley Act (GLBA):

Region: United States

Focus: GLBA applies to financial institutions and regulates the handling of non-public personal information. It mandates measures to protect the privacy and security of consumer financial information.

(9) Personal Information Protection Law (PIPL):

Region: China

Focus: PIPL is China's comprehensive data protection law, aiming to regulate the processing of personal information. It includes provisions for obtaining consent, data subject rights, and restrictions on cross-border data transfers.

(10) National Data Protection Laws:

Region: Various countries have enacted or are in the process of enacting their own national data protection laws, aligning with global trends. Examples include Brazil's LGPD (Lei Geral de Proteção de Dados) and India's Personal Data Protection Bill.

Compliance Challenges and Best Practices:

(1) Understanding Applicability: Organizations must carefully assess which regulatory frameworks apply to their operations based on factors such as the nature of data, the geographic location of data subjects, and industry-specific regulations.

(2) Data Mapping and Classification: Conducting thorough data mapping exercises helps identify the types of data collected, processed, and stored. Classifying data based on sensitivity aids in implementing appropriate security measures.

(3) Consent Management: Ensuring proper consent mechanisms are in place for data collection and processing activities is essential. Organizations should clearly communicate the purpose of data processing and obtain explicit consent from individuals.

(4) Data Security Measures: Implementing robust data security measures, encryption, access controls, and regular security assessments helps safeguard data integrity and prevent unauthorized access.

(5) Data Subject Rights: Establishing processes to honor data subject rights, including the right to access, rectify, or delete personal information, is crucial for compliance.

(6) Documentation and Record-keeping: Maintaining comprehensive records of data processing activities, risk assessments, and compliance efforts is essential for demonstrating adherence to regulatory requirements.

(7) Cross-border Data Transfers: When dealing with international data transfers, organizations should assess the adequacy of data protection in the destination country or implement mechanisms such as Standard Contractual Clauses (SCCs) or Binding Corporate Rules (BCRs).

(8) Continuous Monitoring and Compliance Audits: Regularly monitoring data handling practices, conducting compliance audits, and adapting policies to evolving regulations ensure ongoing adherence to ethical and legal standards.

In summary, compliance with regulatory frameworks is essential for organizations engaged in Big Data analytics. A proactive and comprehensive approach to data protection, privacy, and security is crucial to not only meet legal requirements but also build trust with stakeholders and foster responsible data handling practices.

7.3 Establishing Data Governance in Corporations:

Establishing Data Governance in Corporations:

Data governance is a strategic framework that defines the policies, procedures, and responsibilities for managing and ensuring the quality, availability, integrity, and security of an organization's data. Establishing robust data governance is crucial for corporations as it provides a structured approach to managing data as a valuable asset, enhances data quality, and aligns data practices with organizational objectives. Here are key considerations for establishing data governance in corporations:

(1) Leadership and Sponsorship:

Key Elements: Appointing a data governance leader, often a Chief Data Officer (CDO), and securing executive sponsorship.

Rationale: Leadership buy-in is essential to ensure that data governance is a strategic priority with the necessary resources and organizational support.

(2) Define Data Governance Framework:

Key Elements: Developing a comprehensive data governance framework that includes policies, standards, and procedures.

Rationale: A clear framework provides a common understanding of how data is managed and sets the foundation for consistent practices across the organization.

(3) Data Governance Council:

Key Elements: Establishing a cross-functional data governance council representing different business units.

Rationale: The council ensures collaboration, alignment with business goals, and representation of diverse perspectives in decision-making regarding data management.

(4) Data Stewardship:

Key Elements: Appointing data stewards responsible for data quality, integrity, and compliance within specific business areas.

Rationale: Data stewards play a critical role in implementing and enforcing data policies, ensuring data quality, and serving as advocates for data governance within their respective domains.

(5) Data Management Policies:

Key Elements: Developing and communicating clear data management policies, including data classification, ownership, access controls, and data lifecycle management.

Rationale: Policies provide guidelines for how data should be handled, ensuring consistency and alignment with regulatory requirements.

(6) Data Quality Management:

Key Elements: Implementing processes and tools for monitoring and improving data quality.

Rationale: Data quality management ensures that data is accurate, reliable, and fit for its intended purpose, supporting better decision-making and business operations.

(7) Metadata Management:

Key Elements: Establishing a metadata management program to document and catalog data assets.

Rationale: Metadata management provides insights into the context, lineage, and usage of data, aiding in data discovery, understanding, and governance.

(8) Data Security and Privacy:

Key Elements: Integrating data security and privacy measures into the data governance framework, including encryption, access controls, and compliance with relevant regulations.

Rationale: Safeguarding sensitive information is essential for maintaining trust with stakeholders and ensuring legal compliance.

(9) Data Governance Tools:

Key Elements: Implementing tools and technologies to support data governance processes, such as data cataloging, metadata management, and data quality tools.

Rationale: Tools automate and streamline governance activities, enhancing efficiency and accuracy in managing data assets.

(10) Communication and Training:

Key Elements: Developing communication plans and providing training to ensure that employees understand the importance of data governance and their roles in its implementation.

Rationale: Effective communication and training foster a culture of data awareness and responsibility across the organization.

(11) Continuous Monitoring and Improvement:

Key Elements: Establishing mechanisms for continuous monitoring of data governance practices and periodic reviews to assess effectiveness.

Rationale: Continuous improvement ensures that data governance remains aligned with evolving business needs, technological advancements, and regulatory changes.

(12) Compliance with Regulations:

Key Elements: Ensuring that data governance practices align with relevant data protection and privacy regulations, such as GDPR, HIPAA, or industry-specific requirements.

Rationale: Compliance safeguards organizations from legal consequences and builds trust by demonstrating a commitment to ethical and responsible data handling.

In conclusion, establishing data governance is a multifaceted effort that requires a combination of leadership commitment, organizational alignment, defined frameworks, and ongoing monitoring. A well-implemented data governance program not only ensures the effective management of data assets but also supports informed decision-making, enhances organizational agility, and contributes to long-term business success.

7.4 Teaching Case Study:

7.4.1 Case Study on Importance of Ethical Data Handling:

Case Study: Ethical Data Handling at GlobalHealth Solutions:

Background: GlobalHealth Solutions, a leading healthcare analytics company, has recently faced increased scrutiny regarding its data handling practices. The company processes vast amounts of sensitive patient data to provide valuable insights to healthcare providers. However, concerns have emerged about the ethical implications of its data handling processes, prompting a reassessment of the organization's approach.

Scenario: GlobalHealth Solutions has been entrusted with the responsibility of analyzing patient health records to identify trends, optimize treatments, and enhance overall healthcare outcomes. However, recent media coverage and customer inquiries have shed light on potential ethical lapses in the company's data handling practices. Stakeholders are questioning the transparency, consent mechanisms, and overall ethical framework guiding the use of patient data.

(1) Challenges:

Transparency and Consent: Stakeholders are seeking clarity on how patient data is being used, and there are concerns about the adequacy of consent mechanisms.

Data Security: There are worries about the security measures in place to protect patient data from unauthorized access, breaches, and potential misuse.

Third-party Partnerships: Questions have been raised about GlobalHealth Solutions' partnerships with external entities and how patient data is shared and utilized in collaborative initiatives.

Response: GlobalHealth Solutions acknowledges the concerns raised by stakeholders and is taking proactive steps to address the ethical considerations surrounding its data handling practices. The company is committed to enhancing transparency, fortifying data security measures, and reassessing its partnerships to ensure ethical and responsible data use.

(2) Key Actions:

(i) Enhanced Transparency: GlobalHealth Solutions is revamping its communication strategy to provide stakeholders with clearer insights into how patient data is utilized. This includes transparently outlining the purposes of data usage and the safeguards in place.

(ii) Revised Consent Mechanisms: The company is updating its consent processes to ensure that patients have a better understanding of how their data will be used and have the ability to make informed decisions regarding data sharing.

(iii) Data Security Measures: GlobalHealth Solutions is investing in advanced data security technologies and training programs to fortify its defenses against potential breaches. Regular security audits and assessments will be conducted to ensure compliance with industry best practices.

(iv) Ethics Training: The company is implementing an ethics training program for all employees to instill a culture of responsible data handling. This includes educating staff about the ethical implications of their work and the importance of prioritizing patient privacy.

(3) Conclusion:

GlobalHealth Solutions recognizes the paramount importance of ethical data handling in the healthcare sector. By addressing concerns related to transparency, consent, data security, and partnerships, the company aims to rebuild trust with stakeholders and reaffirm its commitment to the ethical use of patient data. The case demonstrates the evolving landscape of ethical considerations in data handling and the proactive measures organizations must take to align with the highest ethical standards in the industry.

7.4.2 Case Study on Regulatory Frameworks and Compliance:

Case Study: Navigating Regulatory Compliance in Big Data at TechInnovate Corp
Background:
TechInnovate Corp, a multinational technology company, is at the forefront of harnessing Big Data to drive innovation in its products and services. With an increasing reliance on large datasets, the company faces the challenge of navigating complex regulatory frameworks and ensuring compliance in its Big Data initiatives.
Scenario:

TechInnovate Corp has expanded its operations globally, collecting and analyzing vast amounts of data to enhance customer experiences and develop cutting-edge technologies. However, recent developments in data protection and privacy regulations have raised concerns within the company about potential non-compliance risks. There is a growing realization that aligning Big Data practices with regulatory requirements is crucial to maintaining trust and sustaining business growth.

Challenges:

(i) Global Data Protection Laws: TechInnovate Corp operates in multiple countries, each with its own set of data protection laws and regulations. Navigating the diverse landscape poses challenges in ensuring uniform compliance across all jurisdictions.

(ii) Data Security Standards: With the increasing sophistication of cyber threats, ensuring robust data security measures is paramount. TechInnovate Corp needs to assess and enhance its data security protocols to meet evolving standards and safeguard against potential breaches.

(iii) Data Subject Rights: The emergence of data subject rights, such as the right to access, rectify, or erase personal data, requires TechInnovate Corp to establish processes for handling these requests promptly and transparently.

Response: TechInnovate Corp recognizes the importance of proactive compliance and has initiated a comprehensive response to address regulatory challenges.

Key Actions:

(i) Global Compliance Review: TechInnovate Corp is conducting a thorough review of data protection laws in each country where it operates. This includes mapping out the specific requirements, timelines, and implications for Big Data operations.

(ii) Data Security Enhancement: The company is investing in advanced data security technologies and conducting regular audits to identify vulnerabilities. This involves encrypting sensitive data, implementing access controls, and enhancing cybersecurity measures.

(iii) Data Governance Framework: TechInnovate Corp is developing a robust data governance framework that aligns with the principles of transparency, accountability, and ethical data handling. This framework includes policies for data collection, processing, and sharing.

(iv) Employee Training: Recognizing that employees play a crucial role in compliance, TechInnovate Corp is conducting training programs to educate staff on the importance of adhering to regulatory requirements. This includes guidelines on ethical data practices and handling data subject requests.

Conclusion:

In the rapidly evolving landscape of Big Data and data protection regulations, TechInnovate Corp is proactively addressing compliance challenges to ensure the ethical and responsible handling of data. The company's commitment to a global compliance review, enhanced data security measures, the establishment of a robust data governance framework, and ongoing employee training reflects its dedication to meeting regulatory standards and maintaining the trust of its customers and stakeholders. The case illustrates the complexities and importance of navigating regulatory frameworks in the context of Big Data operations.

7.4.3 Case Study on Establishing Data Governance in Corporations:

Case Study: Transforming Data Governance at GlobalTech Solutions:

Background: GlobalTech Solutions, a multinational technology corporation, is on a journey to enhance its data governance practices to align with the company's strategic objectives. The organization recognizes the critical role of effective data governance in managing data as a valuable asset and ensuring its responsible and secure use.

Scenario: GlobalTech Solutions has experienced challenges related to inconsistent data quality, lack of standardized processes, and limited visibility into its diverse data assets. These challenges have hindered the organization's ability to derive meaningful insights, make informed decisions, and comply with regulatory requirements. To address these issues, the leadership has decided to embark on a comprehensive data governance initiative.

Challenges:

(i) Inconsistent Data Quality: GlobalTech Solutions has observed variations in data quality across different business units, impacting the accuracy and reliability of analytics and reporting.

(ii) Lack of Standardized Processes: The absence of standardized data management processes has led to inefficiencies, redundancies, and difficulties in ensuring a consistent approach to data handling.

(iii) Limited Data Visibility: GlobalTech Solutions faces challenges in gaining a holistic view of its data landscape, hindering the organization's ability to leverage data assets strategically.

Response:

GlobalTech Solutions is committed to transforming its data governance practices to overcome existing challenges and harness the full potential of its data.

Key Actions:

(1) Data Quality Assessment: The organization has initiated a comprehensive assessment of data quality across different data sources and business units. This involves identifying data anomalies, inconsistencies, and areas for improvement.

(2) Standardizing Data Management Processes: GlobalTech Solutions is developing and implementing standardized processes for data collection, storage, processing, and sharing. This includes establishing clear data ownership and accountability.

(3) Data Governance Framework: The organization is in the process of developing a robust data governance framework that encompasses policies, procedures, and guidelines for effective data management. This framework is designed to align with industry best practices and regulatory requirements.

(4) Technology Integration: GlobalTech Solutions is investing in data governance tools and technologies to automate and streamline data management processes. This includes data cataloging, metadata management, and data quality monitoring tools.

Conclusion:

GlobalTech Solutions recognizes that establishing a strong data governance foundation is pivotal for unlocking the value of its data assets. The organization's commitment to addressing data quality, standardizing processes, and implementing a comprehensive data governance framework reflects its dedication to promoting responsible and effective data management. As the transformation progresses, GlobalTech Solutions anticipates improved data-driven decision-making, enhanced operational efficiency, and strengthened compliance with regulatory standards. The case exemplifies the importance of proactive data governance in the evolving landscape of data-driven enterprises.

7.5 Learning Questions:

7.5.1 Descriptive Questions:

(1) Discuss the ethical concerns related to privacy in Big Data analytics, emphasizing how ethical data handling safeguards individuals' privacy rights. How does respecting privacy

contribute to building trust with users and customers, and what measures should organizations take to ensure transparent and compliant data collection practices?

(2) Examine the potential discriminatory outcomes resulting from biases in data collection and analysis. How does ethical data handling play a role in recognizing and mitigating biases, promoting fairness in decision-making, and preventing discrimination based on gender, race, or other protected characteristics in the context of Big Data analytics?

(3) Explore the impact of unethical data practices, such as data breaches, on an organization's reputation. Discuss how ethical handling of data contributes to building trust with stakeholders and retaining customer loyalty. Provide examples of how organizations prioritizing ethical considerations can safeguard their brand reputation in the realm of Big Data analytics.

(4) Explain the legal obligations imposed by data privacy laws like GDPR and HIPAA on organizations regarding the handling of personal information. How does adhering to ethical data practices ensure legal compliance, and what potential legal consequences and financial penalties are associated with non-compliance in the context of Big Data analytics?

(5) Discuss the concern of lack of transparency in data collection practices and its potential impact on individuals unknowingly providing personal information. How does ethical data handling involve obtaining informed consent from individuals, empowering them to make informed decisions about their data usage?

(6) Explore the importance of data security in ethical data handling, particularly in preventing data breaches and unauthorized access. How does ethical data handling include implementing robust security measures to protect data confidentiality and integrity, and what are the implications of inadequate data security in the era of Big Data analytics?

(7) Discuss the ethical concerns associated with the potential misuse of data, such as selling or sharing without proper consent. How does ethical data handling ensure responsible data use, and why is transparency about how data is used and shared crucial for organizations in the context of Big Data analytics?

(8) Examine the increasing concern among customers about how their data is handled and used. How do organizations that prioritize ethical data handling build trust with their customers? Discuss the role of trust in customer retention and positive relationships, emphasizing its critical importance for the success of businesses in the context of Big Data analytics.

(9) Explore the risks of unintended consequences, such as unforeseen biases in algorithms, resulting from inadequate ethical considerations. How does ethical data handling involve continuous monitoring and evaluation to identify and address unintended consequences, mitigating the potential negative impacts on individuals or communities in the era of Big Data analytics?

(10) Discuss the role of ethical data handling as a key aspect of Corporate Social Responsibility (CSR). How do organizations that prioritize ethical considerations contribute to the well-being of society by ensuring fair and responsible use of data? Highlight the

broader implications of ethical data handling beyond legal compliance in the context of Big Data analytics.

7.5.2 Fill-up the Blanks Questions:

(1) Big Data often involves the collection of _____ and sensitive information. Ethical data handling safeguards individuals' privacy rights.
- Answer: Personal

(2) Importance: Respecting privacy builds trust with users and customers. Organizations must ensure that data is collected and used transparently, with clear _____, and in compliance with privacy regulations.
- Answer: Consent

(3) Concern: Biases in data collection and analysis can lead to discriminatory outcomes, reinforcing existing _____.
- Answer: Prejudices

(4) Importance: Ethical handling of data builds trust with stakeholders. Organizations that prioritize ethical considerations are more likely to retain customer loyalty and safeguard their _____.
- Answer: Brand Reputation

(5) Concern: Lack of transparency in data collection practices can result in individuals unknowingly providing _____ information.
- Answer: Personal

(6) Importance: Ethical data handling involves obtaining informed consent from individuals before collecting their data. This empowers individuals to make informed decisions about how their information is _____.
- Answer: Used

(7) Concern: Inadequate data security measures can lead to data breaches, exposing sensitive information to _____ access.
- Answer: Unauthorized

(8) Importance: Ethical data handling involves using data responsibly and ensuring that it is used only for the _____ for which it was collected.
- Answer: Purposes

(9) Concern: Customers are increasingly concerned about how their data is handled and used. Organizations that prioritize ethical data handling build _____ with their customers.
- Answer: Trust

(10) Importance: Ethical data handling involves continuous monitoring and evaluation to identify and address _____ consequences. It mitigates the risks of negative impacts on individuals or communities.
- Answer: Unintended

7.5.3 Multiple Choice Questions:

(1) What is the primary concern addressed in the context of Privacy Protection in Big Data analytics?
   A. Financial risks
   B. Collection of personal and sensitive information
   C. Data security measures
   D. Informed consent
- Answer: b. Collection of personal and sensitive information

(2) Why is obtaining clear consent important in ethical data handling?
   A. It speeds up data processing
   B. It ensures legal compliance
   C. It promotes data breaches
   D. It reinforces biases
   - Answer: b. It ensures legal compliance

(3) What potential outcome is associated with biases in data collection and analysis, according to ethical considerations?
   A. Enhanced decision-making
   B. Discriminatory outcomes
   C. Privacy protection
   D. Financial penalties
   - Answer: b. Discriminatory outcomes

(4) What does ethical handling of data contribute to in terms of an organization's reputation?
   A. Increased data breaches
   B. Legal consequences
   C. Trust with stakeholders
   D. Unintended consequences
   - Answer: c. Trust with stakeholders

(5) Which legal obligation is imposed by data privacy laws such as GDPR or HIPAA?
   A. Data breaches
   B. Building customer trust
   C. Ethical data handling
   D. Handling personal information responsibly
   - Answer: d. Handling personal information responsibly

(6) What is the concern associated with lack of transparency in data collection practices?
   A. Building customer trust
   B. Legal compliance
   C. Unintended consequences
   D. Unknowingly providing personal information
   - Answer: d. Unknowingly providing personal information

(7) What does ethical data handling involve in the context of data security?
   A. Promoting data misuse
   B. Implementing robust security measures
   C. Selling or sharing data without consent
   D. Trust with customers
   - Answer: b. Implementing robust security measures

(8) What does responsible data use entail in ethical data handling?
   A. Unethical data practices
   B. Selling or sharing data without consent
   C. Using data only for intended purposes
   D. Avoiding discrimination and bias

- Answer: c. Using data only for intended purposes

(9) What is the primary concern of customers regarding their data in the context of ethical data handling?
   A. Building customer trust
   B. Legal consequences
   C. How data is handled and used
   D. Mitigating unintended consequences
   - Answer: c. How data is handled and used

(10) What is the importance of mitigating unintended consequences in ethical data handling?
   A. Promoting data breaches
   B. Financial penalties
   C. Continuous monitoring and evaluation
   D. Unforeseen biases in algorithms
   - Answer: d. Unforeseen biases in algorithms

(11) In the context of Corporate Social Responsibility (CSR), what does ethical data handling contribute to?
   A. Financial risks
   B. Positive and responsible use of data
   C. Selling or sharing data without consent
   D. Unintended consequences
   - Answer: b. Positive and responsible use of data

(12) Which region does the General Data Protection Regulation (GDPR) primarily focus on?
   A. United States
   B. Singapore
   C. European Union (EU) and European Economic Area (EEA)
   D. China
   - Answer: c. European Union (EU) and European Economic Area (EEA)

(13) What industry does the Health Insurance Portability and Accountability Act (HIPAA) specifically regulate?
   A. Financial institutions
   B. Education
   C. Healthcare
   D. Payment industry
   - Answer: c. Healthcare

(14) Which U.S. state is covered by the California Consumer Privacy Act (CCPA)?
   A. New York
   B. Texas
   C. California
   D. Florida
   - Answer: c. California

(15) What does the Personal Data Protection Act (PDPA) in Singapore govern?
   A. Financial data

B. Personal data
C. Payment card transactions
D. Student education records
- Answer: b. Personal data

(16) Which globally recognized standard focuses on information security management and is applicable to the secure handling of information, including data protection and access controls?
   A. ISO/IEC 27001
   B. HIPAA
   C. CCPA
   D. GLBA
   - Answer: a. ISO/IEC 27001

(17) What does the Family Educational Rights and Privacy Act (FERPA) protect in the United States?
   A. Personal data
   B. Payment card transactions
   C. Privacy of student education records
   D. Non-public personal information
   - Answer: c. Privacy of student education records

(18) Which global standard is designed to secure payment card transactions and is particularly relevant to organizations handling financial data?
   A. PDPA
   B. CCPA
   C. PCI DSS
   D. FERPA
   - Answer: c. PCI DSS

(19) What does the Gramm-Leach-Bliley Act (GLBA) in the United States apply to?
   A. Personal information protection
   B. Financial institutions
   C. Cross-border data transfers
   D. Payment card transactions
   - Answer: b. Financial institutions

(20) Which country does the Personal Information Protection Law (PIPL) primarily focus on?
   A. United States
   B. China
   C. Singapore
   D. European Union (EU)
   - Answer: b. China

****

CHAPTER 8

Data-Driven Decision Making Process

Objectives of the Chapter:

The objective of the chapter is to elucidate the importance of fostering a data-driven culture within organizations in the era of Big Data and analytics. It outlines the key components necessary for cultivating such a culture, including leadership commitment, clear communication, access to data and tools, data literacy programs, data-driven KPIs, empowerment and autonomy, cross-functional collaboration, and continuous learning and adaptation. The chapter further underscores the benefits of a data-driven culture, such as informed decision-making, improved operational efficiency, innovation, enhanced customer experiences, and competitive advantage. Additionally, it addresses challenges in developing such a culture, such as resistance to change, data silos, lack of skills, and insufficient technology infrastructure. The overarching aim is to guide organizations in their transformative journey towards becoming adept in data-driven decision-making, thereby ensuring sustained success in a rapidly evolving business landscape.

8.1 Developing a Data-Driven Culture:

Developing a Data-Driven Culture in Organizations:

In the era of Big Data and analytics, organizations that foster a data-driven culture are better positioned to make informed decisions, innovate, and stay competitive. A data-driven culture involves a mindset where data is not just seen as a byproduct of operations but as a strategic asset that influences decision-making at all levels. Developing such a culture requires a combination of leadership commitment, technology integration, and employee empowerment.

Key Components of a Data-Driven Culture:

(1) Leadership Commitment:

Example: The leadership team consistently emphasizes the importance of data-driven decision-making. Executives lead by example, relying on data insights for strategic planning, and visibly supporting initiatives that promote a data-driven culture.

(2) Clear Communication:

Example: Regular communication channels are established to share the value of data and analytics across the organization. Success stories highlighting instances where data-driven decisions led to positive outcomes are shared to inspire and educate employees.

(3) Access to Data and Tools:

Example: Organizations provide employees with access to user-friendly analytics tools and dashboards. Training programs are conducted to ensure that employees have the necessary skills to interpret and use data effectively in their roles.

(4) Data Literacy Programs:

Example: Companies invest in data literacy programs to enhance employees' understanding of data concepts and methodologies. This includes workshops, online courses, and certifications that empower employees to navigate and analyze data.

(5) Data-Driven KPIs:

Example: Key Performance Indicators (KPIs) are defined and monitored using data-driven metrics. For instance, a marketing team may measure campaign success not just by the number of leads generated but by analyzing conversion rates, customer acquisition costs, and customer lifetime value.

(6) Empowerment and Autonomy:

Example: Employees are encouraged to use data to support their decision-making processes. This includes giving teams the autonomy to experiment with data-driven initiatives and learn from both successes and failures.

(7) Cross-Functional Collaboration:

Example: Departments collaborate across functions to share data and insights. For instance, sales teams may collaborate with marketing to analyze customer behavior data and tailor sales strategies accordingly.

(8) Continuous Learning and Adaptation:

Example: Organizations encourage a culture of continuous learning and adaptation based on data insights. This includes regularly reassessing strategies, updating processes, and iterating based on the feedback generated from data analysis.

Benefits of a Data-Driven Culture:

(1) Informed Decision-Making:

Organizations can make decisions based on real-time, accurate data, reducing reliance on gut feelings or intuition.

(2) Improved Operational Efficiency:

Data-driven processes enable organizations to identify inefficiencies, streamline operations, and optimize resource allocation.

(3) Innovation and Agility:

A culture that values data encourages innovation by allowing employees to experiment, learn, and adapt quickly in response to changing market conditions.

(4) Enhanced Customer Experiences:

Understanding customer behavior through data enables organizations to personalize experiences, predict preferences, and tailor products and services accordingly.

(5) Competitive Advantage:

Companies with a strong data-driven culture gain a competitive edge by being agile, responsive, and capable of anticipating market trends.

Challenges in Developing a Data-Driven Culture:

(1) Resistance to Change:
Employees may resist adopting new data-driven approaches due to fear of change or lack of understanding of the benefits.

(2) Data Silos:
Siloed data within different departments can hinder collaboration and prevent a holistic view of organizational data.

(3) Lack of Skills:
Limited data literacy and analytical skills among employees may impede the successful implementation of a data-driven culture.

(4) Insufficient Technology Infrastructure:
Outdated or inadequate technology infrastructure may hinder the effective collection, processing, and analysis of data.

Conclusion:

Developing a data-driven culture is a transformative journey that requires commitment, investment, and a concerted effort from leadership and employees alike. Organizations that successfully cultivate such a culture position themselves for sustained success in the rapidly evolving landscape of data-driven decision-making. By embracing data as a core asset and fostering a culture of curiosity, experimentation, and continuous learning, companies can harness the power of data to drive innovation and achieve strategic goals.

8.2 Steps in the Decision-Making Process:

Various Steps in the Decision-Making Process as per H. A. Simon:
Herbert A. Simon, a Nobel laureate in Economics, introduced the concept of "bounded rationality" and provided insights into decision-making processes. According to Simon, decision-making is often influenced by cognitive limitations, incomplete information, and organizational constraints. His decision-making model involves the following iterative steps:

(1) Recognition of Need:
Description: The decision-making process begins with the recognition that a decision needs to be made. This recognition can arise from various sources, such as a problem, an opportunity, or a change in the environment.
Simon's Perspective: Simon emphasizes that decision-makers are not always fully aware of all possible alternatives or solutions due to cognitive limitations.

(2) Identification of Alternatives:

Description: Once the need for a decision is recognized, the decision-maker identifies possible alternatives or courses of action. This step involves brainstorming, researching, and considering different options.

Simon's Perspective: Simon acknowledges that individuals have limited cognitive capacity, so they tend to consider a manageable number of alternatives rather than exhaustively examining all possibilities.

(3) Gathering Information:

Description: Decision-makers collect relevant information to assess the feasibility and consequences of each identified alternative. Information may come from internal and external sources, and it helps in understanding the potential outcomes associated with each option.

Simon's Perspective: Due to bounded rationality, decision-makers may only gather a subset of available information, focusing on the most critical aspects of the decision.

(4) Evaluation of Alternatives:

Description: Decision-makers evaluate the pros and cons of each alternative based on the gathered information. This evaluation involves assessing the potential risks, benefits, and consequences associated with each option.

Simon's Perspective: The evaluation is often heuristic, relying on rules of thumb or simplified decision rules due to cognitive limitations.

(5) Selection of Alternative:

Description: After evaluating the alternatives, the decision-maker selects the most suitable course of action. This selection is based on a combination of rational analysis and heuristics.

Simon's Perspective: The decision-maker may not choose the optimal solution but rather a "satisficing" solution—one that meets a satisfactory criterion given the limitations on time and cognitive resources.

(6) Implementation of the Chosen Alternative:

Description: The chosen alternative is implemented in the real-world context. This step involves executing the decision and putting the chosen course of action into practice.

Simon's Perspective: Implementation may be subject to organizational constraints, and adjustments might be necessary based on feedback from the implementation phase.

(7) Monitoring and Feedback:

Description: Decision-makers monitor the outcomes of the implemented decision. Feedback is collected to assess whether the chosen alternative has led to the desired results or if adjustments are needed.

Simon's Perspective: The decision-making process is considered iterative, with the possibility of revisiting and adjusting decisions based on ongoing feedback and learning.

(8) Learning from Experience:

Description: Decision-makers learn from the outcomes of past decisions. This learning contributes to their experience and informs future decision-making processes.

Simon's Perspective: Bounded rationality implies that decision-makers adapt and improve their decision strategies over time but within the constraints of limited cognitive resources.

Simon's model emphasizes that decision-making is a complex and iterative process influenced by cognitive limitations and organizational constraints. It recognizes that decision-makers may not always follow a fully rational path but instead employ heuristics and satisficing strategies to navigate the complexities of decision environments.

Decision-Makingin Data-Driven Environment:

The decision-making process in a data-driven environment involves several key steps that enable organizations to leverage data insights for informed and strategic decision-making. Here are the various steps in the decision-making process within a data-driven environment:

(1) Define the Decision Problem:

Description: Clearly articulate the decision problem or objective that needs to be addressed. This sets the foundation for the entire decision-making process.

Data-driven Aspect: Use data to identify patterns or trends that may highlight the underlying issues or opportunities associated with the decision problem.

(2) Identify Relevant Data Sources:

Description: Determine the data sources that are relevant to the decision problem. This includes internal databases, external datasets, customer feedback, and any other sources that may provide valuable information.

Data-driven Aspect: Prioritize data collection based on its relevance to the decision at hand. Evaluate the quality, accuracy, and timeliness of the data sources.

(3) Data Collection and Integration:

Description: Collect data from the identified sources and integrate it into a centralized repository or data warehouse. Ensure that the data collected is comprehensive and represents the relevant aspects of the decision problem.

Data-driven Aspect: Use data integration tools to streamline the process and maintain data consistency. Perform data cleansing and normalization to enhance data quality.

(4) Data Exploration and Analysis:

Description: Explore the data through descriptive statistics, data visualization, and exploratory data analysis (EDA). Identify patterns, correlations, and trends within the dataset.

Data-driven Aspect: Leverage statistical methods, machine learning algorithms, and data visualization tools to extract meaningful insights. Identify key variables and factors influencing the decision.

(5) Model Development:

Description: Develop predictive or prescriptive models based on the insights gained from data analysis. This may involve creating statistical models, machine learning models, or simulations to predict outcomes or recommend actions.

Data-driven Aspect: Utilize algorithms and models that are best suited for the specific decision problem. Train models on historical data and validate their accuracy and reliability.

(6) Validation and Testing:

Description: Validate the accuracy and effectiveness of the developed models. Test the models using a separate dataset to ensure their generalizability and reliability in real-world scenarios.

Data-driven Aspect: Employ cross-validation techniques and test the models against diverse datasets to identify potential biases or overfitting issues.

(7) Decision Formulation:

Description: Formulate the decision based on the insights generated from data analysis and model results. Consider the implications and risks associated with different decision options.

Data-driven Aspect: Quantify the potential outcomes and risks associated with each decision option. Use data to support the rationale behind the chosen decision.

(8) Implementation and Monitoring:

Description: Implement the chosen decision and monitor its outcomes in the real-world environment. Track key performance indicators (KPIs) to assess the impact of the decision over time.

Data-driven Aspect: Continuously monitor relevant data metrics to ensure that the implemented decision aligns with expected outcomes. Adjust strategies based on ongoing data analysis.

(9) Feedback Loop and Iteration:

Description: Establish a feedback loop to capture the results and lessons learned from the decision implementation. Iterate on the decision-making process based on feedback and evolving data insights.

Data-driven Aspect: Use data feedback to refine models, update assumptions, and enhance decision-making strategies. Embrace a continuous improvement mindset.

(10) Documentation and Communication:

Description: Document the entire decision-making process, including data sources, analyses performed, models developed, and the rationale behind the chosen decision. Communicate the findings and outcomes to relevant stakeholders.

Data-driven Aspect: Provide transparent documentation of data sources, methodologies, and assumptions to ensure reproducibility and accountability.

Use data visualization and storytelling techniques to effectively communicate complex findings.

By following these steps in a data-driven environment, organizations can optimize their decision-making processes, leveraging the power of data to gain insights, reduce uncertainty, and make strategic and informed choices.

8.3 Case Studies on Data-Driven Decision Success:

Case Study: Maximizing Operational Efficiency through Data-Driven Decision Success at TechOptimize Corp

Background: TechOptimize Corp, a global technology solutions provider, faced challenges in optimizing its operational efficiency and delivering timely solutions to clients. The company decided to embark on a data-driven transformation journey to enhance decision-making processes and drive operational excellence.

Challenge: TechOptimize Corp recognized that its operational processes were becoming increasingly complex, leading to bottlenecks and delays in project delivery. The company needed a systematic approach to identify and address inefficiencies, improve resource allocation, and enhance overall operational performance.

Solution: TechOptimize Corp initiated a comprehensive data-driven decision-making strategy to streamline operations and maximize efficiency. The following steps were taken to achieve success:

1. Define Key Performance Indicators (KPIs):

Objective: Identify critical metrics that directly impact operational efficiency, such as project completion times, resource utilization rates, and client satisfaction scores.

Data-Driven Aspect: Leveraging historical data, the organization determined key KPIs that provided insights into current operational performance.

2. Implement Data Integration:

Objective: Integrate data from various operational silos, including project management systems, resource allocation tools, and client feedback platforms.

Data-Driven Aspect: A centralized data repository was established, allowing for a holistic view of operations and breaking down data silos.

3. Conduct Descriptive Analytics:

Objective: Perform descriptive analytics to understand current trends and patterns in operational data.

Data-Driven Aspect: Utilizing data visualization tools, the organization identified areas of improvement, bottlenecks, and potential root causes of delays.

4. Predictive Modeling for Resource Allocation:

Objective: Develop predictive models to forecast resource needs based on project requirements and historical utilization data.

Data-Driven Aspect: Machine learning algorithms were employed to predict resource demands, enabling proactive adjustments to staffing levels for upcoming projects.

5. Real-Time Monitoring Dashboard:

Objective: Implement a real-time monitoring dashboard to track KPIs and operational metrics continuously.

Data-Driven Aspect: The organization deployed a dashboard that provided real-time insights into project timelines, resource allocation, and client feedback.

6. Continuous Improvement Feedback Loop:

- Objective: Establish a continuous improvement feedback loop based on data-driven insights.

- Data-Driven Aspect: Regularly review the performance metrics, seek feedback from project teams, and adjust operational processes based on data-driven findings.
- Results: TechOptimize Corp experienced significant improvements in operational efficiency and decision success through the implementation of its data-driven strategy:
- Reduced Project Completion Times: The organization saw a 20% reduction in project completion times, leading to faster delivery of solutions to clients.
- Optimized Resource Allocation: Predictive modeling resulted in a 15% improvement in resource utilization, ensuring that teams were appropriately staffed for each project.
- Enhanced Client Satisfaction: Real-time monitoring and adjustments based on client feedback led to a 25% increase in client satisfaction scores.
- Cost Savings: Data-driven decision-making resulted in more efficient resource allocation, contributing to a 12% reduction in operational costs.

Lessons Learned:

(1) Cultural Shift: Successful data-driven decision-making required a cultural shift within the organization, emphasizing the importance of leveraging data for operational excellence.

(2) Investment in Technology: The organization needed to invest in advanced analytics tools, machine learning capabilities, and a robust data infrastructure to support its data-driven initiatives.

(3) Continuous Learning: Establishing a culture of continuous learning and adaptation was crucial. Regular training programs ensured that employees were equipped to interpret and act on data-driven insights.

Conclusion: TechOptimize Corp's journey towards data-driven decision success not only optimized its operational processes but also enhanced its ability to deliver value to clients in a dynamic business environment. The case demonstrates the transformative power of leveraging data for decision-making, leading to tangible improvements in operational efficiency and overall organizational success.

8.4 Teaching Case Study:

Teaching Caselet: Leveraging Data for Operational Excellence at TechEnhance Solutions

Introduction: TechEnhance Solutions, a leading technology solutions provider, is committed to achieving operational excellence through the strategic leverage of data. Recognizing the transformative power of data-driven decision-making, the company aims to enhance efficiency, optimize processes, and deliver superior value to its clients.

Current Scenario: TechEnhance Solutions operates in a dynamic and competitive market, offering a diverse range of technology services. However, the company faces challenges in optimizing its internal processes, resource allocation, and project management. There is a need for a comprehensive solution that not only addresses these challenges but also positions TechEnhance as an industry leader in operational efficiency.

The Vision: TechEnhance envisions a future where every decision is backed by actionable insights derived from data. The goal is to establish a data-centric culture that permeates every aspect of the organization, driving continuous improvement and innovation.

Strategic Objectives:

(1) Data-Driven Decision-Making: Implement robust data analytics to empower decision-makers with real-time insights into project performance, resource utilization, and client satisfaction.

(2) Operational Optimization: Utilize data analytics to identify bottlenecks, streamline workflows, and optimize resource allocation, thereby improving overall operational efficiency.

(3) Client-Centric Solutions: Leverage client data to understand their evolving needs, personalize service delivery, and anticipate future requirements, ultimately enhancing client satisfaction and loyalty.

(4) Agile Project Management: Integrate data analytics into project management processes to facilitate agile methodologies, ensuring timely delivery, cost-effectiveness, and adaptability to changing project requirements.

(5) Continuous Improvement: Establish a feedback loop through data analysis, encouraging teams to learn from successes and challenges, and fostering a culture of continuous improvement across the organization.

Implementation Plan:

(1) Data Infrastructure Upgrade: Invest in robust data infrastructure, including data storage, processing capabilities, and analytical tools to support the increased focus on data-driven decision-making.

(2) Skill Development: Provide training and development programs to enhance data literacy and analytical skills across all levels of the organization, ensuring that employees can effectively interpret and use data.

(3) Cross-Functional Collaboration: Foster collaboration between IT, project management, and client-facing teams to break down silos and ensure a holistic approach to leveraging data for operational excellence.

(4) Client Data Security: Implement robust security measures to protect client data, ensuring compliance with data protection regulations and building trust with clients.

(5) Performance Metrics: Define key performance indicators (KPIs) aligned with strategic objectives, regularly monitoring and evaluating performance against these metrics to drive accountability and transparency.

Expected Outcomes:

- Improved decision-making with data-backed insights.
- Enhanced operational efficiency leading to cost savings.
- Increased client satisfaction through personalized solutions.
- Agile project management resulting in quicker project delivery.
- A culture of continuous improvement and innovation.

Analysis Questions:

(1) How can the implementation of data-driven decision-making contribute to TechEnhance Solutions' competitive advantage?

(2) What potential challenges may arise during the transition to a data-centric culture, and how can they be mitigated?

(3) How can TechEnhance Solutions ensure the ethical handling of client data while leveraging it for operational excellence?

(4) In what ways can data analytics be integrated into project management processes to enhance agility and adaptability?

(5) What measures can be taken to ensure that employees at all levels develop the necessary data literacy and analytical skills?

(6) How might the company communicate the benefits of this data-driven initiative to both internal stakeholders and clients?

(7) What strategies can be employed to maintain data security and compliance with relevant regulations throughout the implementation?

(8) How can the company measure and demonstrate the tangible impact of data-driven operational changes on client satisfaction and project success?

(9) What role does cross-functional collaboration play in the successful implementation of data-driven initiatives, and how can it be encouraged?

(10) How might the company foster a culture of continuous improvement and innovation using insights derived from data analysis?

8.5 Learning Questions:

8.5.1 Descriptive Questions:

(1) How does a data-driven culture differentiate from viewing data as a byproduct of operations?

(2) What role does leadership commitment play in fostering a data-driven culture within organizations? Provide an example to illustrate.

(3) How can clear communication channels contribute to the establishment of a data-driven culture? Offer an example of successful communication of the value of data and analytics.

(4) In what ways can organizations ensure that employees have access to user-friendly analytics tools and dashboards?

(5) What are the key components of data literacy programs, and how do they contribute to developing a data-driven culture?

(6) How can organizations define and monitor Data-Driven Key Performance Indicators (KPIs) to measure success? Provide an example of a data-driven KPI in a specific business context.

(7) Explain the significance of empowerment and autonomy in the context of developing a data-driven culture. Provide an example illustrating how employees can use data to support decision-making.

(8) How does cross-functional collaboration contribute to the establishment of a data-driven culture? Provide an example of collaboration between different departments.

(9) What is the role of continuous learning and adaptation in developing and sustaining a data-driven culture?

(10) What benefits do organizations gain from developing a data-driven culture, particularly in terms of informed decision-making, operational efficiency, and innovation?

8.5.2 Fill-up the Blanks Questions:

(1) In the development of a data-driven culture, leadership commitment involves executives leading by example, relying on data insights for _____.
  • Answer: strategic planning

(2) Clear communication channels are established to share the value of data and analytics across the organization. Success stories highlight instances where data-driven decisions led to positive outcomes to inspire and educate _____.
  • Answer: employees

(3) Organizations provide employees with access to user-friendly analytics tools and dashboards. Training programs are conducted to ensure that employees have the necessary skills to interpret and use data effectively in their _____.
  • Answer: roles

(4) Companies invest in data literacy programs to enhance employees' understanding of data concepts and methodologies. This includes workshops, online courses, and certifications that empower employees to navigate and _____ data.

- Answer: analyze

(5) Key Performance Indicators (KPIs) are defined and monitored using data-driven metrics. For instance, a marketing team may measure campaign success not just by the number of leads generated but by analyzing _____, customer acquisition costs, and customer lifetime value.

- Answer: conversion rates

(6) Employees are encouraged to use data to support their decision-making processes. This includes giving teams the autonomy to experiment with data-driven initiatives and learn from both _____ and failures.

- Answer: successes

(7) Departments collaborate across functions to share data and insights. For instance, sales teams may collaborate with marketing to analyze customer behavior data and tailor _____ accordingly.

- Answer: sales strategies

(8) Organizations encourage a culture of continuous learning and adaptation based on data insights. This includes regularly reassessing strategies, updating processes, and iterating based on the feedback generated from _____.

- Answer: data analysis

(9) Informed Decision-Making in a data-driven culture allows organizations to make decisions based on real-time, accurate data, reducing reliance on gut feelings or _____.

- Answer: intuition

(10) Data-driven processes enable organizations to identify inefficiencies, streamline operations, and optimize resource allocation, resulting in improved _____.

- Answer: operational efficiency

8.5.3 Multiple Choice Questions:

(1) What is a key benefit of fostering a data-driven culture in organizations?
   A. Increased reliance on intuition
   B. Improved operational inefficiency
   C. Enhanced decision-making
   D. Limited access to data
   - Answer: C) Enhanced decision-making

(2) Which component of a data-driven culture involves executives leading by example in relying on data insights for strategic planning?
   A. Clear Communication
   B. Access to Data and Tools
   C. Leadership Commitment
   D. Empowerment and Autonomy

- Answer: C) Leadership Commitment

(3) What is an example of a data-driven Key Performance Indicator (KPI) for a marketing team?

    A. Number of employees trained

    B. Customer satisfaction scores

    C. Conversion rates, customer acquisition costs, and customer lifetime value

    D. Quantity of data collected

- Answer: C) Conversion rates, customer acquisition costs, and customer lifetime value

(4) How can organizations overcome the challenge of employees resisting new data-driven approaches?

    A. Limiting access to data

    B. Avoiding communication about data benefits

    C. Providing leadership commitment

    D. Emphasizing data silos

- Answer: C) Providing leadership commitment

(5) In a data-driven environment, what is the purpose of data exploration and analysis during the decision-making process?

    A. To avoid data collection

    B. To identify patterns, correlations, and trends within the dataset

    C. To restrict access to data

    D. To eliminate the need for models

- Answer: B) To identify patterns, correlations, and trends within the dataset

(6) What is the main advantage of a culture that values data in terms of innovation and agility?

    A. Stagnation in response to market changes

    B. Limitation of employee experimentation

    C. Encouragement of innovation and quick adaptation

    D. Dependence on outdated strategies

- Answer: C) Encouragement of innovation and quick adaptation

(7) What is a potential consequence of having siloed data within different departments in an organization?

    A. Improved collaboration

    B. A holistic view of organizational data

    C. Hindered collaboration and lack of a holistic view

    D. Enhanced data literacy

- Answer: C) Hindered collaboration and lack of a holistic view

(8) What is Herbert A. Simon's perspective on the decision-making process?

    A. Decision-makers are fully aware of all possible alternatives.

    B. Decision-makers tend to consider an exhaustive number of alternatives.

    C. Decision-makers may only gather a subset of available information.

    D. Decision-makers always choose the optimal solution.

- Answer: C) Decision-makers may only gather a subset of available information.

(9) What step in the decision-making process involves formulating the decision based on insights generated from data analysis and model results?

    A. Decision Formulation

    B. Identification of Alternatives

    C. Gathering Information

    D. Implementation and Monitoring

- Answer: A) Decision Formulation

(10) How can organizations benefit from the continuous learning and adaptation component of a data-driven culture?

   A. By avoiding reassessment of strategies
   B. By limiting process updates
   C. By embracing a culture of curiosity and experimentation
   D. By disregarding feedback from data analysis
   - Answer: C) By embracing a culture of curiosity and experimentation

CHAPTER 9

Business Intelligence in Marketing

Objectives of the Chapter:

The objective of the chapter is to provide a comprehensive understanding of the integral role of business intelligence in marketing, specifically focusing on customer segmentation and targeting, personalization, marketing automation, and the analysis of marketing campaign effectiveness. It emphasizes the significance of using advanced analytics tools to segment diverse customer bases, target specific segments strategically, and personalize marketing efforts based on individual preferences. The chapter also highlights the benefits of these practices, such as enhanced marketing ROI, improved customer satisfaction, and increased conversion rates. Furthermore, it delves into the challenges and considerations associated with data quality, ethical concerns, and the need for adaptability in response to evolving markets. The subsequent sections explore how personalization and marketing automation work in tandem, leveraging business intelligence to create targeted, relevant interactions. The chapter concludes by emphasizing the continuous and iterative nature of analyzing marketing campaign effectiveness through business intelligence, enabling data-driven decision-making, optimization, and long-term success in the dynamic landscape of marketing.

9.1 Customer Segmentation and Targeting:

Customer Segmentation and Targeting in Business Intelligence for Marketing:

Customer segmentation and targeting are crucial components of business intelligence in marketing. These practices involve dividing a diverse customer base into distinct segments based on shared characteristics and preferences. Business intelligence tools and analytics play a vital role in identifying patterns, extracting insights, and enabling marketers to tailor their strategies for maximum impact.

1. Customer Segmentation:

Definition: Customer segmentation is the process of categorizing a heterogeneous customer base into distinct groups with similar characteristics, behaviors, or needs.

Key Variables for Segmentation:

- Demographic: Age, gender, income, education.
- Psychographic: Interests, lifestyle, values.
- Behavioral: Purchase history, brand loyalty, product usage.
- Geographic: Location, climate, population density.

Role of Business Intelligence:
- Utilizes advanced analytics to identify patterns and relationships within large datasets.
- Allows for dynamic segmentation based on real-time data, ensuring up-to-date customer profiles.
- Enables predictive modeling to anticipate future customer behavior and preferences.

2. Targeting:

Definition: Targeting involves selecting specific customer segments to focus marketing efforts, resources, and campaigns on, ensuring a more personalized and effective approach.

Criteria for Targeting:
- Size and Potential: Evaluate the size and growth potential of each segment.
- Accessibility: Assess the accessibility and reachability of the segment through marketing channels.
- Compatibility: Ensure that the segment aligns with the company's products, values, and marketing goals.

Role of Business Intelligence:
- Provides insights into the profitability and lifetime value of different customer segments.
- Facilitates A/B testing and experimentation to determine the most effective marketing messages for each segment.
- Enables real-time monitoring of campaign performance, allowing for quick adjustments based on customer responses.

3. Personalization:

Definition: Personalization involves tailoring marketing messages, content, and offerings to individual customers within targeted segments, enhancing the customer experience.

Methods of Personalization:
- Content Personalization: Customizing website content, emails, and advertisements based on customer preferences.
- Product Recommendations: Using algorithms to suggest products or services based on past purchases and browsing behavior.
- Communication Personalization: Tailoring communication channels and frequency to match customer preferences.

Role of Business Intelligence:
- Leverages data analytics to understand individual customer behavior and preferences.
- Utilizes machine learning algorithms to predict the most relevant content and products for each customer.

- Monitors real-time customer interactions to dynamically adjust personalization strategies.

4. Benefits of Customer Segmentation and Targeting:

- Enhanced Marketing ROI: By focusing efforts on high-potential segments, marketing resources are allocated more efficiently, leading to a better return on investment.
- Improved Customer Satisfaction: Personalized and relevant marketing messages enhance the overall customer experience, fostering satisfaction and loyalty.
- Increased Conversion Rates: Targeting specific segments with tailored messages increases the likelihood of conversions and customer engagement.

5. Challenges and Considerations:

- Data Quality and Integration: Ensuring the accuracy and integration of customer data from various sources is crucial for effective segmentation.
- Ethical Considerations: Balancing personalization with privacy concerns and ethical practices is essential to maintain customer trust.
- Adaptability: Markets and customer behaviors evolve; continuous monitoring and adjustment of segmentation and targeting strategies are necessary.

Conclusion: In the realm of business intelligence for marketing, customer segmentation and targeting empower organizations to move beyond one-size-fits-all approaches. Leveraging data analytics and business intelligence tools, marketers can identify, understand, and engage with specific customer segments in a more meaningful and personalized manner, ultimately driving business success and customer satisfaction.

9.2 Personalization and Marketing Automation:

Personalization and Marketing Automation in Business Intelligence for Marketing:

In the dynamic landscape of marketing, personalization and marketing automation are pivotal components that leverage business intelligence to create targeted, relevant, and timely interactions with customers. These strategies, empowered by data analytics and business intelligence tools, enable marketers to optimize their campaigns, enhance customer engagement, and drive business growth.

1. Personalization:

Definition: Personalization in marketing refers to the customization of content, messages, and experiences to meet the specific needs, preferences, and behaviors of individual customers.

Key Elements of Personalization:

- Content Personalization: Tailoring website content, emails, and advertisements to match individual customer preferences and behaviors.
- Product Recommendations: Using data analytics to suggest products or services based on past purchase history and browsing patterns.
- Communication Personalization: Customizing communication channels, timing, and frequency to align with individual preferences.

Role of Business Intelligence:
- Customer Segmentation: Business intelligence tools analyze customer data to identify segments with shared characteristics, enabling more targeted personalization.
- Predictive Analytics: Leveraging predictive modeling to anticipate customer preferences and behaviors, facilitating proactive personalization.
- Real-time Insights: Continuous monitoring and analysis of customer interactions in real-time, allowing for dynamic adjustments in personalization strategies.

2. Marketing Automation:

Definition: Marketing automation involves the use of technology and software to streamline, automate, and measure marketing tasks and workflows, reducing manual efforts and increasing efficiency.

Key Components of Marketing Automation:
- Email Marketing Automation: Triggered and automated email campaigns based on customer actions or predefined workflows.
- Lead Scoring: Automated processes for assigning scores to leads based on their interactions, indicating their readiness for sales engagement.
- Social Media Automation: Scheduling and automating social media posts, tracking engagement, and responding to interactions.
- Workflow Automation: Automating repetitive marketing tasks, such as data entry, lead nurturing, and segmentation.

Role of Business Intelligence:
- Data Integration: Business intelligence ensures seamless integration of data from various sources, providing a unified view for marketing automation processes.
- Analytics for Optimization: Analyzing campaign performance, customer behaviors, and conversion metrics to optimize marketing automation workflows.
- Segmentation for Targeting: Utilizing customer segmentation insights to design targeted and personalized marketing automation campaigns.

3. Benefits of Personalization and Marketing Automation:
- Enhanced Customer Experience: Personalization creates a more personalized and relevant experience, leading to increased customer satisfaction and loyalty.

- Operational Efficiency: Marketing automation streamlines workflows, reducing manual efforts and enabling marketers to focus on strategic initiatives.
- Improved Conversion Rates: Targeted and timely communications through personalization and marketing automation contribute to higher conversion rates.
- Data-Driven Decision Making: The integration of business intelligence facilitates data-driven decision-making, allowing marketers to refine strategies based on analytics.

4. Integration of Personalization and Marketing Automation:

- Dynamic Content Delivery: Integrating personalization into marketing automation allows for the dynamic delivery of content based on individual preferences and behaviors.
- Behavior-Driven Automation: Using customer behavior data to trigger specific automation workflows, ensuring relevance and timeliness in communications.
- A/B Testing for Optimization: Employing A/B testing within marketing automation to evaluate the effectiveness of different personalization strategies.

5. Challenges and Considerations:

- Data Privacy and Compliance: Balancing the benefits of personalization with the need to adhere to data privacy regulations and customer consent.
- Data Quality: Ensuring the accuracy and completeness of customer data to avoid errors and inaccuracies in personalization efforts.
- Striking the Right Balance: Achieving a balance between automation and maintaining a human touch in customer interactions to avoid appearing overly mechanized.

Conclusion: In the realm of business intelligence for marketing, the synergies between personalization and marketing automation are transformative. By leveraging data analytics, marketers can create tailored experiences, automate workflows, and engage with customers in a more meaningful way. This not only enhances customer satisfaction and loyalty but also drives operational efficiency and business success in an increasingly competitive market.

9.3 Analyzing Marketing Campaign Effectiveness:

Analyzing Marketing Campaign Effectiveness through Business Intelligence in Marketing:

Analyzing marketing campaign effectiveness is a critical aspect of leveraging business intelligence in marketing. It involves the systematic evaluation of various metrics and key performance indicators (KPIs) to measure the success of marketing initiatives. Business intelligence tools play a central role in collecting, processing, and analyzing data to provide insights that inform decision-making and optimize future campaigns.

1. Key Metrics for Analyzing Marketing Campaigns:

- Conversion Rates: Measure the percentage of individuals who took a desired action, such as making a purchase or filling out a form, in response to the campaign.
- Click-Through Rates (CTR): Evaluate the percentage of individuals who clicked on a specific link or call-to-action within the campaign.
- Return on Investment (ROI): Calculate the financial return generated relative to the cost of the marketing campaign.
- Customer Acquisition Cost (CAC): Assess the cost incurred to acquire a new customer through the campaign.
- Lead Generation Metrics: Evaluate the number and quality of leads generated by the campaign.

2. Role of Business Intelligence in Analyzing Campaigns:

- Data Integration: Business intelligence tools integrate data from various sources, including marketing automation platforms, CRM systems, and web analytics tools, providing a unified dataset for analysis.
- Data Visualization: Utilize dashboards and visualizations to present complex marketing data in a comprehensible and actionable format.
- Predictive Analytics: Leverage predictive modeling to forecast future campaign performance and identify factors influencing success.
- Attribution Modeling: Analyze the customer journey to attribute conversions and interactions to specific touchpoints within the campaign.
- A/B Testing: Conduct A/B testing to experiment with different elements of the campaign and determine which variations are more effective.

3. Steps in Analyzing Marketing Campaign Effectiveness:

- Data Collection: Gather relevant data from multiple sources, including website analytics, social media platforms, and email marketing tools.
- Data Cleaning and Preprocessing: Ensure data quality by cleaning and preprocessing the data to eliminate errors and inconsistencies.
- Performance Metrics Calculation: Calculate key performance metrics, such as conversion rates, CTR, ROI, and customer acquisition cost.
- Comparative Analysis: Compare the performance of the current campaign with historical data or benchmarks to assess its relative success.
- Segmentation Analysis: Segment the audience to understand how different segments respond to the campaign, enabling targeted optimizations.

4. Interpretation of Results:

- Identify Successful Channels: Determine which marketing channels contributed most significantly to the campaign's success.
- Understand Audience Behavior: Gain insights into customer behavior, preferences, and interactions with the campaign.

- Discover Opportunities: Identify opportunities for improvement or expansion based on areas of success and areas that underperformed.
- Benchmark Against Goals: Compare the campaign's performance against predefined goals and objectives.

5. Continuous Optimization:
- Iterative Testing: Continuously test and iterate campaign elements based on insights gained from the analysis.
- Feedback Loop: Establish a feedback loop between marketing analytics and campaign execution to implement real-time adjustments.
- Dynamic Adaptation: Adapt marketing strategies dynamically based on changing market conditions, customer behavior, and emerging trends.

6. Challenges and Considerations:
- Data Accuracy and Consistency: Ensuring the accuracy and consistency of data across various platforms and systems.
- Attribution Challenges: Addressing the complexity of attributing conversions to multiple touchpoints within the customer journey.
- Interpreting Causation vs. Correlation: Distinguishing between causation and correlation to make informed decisions rather than relying solely on statistical relationships.

Analyzing marketing campaign effectiveness through business intelligence is a continuous process that empowers marketers to make data-driven decisions, optimize strategies, and maximize return on investment. By leveraging sophisticated analytics tools and methodologies, businesses can gain actionable insights that not only measure the success of current campaigns but also inform future marketing initiatives for sustained growth and customer engagement.

9.4 Teaching Case Study:

Caselet: Unlocking Marketing Potential with Business Intelligence at XYZ Electronics

Background: XYZ Electronics, a leading consumer electronics company, was facing challenges in understanding customer behaviour, optimizing marketing campaigns, and staying competitive in the rapidly evolving market. Recognizing the need for data-driven insights, the company decided to implement a business intelligence solution to enhance its marketing strategies.

Situation: XYZ Electronics had diverse product offerings, and their marketing efforts spanned multiple channels, including online and offline platforms. However, the lack of a unified view of customer data and ineffective analysis hindered their ability to make informed decisions.

Implementation of Business Intelligence:
- Data Integration: XYZ Electronics integrated data from various sources, including online sales platforms, customer relationship management (CRM) systems, and social media, to create a comprehensive dataset.

- Customer Segmentation: Utilizing business intelligence tools, XYZ Electronics segmented its customer base based on demographics, purchase history, and online behavior.
- Campaign Optimization: The marketing team analyzed historical campaign data, identified successful elements, and used predictive analytics to optimize future campaigns.
- Real-Time Dashboards: Business intelligence dashboards were implemented to provide real-time insights into campaign performance, customer interactions, and market trends.

Results:
- XYZ Electronics experienced a 15% increase in online sales within the first quarter of implementing business intelligence.
- Customer satisfaction scores improved by 20%, reflecting the impact of personalized marketing strategies.
- Marketing expenses were optimized, leading to a 10% reduction in customer acquisition costs.

Questions for Discussion:

(1) What were the key challenges faced by XYZ Electronics in their marketing efforts before implementing business intelligence?

(2) How did the integration of data from various sources contribute to XYZ Electronics' ability to make more informed marketing decisions?

(3) Explain the significance of customer segmentation in the context of enhancing marketing strategies. What benefits can businesses derive from a well-executed segmentation strategy?

(4) Discuss the role of predictive analytics in optimizing future marketing campaigns. How can businesses leverage predictive modeling to stay ahead in a competitive market?

(5) What impact did real-time dashboards have on XYZ Electronics' ability to monitor and adjust marketing strategies? How can real-time insights contribute to more agile decision-making?

(6) Considering the positive outcomes observed, how might other businesses, irrespective of their industry, benefit from incorporating business intelligence into their marketing strategies?

(7) What ethical considerations should companies keep in mind when using business intelligence in marketing, especially concerning customer data and privacy?

This caselet provides a foundation for discussing the practical applications and benefits of business intelligence in the context of marketing. Students can explore how data-driven insights contribute to improved decision-making, enhanced customer satisfaction, and the overall success of marketing initiatives.

9.5 Learning Questions:

9.5.1 Descriptive Questions:

(1) What is the role of business intelligence in customer segmentation, particularly in terms of real-time data?

(2) How does personalization contribute to enhanced customer satisfaction in marketing, and what role does business intelligence play in achieving this?

(3) Explain the significance of A/B testing in marketing automation and how it helps in optimizing personalization strategies.

(4) What challenges and considerations are associated with data privacy and compliance when implementing personalization and marketing automation strategies?

(5) In the context of business intelligence for marketing, how does segmentation analysis contribute to the optimization of marketing campaigns?

(6) What is the primary purpose of analyzing conversion rates, click-through rates, return on investment (ROI), and customer acquisition cost (CAC) in marketing campaign effectiveness?

(7) Describe the steps involved in the continuous optimization of marketing campaigns using business intelligence tools.

(8) How does business intelligence aid in identifying successful marketing channels and understanding audience behavior during the interpretation of marketing campaign results?

(9) Explain the iterative testing approach and feedback loop in the context of continuous optimization of marketing campaigns through business intelligence.

(10) What is the role of predictive analytics in personalization and marketing automation, and how does it contribute to proactive personalization efforts?

9.5.2 Fill-up the Blanks Questions:

(1) Customer segmentation is the process of categorizing a _____ customer base into distinct groups with similar characteristics, behaviors, or needs.
Answer: Heterogeneous

(2) Business intelligence tools utilize advanced analytics to identify patterns and relationships within large datasets, allowing for dynamic segmentation based on _____ data.
Answer: Real-time

(3) Targeting in marketing involves selecting specific customer segments based on criteria such as size, potential, and _____ to focus marketing efforts and campaigns on.
Answer: Accessibility

(4) Personalization in marketing refers to the customization of content, messages, and offerings to individual customers within targeted segments, enhancing the overall _____.
Answer: Customer experience

(5) The role of business intelligence in personalization includes leveraging data analytics to understand individual customer behavior and preferences, as well as utilizing machine learning algorithms to predict the most relevant _____ for each customer.
Answer: Content and products

(6) Enhanced marketing ROI is achieved by focusing marketing efforts on high-potential segments, leading to more efficient allocation of marketing _____.
Answer: Resources

(7) Challenges in customer segmentation and targeting include ensuring the accuracy and integration of customer data from various sources, addressing _____ concerns, and adapting strategies to evolving markets and customer behaviors.
Answer: Ethical

(8) Marketing automation involves the use of technology and software to streamline, automate, and measure marketing tasks, reducing manual efforts and increasing _____.
Answer: Efficiency

(9) Data integration in marketing automation is facilitated by business intelligence tools, providing a unified view by integrating data from various sources, including marketing automation platforms, CRM systems, and _____ tools.
Answer: Web analytics

(10) Continuous optimization of marketing campaigns involves establishing a feedback loop between marketing analytics and campaign execution to implement real-time adjustments and dynamically adapting marketing _____ based on changing market conditions and customer behavior.
Answer: Strategies

9.5.3 Multiple Choice Questions:

(1) What is the role of business intelligence in customer segmentation?
  A. Conducting market research
  B. Identifying patterns and relationships within large datasets
  C. Creating personalized content
  D. Implementing A/B testing
  - Answer: b) Identifying patterns and relationships within large datasets

(2) Which of the following is a demographic variable used in customer segmentation?
  A. Interests
  B. Purchase history
  C. Age
  D. Communication channels
  - Answer: c) Age

(3) What does targeting in marketing involve?
  A. Customizing content based on customer preferences
  B. Selecting specific customer segments for focused efforts
  C. Analyzing conversion rates
  D. Conducting A/B testing
  - Answer: b) Selecting specific customer segments for focused efforts

(4) How does personalization enhance the customer experience?
  A. By focusing on high-potential segments
  B. By conducting A/B testing
  C. By tailoring messages and offerings to individual customers
  D. By integrating data from various sources
  - Answer: c) By tailoring messages and offerings to individual customers

(5) What is a key benefit of customer segmentation and targeting?
   A. Increased data privacy
   B. Improved customer satisfaction
   C. Higher A/B testing efficiency
   D. Reduced marketing ROI
   - Answer: b) Improved customer satisfaction

(6) Which challenge is associated with customer segmentation and targeting?
   A. Increased conversion rates
   B. Ethical considerations
   C. Improved data quality
   D. Compatibility with marketing goals
   - Answer: b) Ethical considerations

(7) What is the main goal of marketing automation?
   A. Enhancing customer experience
   B. Streamlining and automating marketing tasks
   C. Conducting A/B testing
   D. Analyzing campaign performance
   - Answer: b) Streamlining and automating marketing tasks

(8) Which role does business intelligence play in personalization?
   A. Scheduling social media posts
   B. Analyzing customer data for segmentation
   C. Automating email campaigns
   D. Conducting A/B testing
   - Answer: b) Analyzing customer data for segmentation

(9) What is a benefit of personalization and marketing automation?
   A. Reduced customer satisfaction
   B. Decreased operational efficiency
   C. Lower conversion rates
   D. Enhanced customer experience
   - Answer: d) Enhanced customer experience

(10) How can personalization be integrated into marketing automation?
   A. By conducting A/B testing
   B. Through dynamic content delivery
   C. Scheduling social media posts
   D. Analyzing campaign performance
   - Answer: b) Through dynamic content delivery

(11) Which challenge is associated with personalization and marketing automation?
   A. Operational efficiency
   B. Data privacy and compliance
   C. Conducting A/B testing
   D. Analyzing customer interactions
   - Answer: b) Data privacy and compliance

(12) What is a key metric for analyzing marketing campaigns?
    A. Social media engagement
    B. Customer acquisition cost (CAC)
    C. Workflow automation
    D. Lead scoring
    • Answer: b) Customer acquisition cost (CAC)

(13) How does business intelligence contribute to analyzing marketing campaigns?
    A. Conducting A/B testing
    B. Scheduling social media posts
    C. Integrating data from various sources
    D. Automating email campaigns
    • Answer: c) Integrating data from various sources

(14) What does A/B testing involve in the context of marketing campaigns?
    A. Analyzing customer interactions
    B. Conducting segmentation analysis
    C. Comparing different campaign variations
    D. Calculating conversion rates
    • Answer: c) Comparing different campaign variations

(15) What is a step in analyzing marketing campaign effectiveness?
    A. Conducting A/B testing
    B. Data collection
    C. Automating email campaigns
    D. Scheduling social media posts
    • Answer: b) Data collection

(16) How can successful channels be identified in marketing campaigns?
    A. Through dynamic content delivery
    B. By analyzing campaign performance
    C. Conducting A/B testing
    D. Segmenting the audience
    • Answer: b) By analyzing campaign performance

(17) What is the continuous optimization of marketing campaigns based on?
    A. Static strategies
    B. Real-time adjustments from A/B testing
    C. Customer acquisition cost (CAC)
    D. Lead generation metrics
    • Answer: b) Real-time adjustments from A/B testing

(18) Which challenge is associated with analyzing marketing campaign effectiveness?
    A. Increased conversion rates
    B. Operational efficiency
    C. Data accuracy and consistency
    D. Improved customer satisfaction
    • Answer: c) Data accuracy and consistency

(19) What is the goal of interpreting results in marketing campaign analysis?
   A. Scheduling social media posts
   B. Understanding audience behavior
   C. Conducting A/B testing
   D. Calculating customer acquisition cost (CAC)
   - Answer: b) Understanding audience behavior

(20) What is emphasized in the conclusion regarding business intelligence for marketing?
   A. Decreased customer satisfaction
   B. Reduced operational efficiency
   C. Increased reliance on A/B testing
   D. Data-driven decisions for sustained growth
   - Answer: d) Data-driven decisions for sustained growth

****

CHAPTER 10

Financial Analytics and Business Intelligence

The objective of the chapter is to provide a comprehensive understanding of financial analytics and business intelligence, highlighting their pivotal roles in modern business environments. The chapter introduces the synergies between data analysis, technology, and strategic thinking, emphasizing their transformative impact on converting raw data into actionable intelligence. It delves into the key components of financial analytics, encompassing financial modeling, performance analytics, risk analytics, and predictive analytics. Simultaneously, it explores business intelligence, covering data warehousing, data visualization, querying and reporting, and performance management. The integration of financial analytics and business intelligence is elucidated, underscoring the benefits of informed decision-making, comprehensive performance evaluation, real-time monitoring, and scenario planning. Ultimately, the chapter aims to equip organizations with the knowledge needed to leverage financial analytics and business intelligence for strategic decision-making, ensuring a competitive edge in the dynamic business landscape.

10.1 Financial Forecasting and Risk Management:

Introduction to Financial Analytics and Business Intelligence:
Financial Analytics and Business Intelligence (BI) have emerged as pivotal disciplines in the modern business landscape, providing organizations with powerful tools and insights to drive informed decision-making. These fields synergize data analysis, technology, and strategic thinking to transform raw data into actionable intelligence, fostering a deeper understanding of financial trends, performance, and risks.

Financial Analytics:
Definition: Financial analytics involves the use of data analysis tools and techniques to gain insights into an organization's financial performance, facilitate forecasting, and support strategic decision-making. It encompasses a wide range of activities, from historical data analysis to predictive modeling, with the overarching goal of enhancing financial performance.

Key Components:
1. Financial Modeling: Creating mathematical representations of financial scenarios to aid decision-making.
2. Performance Analytics: Evaluating key performance indicators (KPIs) to assess and optimize financial performance.

3. Risk Analytics: Identifying, assessing, and mitigating potential financial risks.
4. Predictive Analytics: Using statistical algorithms and machine learning to forecast future financial outcomes.

Business Intelligence:

Definition: Business Intelligence refers to the technologies, processes, and tools that help organizations collect, analyze, and present business data to support decision-making. BI encompasses a broader spectrum, including financial data, operational metrics, and strategic insights, with the aim of improving overall business performance.

Key Components:
1. Data Warehousing: Centralizing and organizing data from various sources for comprehensive analysis.
2. Data Visualization: Transforming complex data sets into visually accessible and understandable formats, such as charts and dashboards.
3. Querying and Reporting: Enabling users to extract relevant information through queries and generate reports.
4. Performance Management: Monitoring and evaluating organizational performance against predefined goals and benchmarks.

Integration of Financial Analytics and Business Intelligence:

Financial Analytics and Business Intelligence are often integrated to provide a holistic view of an organization's performance. This integration offers several benefits:
1. Informed Decision-Making: Combining financial insights with broader business data ensures that decisions are well-informed and aligned with overall strategic objectives.
2. Comprehensive Performance Evaluation: BI tools facilitate the integration of financial metrics with operational and strategic data, enabling a comprehensive evaluation of organizational performance.
3. Real-time Monitoring: The integration allows for real-time monitoring of financial and business metrics, enabling swift responses to emerging trends and challenges.
4. Scenario Planning: The combined power of financial analytics and BI supports scenario planning by providing a dynamic and adaptable framework for decision-makers.

In conclusion, Financial Analytics and Business Intelligence are indispensable for organizations seeking a competitive edge in today's data-driven environment. By harnessing the insights derived from these disciplines, businesses can navigate complexities, uncover hidden opportunities, and optimize their overall performance in an ever-evolving marketplace.

Financial Forecasting:

Financial forecasting and risk management are critical components of financial analytics and business intelligence. These practices help organizations make informed decisions by predicting future financial trends and identifying potential risks. In this note, we'll explore the concepts of financial forecasting and risk management, their importance, and how they are implemented in the realm of financial analytics and business intelligence.

Definition: Financial forecasting involves predicting future financial outcomes based on historical data, market analysis, and other relevant factors. It helps organizations plan and allocate resources effectively.

Importance:

1. Strategic Planning: Enables organizations to develop long-term strategies and set realistic goals.
2. Resource Allocation: Helps in allocating resources efficiently by anticipating future financial needs.
3. Investor Confidence: Builds confidence among investors by providing a clear picture of the company's financial health.

Methods of Financial Forecasting:

1. Time Series Analysis: Analyzing historical data to identify patterns and trends.
2. Regression Analysis: Examining the relationship between variables to make predictions.
3. Scenario Analysis: Evaluating different scenarios and their potential impact on financial outcomes.
4. Budgeting: Creating a financial plan that outlines expected revenues and expenses.

Example: A retail company might use financial forecasting to predict future sales based on historical sales data, market trends, and economic indicators. This allows the company to adjust inventory levels, staffing, and marketing strategies to meet anticipated demand.

Risk Management:

Definition: Risk management involves identifying, assessing, and mitigating potential risks that could impact the achievement of organizational objectives.

Importance:

1. Preserving Value: Protects the organization's value by minimizing the impact of potential risks.
2. Compliance: Ensures compliance with regulations and ethical standards.
3. Decision Support: Facilitates better decision-making by considering potential risks.

Methods of Risk Management:

1. Risk Identification: Identifying and categorizing potential risks.
2. Risk Assessment: Evaluating the likelihood and impact of identified risks.
3. Risk Mitigation: Implementing strategies to reduce or eliminate risks.

4. Monitoring and Review: Continuously monitoring and reviewing the effectiveness of risk management strategies.

Example: A technology company may identify the risk of a cybersecurity breach. To mitigate this risk, the company may invest in robust cybersecurity measures, conduct regular audits, and train employees on security protocols.

Integration with Financial Analytics and Business Intelligence:

1. Data Integration: Financial analytics and business intelligence platforms integrate data from various sources, allowing for comprehensive analysis and forecasting.
2. Advanced Analytics: Utilizing predictive analytics to enhance financial forecasting accuracy and identify emerging risks.
3. Real-time Monitoring: Implementing tools that provide real-time insights into financial metrics and potential risks.
4. Visualization: Using data visualization to communicate financial forecasts and risk assessments effectively.

In conclusion, financial forecasting and risk management are indispensable components of financial analytics and business intelligence. By leveraging these practices, organizations can navigate uncertainties, make informed decisions, and achieve sustainable financial success.

10.2 Fraud Detection and Prevention:

Fraud Detection and Prevention in Financial Analytics and Business Intelligence:

Fraud detection and prevention are critical components of financial analytics and business intelligence, aimed at identifying and mitigating fraudulent activities within an organization. As technology advances, so do the methods employed by fraudsters, making it imperative for businesses to leverage sophisticated analytics and BI tools to safeguard their assets. This comprehensive approach involves proactive monitoring, data analysis, and the implementation of preventive measures.

1. Detection Techniques:

a. Anomaly Detection:

- Definition: Anomaly detection involves identifying deviations from expected patterns or behaviors in data.
- Example: In credit card transactions, if a card is typically used for small, local purchases, a sudden large transaction from a different geographic location may trigger an anomaly alert.

b. Pattern Recognition:

- Definition: Recognizing patterns of fraudulent behavior based on historical data and known fraud cases.

- Example: Identifying patterns where multiple accounts are created from the same IP address in a short time span, suggesting potential fraudulent account creation.

c. Predictive Modeling:
- Definition: Utilizing machine learning algorithms to predict and prevent fraudulent activities.
- Example: Predictive models can analyze transaction data to identify potential fraud before it occurs, based on historical patterns.

2. Data Sources:

a. Transactional Data:
- Description: Analyzing transactional data for irregularities or patterns indicative of fraudulent activities.
- Example: Unusual spending patterns, frequent small transactions, or transactions outside normal business hours can be red flags.

b. User Behavior Data:
- Description: Monitoring user behavior to detect unusual activity or access patterns.
- Example: An employee accessing sensitive financial information outside their usual working hours may raise suspicions.

c. External Data Sources:
- Description: Integrating external data sources, such as public records or watchlists, to enhance fraud detection capabilities.
- Example: Checking customer details against known fraud databases to identify individuals with a history of fraudulent activities.

3. Implementation of Preventive Measures:

a. Authentication and Authorization Controls:
- Description: Implementing robust authentication processes and strict authorization controls to ensure only authorized individuals access sensitive data.
- Example: Multi-factor authentication for online transactions or limiting access to financial data based on job roles.

b. Real-time Monitoring:
- Description: Continuously monitoring transactions and user activities in real-time to promptly identify and respond to potential fraud.
- Example: Setting up alerts for suspicious activities, such as large transactions or multiple failed login attempts.

c. Machine Learning Models for Prevention:
- Description: Utilizing machine learning models not only for detection but also for preventing fraud by predicting and blocking potentially fraudulent activities.

- Example: Automatically blocking a transaction that the model predicts as high-risk based on historical fraud patterns.

4. Case Study:

Example: A financial institution uses advanced analytics to detect credit card fraud. By analyzing transactional data, user behavior, and external data sources, the system identifies unusual spending patterns and flags transactions that deviate from the customer's typical behavior. Real-time monitoring allows the institution to block suspicious transactions immediately, preventing potential financial losses and ensuring the security of their customers' accounts.

In conclusion, fraud detection and prevention in financial analytics and business intelligence involve a multi-faceted approach that combines advanced analytics, data from various sources, and proactive measures. Implementing these strategies is crucial for organizations to stay one step ahead of evolving fraudulent activities and safeguard their financial assets and reputation.

10.3 Using BI for Financial Performance Analysis:

Financial Performance Analysis: A Comprehensive Overview

Financial performance analysis is a crucial aspect of assessing how well a business is performing financially. It involves the evaluation of an organization's financial statements, ratios, and other metrics to gain insights into its profitability, efficiency, liquidity, solvency, and overall financial health. This analysis is essential for both internal management decision-making and external stakeholders, including investors, creditors, and regulatory bodies.

Components of Financial Performance Analysis:

1. Financial Statements Analysis:

Income Statement:
- Examining revenue, expenses, and profits to assess the company's ability to generate income.
- Key metrics include gross profit margin, operating profit margin, and net profit margin.

Balance Sheet:
- Evaluating assets, liabilities, and equity to understand the organization's financial position.
- Key ratios include the current ratio and quick ratio for liquidity assessment.

Cash Flow Statement:
- Analyzing cash inflows and outflows to assess the company's ability to generate cash and meet its obligations.

2. Ratio Analysis:

Liquidity Ratios:
- Current Ratio: Indicates the company's ability to cover short-term liabilities with short-term assets.
- Quick Ratio: Measures the ability to meet short-term obligations with the most liquid assets.

Profitability Ratios:
- Return on Equity (ROE): Assesses how efficiently the company is utilizing shareholders' equity to generate profits.
- Gross Margin: Indicates the profitability of goods sold.

Efficiency Ratios:
- Inventory Turnover: Measures how quickly inventory is sold.
- Accounts Receivable Turnover: Evaluates how efficiently the company collects receivables.

Solvency Ratios:
- Debt-to-Equity Ratio: Assesses the proportion of debt used to finance the company's assets.
- Interest Coverage Ratio: Indicates the ability to meet interest obligations.

3. Trend Analysis:
- Analyzing financial data over multiple periods to identify trends, changes, or anomalies.
- Understanding the direction and magnitude of changes in key financial metrics.

4. Comparative Analysis:
- Comparing the financial performance of the company against industry benchmarks, competitors, or its own historical performance.
- Identifying areas of strength or weakness relative to peers.

Importance of Financial Performance Analysis:
1. Decision-Making: Enables informed decision-making by providing insights into the financial health of the organization.
2. Investor Confidence: Builds confidence among investors by demonstrating the company's ability to generate profits and manage its finances effectively.
3. Creditworthiness: Affects the company's credit rating and its ability to secure financing.
4. Strategic Planning: Guides strategic planning by identifying areas for improvement or investment.

Case Example:

Consider a manufacturing company that wants to assess its financial performance. By analyzing its income statement, balance sheet, and cash flow statement, the company identifies a decline in profitability over the last quarter. Ratio analysis reveals a decreasing gross margin and a rising debt-to-equity ratio. Trend analysis indicates a consistent decline in net income. The company decides to implement cost-cutting measures, renegotiate supplier contracts, and focus on improving operational efficiency to reverse the negative trend.

Challenges:

1. Data Quality: Dependence on accurate and reliable financial data for meaningful analysis.
2. Industry Variability: Different industries may have distinct financial metrics, making comparisons challenging.
3. Economic Factors: External economic conditions can impact financial performance independent of managerial decisions.

In conclusion, financial performance analysis is a comprehensive evaluation of an organization's financial statements and key metrics. It provides valuable insights for decision-making, strategic planning, and stakeholder confidence, making it an indispensable tool for businesses seeking sustainable growth and success.

Financial performance analysis using Business Intelligence (BI) involves leveraging advanced analytics tools and technologies to gather, process, and analyze financial data in a dynamic and interactive manner. BI tools enable organizations to transform raw financial data into actionable insights, facilitating informed decision-making. Here's how financial performance analysis can be conducted using BI, along with examples:

(1) Data Integration:
- BI tools aggregate financial data from various sources, such as ERP systems, accounting software, and external databases, into a centralized data warehouse.
- Example: Integrating data from sales, expenses, and inventory systems to provide a holistic view of financial performance.

(2) Interactive Dashboards:
- BI platforms create visually appealing dashboards that allow users to monitor key financial metrics in real time.
- Example: A financial dashboard displaying revenue trends, expenses breakdown, and profit margins over different periods.

(3) Drill-Down Analysis:
- Users can drill down into specific details of financial data, uncovering insights at a granular level.
- Example: Investigating a decline in sales by drilling down to regional or product-specific data to identify the root cause.

(4) Key Performance Indicators (KPIs):
- Defining and tracking KPIs relevant to financial performance, such as return on investment (ROI), gross profit margin, and liquidity ratios.
- Example: A BI dashboard featuring KPI widgets that dynamically update to reflect real-time changes in financial metrics.

(5) Predictive Analytics:

- BI tools equipped with predictive analytics capabilities can forecast future financial trends based on historical data.
- Example: Predicting future sales based on historical patterns, seasonality, and market trends to assist in inventory planning.

(6) Ad Hoc Reporting:
- BI platforms allow users to create ad hoc reports, enabling on-the-fly analysis of specific financial questions.
- Example: Generating a report to analyze the impact of a new marketing campaign on sales and customer acquisition costs.

(7) Benchmarking and Comparison:
- BI tools facilitate benchmarking financial performance against industry standards or competitors.
- Example: Comparing the company's profit margins to industry averages to identify areas for improvement.

(8) Scenario Analysis:
- BI enables scenario planning by modeling the impact of various financial scenarios on the organization.
- Example: Analyzing the financial implications of entering new markets, introducing new products, or facing economic downturns.

(9) Geospatial Analysis:
- BI tools with geospatial capabilities can analyze financial data based on geographic locations.
- Example: Mapping sales performance across regions to identify high-performing and underperforming areas.

(10) Data Visualization:
- BI tools use visualization techniques such as charts, graphs, and heatmaps to present financial data in a comprehensible and insightful manner.
- Example: Visualizing cash flow trends over time through a line chart, making it easier to identify patterns and anomalies.

Case Example:

A retail company uses a BI platform to analyze its financial performance. The interactive dashboard provides real-time insights into sales, inventory turnover, and customer acquisition costs. The company notices a decline in profit margins and uses drill-down analysis to identify that increased marketing expenses are not resulting in proportional revenue growth. This prompts the management to reevaluate the marketing strategy and optimize spending to improve profitability.

In conclusion, BI plays a pivotal role in enhancing financial performance analysis by providing dynamic, interactive, and visually appealing tools for extracting valuable insights from financial data. These tools empower organizations to make data-driven decisions and respond promptly to changing financial conditions.

10.4 Teaching Case Study:

Case Study on Financial Analytics and Business Intelligence

Learning Case Study: Enhancing Financial Decision-Making with Financial Analytics and Business Intelligence

Background: ABC Corporation, a multinational manufacturing company, has recently implemented Financial Analytics and Business Intelligence solutions to improve its financial decision-making processes. The goal is to leverage data-driven insights to enhance profitability, mitigate risks, and optimize resource allocation.

Scenario: The company faced challenges in accurately predicting demand, managing costs, and optimizing financial performance. To address these issues, ABC Corporation decided to adopt advanced Financial Analytics and Business Intelligence tools to harness the power of data and analytics.

Implementation:

1. Data Integration: ABC Corporation integrated financial data from various sources, including sales, expenses, and supply chain, into a centralized data warehouse.
2. BI Dashboards: The company created interactive dashboards displaying key financial metrics such as revenue, costs, and profit margins. These dashboards allowed executives to monitor real-time financial performance.
3. Predictive Analytics: ABC Corporation employed predictive analytics to forecast future demand, identify cost-saving opportunities, and optimize pricing strategies.
4. Ad Hoc Reporting: The finance team utilized ad hoc reporting features to generate on-the-fly reports for specific financial queries, aiding in quick decision-making.
5. Benchmarking: The BI tools enabled benchmarking against industry standards, allowing ABC Corporation to assess its financial performance relative to competitors.

Results: The implementation of Financial Analytics and Business Intelligence solutions led to improved financial visibility, better decision-making, and enhanced overall performance. The company experienced increased profitability, optimized operational efficiency, and improved resource allocation.

Learning Questions:

(1) Data Integration and Centralization:

(2) What benefits can ABC Corporation derive from centralizing financial data using Business Intelligence tools?

(3) How does data integration contribute to a more comprehensive financial analysis?

(4) Interactive Dashboards:
   - How can interactive dashboards enhance the decision-making process for financial executives?
   - Provide examples of key financial metrics that can be monitored using BI dashboards.

(5) Predictive Analytics:
   - Explain how predictive analytics can be utilized in financial decision-making.
   - What are the potential challenges of relying solely on historical data without incorporating predictive analytics?

(6) Ad Hoc Reporting:
   - Discuss the importance of ad hoc reporting in responding to immediate financial inquiries.
   - Provide examples of scenarios where ad hoc reporting can be particularly beneficial.

(7) Benchmarking:
   - How can benchmarking against industry standards contribute to strategic financial planning?

- In what ways does benchmarking support ABC Corporation in gaining a competitive edge?

Conclusion: The implementation of Financial Analytics and Business Intelligence has transformed ABC Corporation's financial decision-making processes. Through this case study, participants can gain insights into the practical application of these tools and understand their impact on financial performance. The learning questions encourage reflection on key concepts and their relevance to real-world scenarios.

10.5 Learning Questions:

10.5.1 Descriptive Questions:

(1) What is the definition of Financial Analytics, and how does it contribute to informed decision-making in organizations? Provide examples.

(2) Describe the key components of Financial Analytics, including Financial Modeling, Performance Analytics, Risk Analytics, and Predictive Analytics. How do these components collectively enhance an organization's financial performance?

(3) Explain the role of Business Intelligence in Financial Analytics. What are the key components of Business Intelligence, and how do they contribute to overall business performance?

(4) How does the integration of Financial Analytics and Business Intelligence benefit organizations? Provide specific examples of the advantages gained through this integration.

(5) What is Financial Forecasting, and why is it considered a critical component of Financial Analytics and Business Intelligence? Provide examples of methods used in Financial Forecasting.

(6) Define Risk Management in the context of Financial Analytics and Business Intelligence. Explain the importance of Risk Management and the methods involved in identifying, assessing, and mitigating risks.

(7) How do businesses use Data Integration, Advanced Analytics, Real-time Monitoring, and Visualization to enhance Financial Forecasting and Risk Management in the context of Business Intelligence? Provide practical examples.

(8) Explain the various techniques used in Fraud Detection, such as Anomaly Detection, Pattern Recognition, and Predictive Modeling. How do these techniques contribute to safeguarding organizations against fraudulent activities?

(9) Describe the significance of Data Sources, including Transactional Data, User Behavior Data, and External Data Sources, in Fraud Detection and Prevention. Provide real-world examples of how these data sources are utilized.

(10) In the context of Financial Performance Analysis, elaborate on the importance of Trend Analysis, Comparative Analysis, and the challenges associated with Data Quality, Industry Variability, and Economic Factors. Provide examples illustrating these concepts.

10.5.2 Fill-up the Blanks Questions:

(1) Financial analytics involves the use of data analysis tools and techniques to gain insights into an organization's _____, facilitate forecasting, and support strategic decision-making.
Answer: Financial performance.

(2) Financial modeling is a key component of financial analytics and involves creating mathematical representations of _____ to aid decision-making.
Answer: Financial scenarios.

(3) Business Intelligence refers to the technologies, processes, and tools that help organizations collect, analyze, and present business data to support _____.
Answer: Decision-making.

(4) Data warehousing is a key component of Business Intelligence, involving centralizing and organizing data from various sources for comprehensive _____.
Answer: Analysis.

(5) Integration of Financial Analytics and Business Intelligence ensures real-time monitoring of financial and business metrics, enabling swift responses to _____.
Answer: Emerging trends and challenges.

(6) Financial forecasting involves predicting future financial outcomes based on historical data, market analysis, and other relevant factors, facilitating effective _____.
Answer: Resource allocation.

(7) Risk management in financial analytics involves identifying, assessing, and mitigating potential risks that could impact the achievement of _____.
Answer: Organizational objectives.

(8) Anomaly detection in fraud prevention involves identifying deviations from expected patterns or behaviours in _____.
Answer: Data.

(9) BI tools with geospatial capabilities can analyze financial data based on _____, helping identify high-performing and underperforming areas.
Answer: Geographic locations.

(10) BI platforms enable users to create ad hoc reports for on-the-fly analysis, such as analyzing the impact of a new marketing campaign on sales and _____.
Answer: Customer acquisition costs.

10.5.3 Multiple Choice Questions:

1. What is the primary goal of Financial Analytics?
    A. Enhancing social performance
    B. Transforming raw data into actionable intelligence
    C. Developing cutting-edge technologies
    D. Predicting global economic trends
    - Answer: B. Transforming raw data into actionable intelligence

2. Which component of Financial Analytics involves creating mathematical representations of financial scenarios?
    A. Risk Analytics
    B. Performance Analytics
    C. Financial Modeling
    D. Predictive Analytics
    - Answer: c. Financial Modeling

3. What is the overarching goal of Business Intelligence (BI)?

a. Enhancing personal skills
b. Improving overall business performance
c. Building advanced technologies
d. Predicting market fluctuations
Answer: b. Improving overall business performance

4. Which key component of BI involves centralizing and organizing data for comprehensive analysis?
a. Data Warehousing
b. Data Visualization
c. Querying and Reporting
d. Performance Management
Answer: a. Data Warehousing

5. In the integration of Financial Analytics and BI, what benefit does real-time monitoring provide?
a. Historical analysis
b. Swift responses to emerging trends and challenges
c. Predictive modeling
d. Scenario planning
Answer: b. Swift responses to emerging trends and challenges

6. What does Financial Forecasting primarily involve?
a. Analyzing historical data
b. Predicting future financial outcomes
c. Developing strategic tools
d. Enhancing risk analytics
Answer: b. Predicting future financial outcomes

7. How does financial forecasting contribute to strategic planning?
a. By predicting market trends
b. By assessing and optimizing financial performance
c. By anticipating future financial needs
d. By facilitating decision support
Answer: c. By anticipating future financial needs

8. What is the primary goal of Risk Management?
a. Maximizing profits
b. Minimizing the impact of potential risks
c. Predicting market fluctuations
d. Enhancing data visualization
Answer: b. Minimizing the impact of potential risks

9. What method of risk management involves evaluating the likelihood and impact of identified risks?
a. Risk Identification
b. Risk Assessment
c. Risk Mitigation
d. Monitoring and Review
Answer: b. Risk Assessment

10. In the context of Fraud Detection, what does Anomaly Detection involve?
a. Identifying deviations from expected patterns in data
b. Recognizing patterns of ethical behavior
c. Utilizing predictive models for detection
d. Integrating external data sources
Answer: a. Identifying deviations from expected patterns in data

11. What data source is commonly analyzed for irregularities in fraud detection?
a. Historical data
b. User behavior data
c. External data sources
d. Transactional data
Answer: d. Transactional data

12. How can Preventive Measures be implemented in fraud prevention?
a. By creating mathematical representations
b. Through real-time monitoring
c. By evaluating key performance indicators
d. Using machine learning algorithms
Answer: b. Through real-time monitoring

13. What does Geospatial Analysis in BI involve?
a. Evaluating key performance indicators
b. Analyzing financial statements
c. Mapping financial data based on geographic locations
d. Assessing and optimizing financial performance
Answer: c. Mapping financial data based on geographic locations

14. What does Trend Analysis in Financial Performance involve?
a. Analyzing transactional data
b. Mapping sales performance
c. Evaluating financial data over multiple periods
d. Predicting future financial outcomes
Answer: c. Evaluating financial data over multiple periods

15. Why is Comparative Analysis important in Financial Performance Analysis?
a. To predict market fluctuations
b. To build advanced technologies
c. To identify areas of strength or weakness relative to peers
d. To enhance data visualization
Answer: c. To identify areas of strength or weakness relative to peers

16. What is the main purpose of Data Integration in BI?
a. Analyzing transactional data
b. Creating mathematical representations
c. Aggregating data from various sources for comprehensive analysis
d. Monitoring user behavior
Answer: c. Aggregating data from various sources for comprehensive analysis

17. How do Interactive Dashboards contribute to Financial Performance Analysis in BI?
a. By predicting market trends
b. By creating mathematical representations
c. By allowing users to monitor key financial metrics in real time
d. By evaluating key performance indicators
Answer: c. By allowing users to monitor key financial metrics in real time

18. What does Ad Hoc Reporting in BI enable users to do?
a. Predict future financial outcomes
b. Analyze the impact of a new marketing campaign
c. Evaluate the likelihood and impact of identified risks
d. Implement scenario planning
Answer: b. Analyze the impact of a new marketing campaign

19. How does BI contribute to Scenario Analysis in Financial Performance?
a. By creating mathematical representations
b. By analyzing historical data
c. By modeling the impact of various financial scenarios
d. By integrating external data sources
Answer: c. By modeling the impact of various financial scenarios

20. What role does Data Visualization play in Financial Performance Analysis using BI?
a. Creating mathematical representations
b. Mapping financial data based on geographic locations
c. Transforming complex data sets into visually accessible formats
d. Identifying deviations from expected patterns in data
Answer: c. Transforming complex data sets into visually accessible formats

****

CHAPTER 11

Operational Excellence through Data Analytics

Objectives of the Chapter:

This chapter aims to elucidate the significance of operational excellence in modern organizations and how data analytics acts as a catalyst in achieving superior efficiency, effectiveness, and agility. The chapter delves into various aspects of operational enhancement, including process optimization, predictive maintenance, inventory management, customer experience enhancement, quality control, cost reduction, and employee productivity, each supported by real-world examples. It emphasizes the transformative impact of leveraging data analytics for informed decision-making and explores how organizations can harness the power of data to optimize processes, reduce costs, and ultimately achieve operational excellence. The provided examples serve to illustrate the practical applications of data analytics across different operational facets, demonstrating its tangible benefits in fostering efficiency and performance improvements.

11.1 Operational Excellence through Data Analytics: Transforming Efficiency and Performance

Operational excellence refers to the continuous improvement of business operations to achieve superior efficiency, effectiveness, and agility. In today's data-driven era, organizations are leveraging data analytics to enhance operational excellence across various functions. By harnessing the power of data, companies can optimize processes, reduce costs, and make informed decisions. Here, we explore how data analytics contributes to operational excellence, supported by real-world examples.

1. Process Optimization:

Data analytics allows organizations to analyze operational processes, identify bottlenecks, and streamline workflows for enhanced efficiency.

Example: A logistics company uses data analytics to optimize its supply chain. By analyzing historical shipment data, they identify optimal routes, reduce delivery times, and minimize fuel costs, ultimately improving overall operational efficiency.

2. Predictive Maintenance:

Utilizing data analytics for predictive maintenance helps organizations anticipate equipment failures, reducing downtime and extending the lifespan of assets.

Example: A manufacturing plant employs sensor data and predictive analytics to monitor the health of machinery. By predicting when equipment is likely to fail, the organization can schedule maintenance proactively, avoiding unplanned downtime and optimizing production schedules.

3. Inventory Management:

Data analytics aids in optimizing inventory levels by analyzing historical sales data, demand patterns, and supply chain dynamics.

Example: A retail company uses data analytics to forecast demand for different products. By adjusting inventory levels based on real-time insights, the company minimizes overstock and stockouts, leading to improved cash flow and customer satisfaction.

4. Customer Experience Enhancement:

Analyzing customer data helps organizations tailor their services, personalize experiences, and improve overall customer satisfaction.

Example: An e-commerce platform uses data analytics to analyze customer behavior. By understanding preferences and purchase patterns, the platform provides personalized recommendations, enhancing the customer shopping experience.

5. Quality Control:

Data analytics plays a crucial role in maintaining and improving product or service quality by identifying patterns and anomalies in production processes.

Example: A manufacturing company utilizes data analytics to monitor product quality in real time. By analyzing production data, they can identify defects early in the process, ensuring higher quality outputs and reducing waste.

6. Cost Reduction:

Analyzing operational data helps identify areas of inefficiency, allowing organizations to reduce costs and optimize resource allocation.

Example: A financial institution employs data analytics to analyze transaction processes. By identifying redundant steps and streamlining operations, they reduce operational costs and improve the overall cost-efficiency of the organization.

7. Employee Productivity:

Data analytics can be applied to analyze employee performance, identify training needs, and optimize workforce management.

Example: A call center uses data analytics to analyze employee performance metrics. By identifying areas for improvement and providing targeted training, they enhance employee productivity and customer service.

Conclusion:

Operational excellence through data analytics is a strategic imperative for organizations aiming to stay competitive in today's fast-paced business environment. By leveraging insights derived from data, companies can optimize processes, reduce costs, and enhance overall performance, ultimately achieving operational excellence. The examples provided illustrate the tangible benefits of incorporating data analytics into various operational facets, showcasing its transformative impact on business operations.

11.1 Supply Chain Optimization:

Supply Chain Optimization using Data Analytics and Business Intelligence: Driving Efficiency and Resilience

Supply chain optimization is crucial for businesses aiming to enhance efficiency, reduce costs, and respond effectively to market dynamics. Data analytics and Business Intelligence (BI) play a pivotal role in transforming traditional supply chains into agile and data-driven systems. This note explores how organizations leverage these tools for supply chain optimization, supported by real-world examples.

1. Demand Forecasting:

Data analytics enables organizations to analyze historical data, market trends, and external factors to predict future demand accurately.

Example: A consumer goods company uses predictive analytics to analyze historical sales data, seasonality, and market trends. This allows them to forecast demand accurately, optimize inventory levels, and reduce the risk of stockouts or overstock.

2. Inventory Management:

Business Intelligence tools provide real-time visibility into inventory levels, helping organizations optimize stock levels, reduce carrying costs, and enhance order fulfillment.

Example: An e-commerce company uses BI dashboards to monitor inventory turnover rates, supplier performance, and order fulfillment metrics. By making data-driven decisions, they ensure optimal stock levels, minimize holding costs, and improve order accuracy.

3. Supplier Performance Analytics:

Analyzing supplier data helps organizations identify high-performing suppliers, negotiate better terms, and mitigate risks associated with supply chain disruptions.

Example: An automotive manufacturer uses BI to assess supplier performance metrics such as on-time deliveries, quality, and pricing. This allows them to optimize their supplier network, reduce costs, and enhance overall supply chain resilience.

4. Route Optimization:

Data analytics aids in optimizing transportation routes, reducing transit times, and minimizing transportation costs.

Example: A logistics company utilizes data analytics to analyze traffic patterns, delivery schedules, and fuel consumption. By optimizing delivery routes, they reduce transportation costs, improve delivery times, and enhance overall operational efficiency.

5. Warehouse Management:

Business Intelligence tools help organizations optimize warehouse operations by providing insights into inventory turnover, storage utilization, and order processing times.

Example: A retail chain uses BI analytics to monitor warehouse performance, track order processing times, and optimize storage space. This leads to improved order fulfillment, reduced operational costs, and enhanced customer satisfaction.

6. Real-Time Visibility:

BI dashboards provide real-time visibility into the entire supply chain, allowing organizations to quickly respond to disruptions and make informed decisions.

Example: A global electronics manufacturer employs real-time BI dashboards to monitor the movement of goods across its supply chain. When unexpected delays occur, the organization can quickly reroute shipments and mitigate potential disruptions.

7. Risk Management:

Data analytics assists in identifying and mitigating risks within the supply chain, such as geopolitical issues, natural disasters, or supplier instability.

Example: A pharmaceutical company uses data analytics to assess geopolitical risks, monitor the stability of suppliers, and identify alternative sourcing options. This allows them to proactively manage risks and ensure a stable supply chain.

Conclusion:

Supply chain optimization through data analytics and Business Intelligence is imperative for organizations seeking to build resilient and efficient supply chain ecosystems. By leveraging these tools, businesses can enhance demand forecasting, improve inventory management, optimize logistics, and respond swiftly to changing market conditions. The examples provided illustrate the tangible benefits of incorporating data analytics and BI into supply chain processes, ultimately driving efficiency and ensuring a competitive edge in today's dynamic business landscape.

11.2 Process Improvement using Analytics

Operational Process Improvement using Analytics and Business Intelligence: Enhancing Efficiency and Effectiveness

Operational process improvement is a continuous effort to enhance the efficiency and effectiveness of business processes. Leveraging analytics and Business Intelligence (BI) tools provides organizations with valuable insights into their operations, enabling data-driven decision-making and optimization of key processes. This note explores how analytics and BI contribute to operational process improvement, supported by examples.

1. Data-Driven Decision-Making:

Analytics and BI empower organizations to make informed decisions by transforming raw data into actionable insights. This aids in identifying areas of improvement within operational processes.

Example: A manufacturing company uses BI dashboards to analyze production data, identifying bottlenecks and inefficiencies. With real-time insights, the company can make data-driven decisions to optimize production schedules and resource allocation.

2. Process Visibility and Monitoring:

BI tools provide visibility into various operational processes, allowing organizations to monitor key performance indicators (KPIs) and track process metrics.

Example: A customer service center uses BI dashboards to monitor call volumes, average handling times, and customer satisfaction scores. This visibility enables them to identify areas for improvement, such as optimizing staffing levels during peak hours.

3. Root Cause Analysis:

Analytics facilitates root cause analysis by identifying the underlying factors contributing to process issues or inefficiencies.

Example: A financial institution uses analytics to investigate the root causes of loan approval delays. By analyzing historical data, they identify specific steps in the approval process that contribute to delays and implement targeted improvements.

4. Predictive Analytics for Process Optimization:

Predictive analytics allows organizations to forecast potential process issues, enabling proactive optimization and resource planning.

Example: An e-commerce company uses predictive analytics to forecast website traffic during promotional events. By anticipating increased demand, they can optimize server capacity and prevent potential website outages.

5. Workflow Automation:

BI tools can integrate with workflow automation systems to streamline and automate repetitive tasks, reducing manual effort and improving process efficiency.

Example: An HR department uses BI to analyze employee onboarding processes. By identifying repetitive tasks suitable for automation, they implement workflow automation solutions, reducing onboarding times and minimizing errors.

6. Continuous Monitoring and Feedback:

Analytics and BI enable continuous monitoring of operational processes, providing real-time feedback that allows organizations to adapt quickly to changing conditions.

Example: A retail chain uses BI to monitor inventory levels and sales data. When inventory levels drop below a predefined threshold, automated alerts trigger reordering processes, ensuring products are always available for customers.

7. Benchmarking and Best Practices:

BI tools allow organizations to benchmark their processes against industry best practices, facilitating the identification of areas for improvement.

Example: A logistics company compares its delivery times against industry benchmarks using BI analytics. By identifying areas where their performance lags, they implement changes to improve delivery efficiency.

Conclusion:

Operational process improvement through analytics and BI is a dynamic and iterative process that enables organizations to adapt to changing business environments. By leveraging these tools, businesses can enhance decision-making, optimize workflows, and continuously monitor and refine their operational processes. The examples provided demonstrate how analytics and BI contribute to tangible improvements, fostering efficiency, and effectiveness within organizations.

11.3 Enhancing Operational Efficiency:

How Data Analytics and Business Intelligence Enhance Operational Efficiency: A Detailed Overview

Data Analytics and Business Intelligence (BI) have become integral components for organizations seeking to enhance operational efficiency. These tools provide valuable insights, facilitate data-driven decision-making, and optimize business processes across various functions. Here's a detailed exploration of how Data Analytics and BI contribute to operational efficiency:

(1) Data Integration and Centralization:

Objective: Centralizing and integrating data from diverse sources to create a unified, comprehensive view.

Benefits:

- Holistic Insights: Centralized data allows organizations to gain a holistic view of operations, breaking down silos and providing a comprehensive understanding of processes.

Example: An e-commerce company integrates data from sales, inventory, and customer service systems into a centralized data warehouse. This integration enables them to analyze the entire customer journey, from browsing to purchase, for more informed decision-making.

(2) Real-Time Monitoring with BI Dashboards:

Objective: Utilizing BI dashboards for real-time visualization of key performance indicators (KPIs) and operational metrics.

Benefits:

- Quick Decision-Making: BI dashboards offer instant insights, enabling faster decision-making by providing a real-time snapshot of operational performance.

Example: A manufacturing plant uses BI dashboards to monitor production line efficiency, equipment uptime, and quality metrics. This real-time monitoring helps identify issues promptly and minimize downtime.

3. Predictive Analytics for Proactive Decision-Making:

Objective: Implementing predictive analytics to forecast trends, anticipate issues, and proactively address potential challenges.

Benefits:

- Proactive Decision-Making: Predictive analytics enables organizations to address issues before they escalate, allowing for proactive decision-making.

Example: A logistics company uses predictive analytics to forecast delivery times based on historical data, weather patterns, and traffic conditions. This helps them proactively adjust routes to optimize delivery schedules.

4. Process Optimization through Advanced Analytics:

Objective: Applying advanced analytics to identify inefficiencies, bottlenecks, and areas for improvement within operational processes.

Benefits:

- Efficiency Gains: Advanced analytics help organizations identify and eliminate inefficiencies, leading to streamlined processes and improved overall efficiency.

Example: A financial institution uses advanced analytics to analyze loan approval processes. By identifying bottlenecks, they optimize the workflow, reducing approval times and improving customer satisfaction.

(5) Root Cause Analysis:

Objective: Employing data analytics to investigate the root causes of operational issues, enabling targeted solutions.

Benefits:

- Sustainable Solutions: Root cause analysis ensures that solutions are targeted at the underlying issues, preventing the recurrence of problems.

Example: An IT department uses data analytics to identify the root causes of system outages. By addressing the core issues, they enhance system stability and reduce downtime.

(6) Workflow Automation Integration:

Objective: Integrating BI with workflow automation tools to automate routine tasks, reducing manual effort and minimizing errors.

Benefits:

- Efficiency and Accuracy: Workflow automation reduces manual effort, minimizes errors, and accelerates routine processes, contributing to operational efficiency.

Example: HR processes, such as employee onboarding, are streamlined through workflow automation integrated with BI tools, ensuring a smoother and error-free onboarding experience.

(7) Continuous Monitoring and Feedback Loop:

Objective: Establishing a continuous monitoring system with feedback loops to adapt to changing conditions.
Benefits:

- Adaptability: Continuous monitoring allows organizations to adapt quickly to changing circumstances, ensuring ongoing operational efficiency.

Example: An online retailer continuously monitors website performance metrics. If a sudden increase in traffic is detected, automated alerts trigger additional server capacity to maintain website responsiveness.

(8) Benchmarking and Best Practices:

Objective: Utilizing BI to benchmark operational processes against industry best practices for continuous improvement.
Benefits:

- Optimization: Benchmarking against industry best practices helps identify areas for improvement and optimization.

Example: A manufacturing company uses BI to benchmark production processes against industry standards, implementing changes to align with best practices and enhance operational efficiency.

In conclusion, Data Analytics and Business Intelligence play a pivotal role in enhancing operational efficiency by providing organizations with actionable insights, real-time monitoring capabilities, and tools for continuous improvement. These technologies enable organizations to not only react to current challenges but also to proactively optimize processes, leading to sustained operational excellence. The examples provided illustrate the diverse ways in which analytics and BI contribute to operational efficiency across various industries and functions.

11.4 Teaching Case Study:

Teaching Case Study: Operational Excellence through Data Analytics
Background: XYZ Corporation, a manufacturing company, is striving to achieve operational excellence by leveraging data analytics. The company has recognized the potential of data-driven insights in enhancing efficiency, reducing costs, and improving overall operational

performance. The leadership has initiated a strategic plan to integrate data analytics into various operational processes.

Scenario: The manufacturing processes at XYZ Corporation involve complex workflows, inventory management, and production scheduling. The company aims to use data analytics to optimize these processes, reduce downtime, and enhance overall operational efficiency.

Implementation Steps:

1. Data Integration: XYZ Corporation begins by integrating data from various sources, including production machines, supply chain systems, and quality control processes, into a centralized data warehouse.

2. Real-time Monitoring: The company implements real-time monitoring using data analytics dashboards to track key performance indicators (KPIs) such as machine utilization, production output, and inventory levels.

3. Predictive Maintenance: Utilizing predictive analytics, XYZ Corporation establishes a system to predict equipment failures, allowing proactive maintenance to minimize downtime.

4. Process Optimization: Data analytics is applied to identify bottlenecks and inefficiencies in the production process, enabling targeted optimizations for increased throughput.

5. Inventory Management: By analyzing historical sales data and market trends, the company optimizes inventory levels to prevent stockouts and reduce excess inventory carrying costs.

6. Quality Control: Data analytics tools are used to monitor and analyze quality control data, ensuring that defective products are identified early in the process.

7. Continuous Improvement: The organization establishes a culture of continuous improvement by using data analytics insights to regularly review and enhance operational processes.

Results:

After the implementation of data analytics in operational processes, XYZ Corporation observes improvements in production efficiency, reduction in downtime, and optimized inventory management. The leadership is pleased with the positive impact on operational excellence.

Questions for Analysis of Decisions:

Data Integration Strategy:

(1) How does the integration of data from various sources contribute to a more comprehensive understanding of operational processes?

(2) What challenges might XYZ Corporation face in integrating data from diverse sources, and how can they address these challenges?

Real-time Monitoring:

(3) In what ways can real-time monitoring using data analytics dashboards enhance decision-making at XYZ Corporation?

(4) What specific KPIs should be prioritized in the real-time monitoring dashboards to ensure effective oversight of operational processes?

Predictive Maintenance Implementation:

(5) How does predictive maintenance contribute to minimizing downtime and optimizing equipment performance?

(6) What potential risks and challenges might arise in the implementation of predictive maintenance, and how can XYZ Corporation mitigate them?

Process Optimization Using Data Analytics:

(7) How can data analytics be leveraged to identify and optimize bottlenecks in the production process?

(8) What strategies can XYZ Corporation employ to ensure that the optimization efforts are sustained and continually improved?

Inventory Management:

(9) Explain how analyzing historical sales data and market trends contributes to optimized inventory management.

(10) What considerations should XYZ Corporation take into account when implementing changes to optimize inventory levels?

Quality Control Measures:

(11) In what ways does data analytics enhance quality control processes?

(12) How can XYZ Corporation use insights from quality control data to continuously improve product quality?

Sustaining Continuous Improvement:

(13) Discuss the role of data analytics in fostering a culture of continuous improvement.

(14) What mechanisms can XYZ Corporation establish to ensure that the organization consistently embraces and acts upon insights from data analytics for continuous improvement?

This teaching case study provides a practical illustration of how data analytics can be strategically applied to achieve operational excellence. The questions for analysis encourage students or participants to critically assess the decisions made during the implementation of data analytics and consider potential challenges and improvements.

11.5 Learning Questions:

11.5.1 Descriptive Questions:

(1) How does data analytics contribute to Process Optimization in achieving operational excellence? Provide a real-world example to illustrate its impact.

(2) Explain the role of Predictive Maintenance in enhancing operational efficiency, supported by a real-world example from a manufacturing context.

(3) In what ways does data analytics contribute to Inventory Management, and how can it positively impact cash flow and customer satisfaction? Provide a relevant example from the retail industry.

(4) How does analyzing customer data through data analytics enhance Customer Experience, and how can this be applied in the context of an e-commerce platform? Provide a specific example.

(5) Discuss the role of Data Analytics in maintaining and improving Quality Control in manufacturing processes. Offer a real-world example showcasing the impact on product quality.

(6) Explain how organizations can achieve Cost Reduction by leveraging operational data analytics, with a specific example from the financial sector.

(7) How can data analytics be applied to enhance Employee Productivity? Provide an example of a company utilizing data analytics to optimize workforce management in a call center setting.

(8) Discuss the strategic importance of Supply Chain Optimization using Data Analytics and Business Intelligence, illustrating the impact through an example from the logistics industry.

(9) Explain how Data Integration and Centralization contribute to operational efficiency, providing a real-world example of an organization benefiting from this approach.

(10) Describe the significance of Continuous Monitoring and Feedback Loops in achieving operational excellence. Provide an example of an organization using BI to adapt quickly to changing conditions.

11.5.2 Fill-up the Blanks Questions:

(1) Operational excellence involves the continuous improvement of business operations to achieve superior _____, _____, and agility.
Answer: efficiency, effectiveness

(2) Organizations leverage data analytics to enhance operational excellence by optimizing processes, reducing costs, and making _____ decisions.
Answer: informed

(3) In Process Optimization, data analytics helps identify bottlenecks and streamline workflows for enhanced _____.
Answer: efficiency

(4) Predictive Maintenance, using data analytics, enables organizations to anticipate equipment failures, reducing downtime and extending the lifespan of _____.
Answer: assets

(5) Data analytics aids in optimizing inventory levels by analyzing historical sales data, demand patterns, and supply chain _____.
Answer: dynamics

(6) Analyzing customer data helps organizations tailor their services, personalize experiences, and improve overall _____ satisfaction.
Answer: customer

(7) Data analytics plays a crucial role in maintaining and improving product or service quality by identifying patterns and anomalies in _____ processes.
Answer: production

(8) Analyzing operational data helps identify areas of inefficiency, allowing organizations to reduce costs and optimize _____ allocation.
Answer: resource

(9) Data analytics can be applied to analyze employee performance, identify training needs, and optimize _____ management.
Answer: workforce

(10) Operational excellence through data analytics is a strategic imperative for organizations aiming to stay competitive in today's _____ business environment.
Answer: fast-paced

11.5.3 Multiple Choice Questions:

(1) What is the primary goal of operational excellence?
   A. Profit maximization
   B. Continuous improvement of business operations
   C. Market dominance
   D. Resource allocation
   • Answer: b) Continuous improvement of business operations

(2) How does data analytics contribute to process optimization?

A. By increasing production costs
B. By identifying bottlenecks and streamlining workflows
C. By reducing data accuracy
D. By minimizing fuel costs
- Answer: b) By identifying bottlenecks and streamlining workflows

(3) In predictive maintenance, what is the goal of using sensor data and predictive analytics?
A. Increasing equipment downtime
B. Reducing the lifespan of assets
C. Anticipating equipment failures and extending asset lifespan
D. Eliminating scheduled maintenance
- Answer: c) Anticipating equipment failures and extending asset lifespan

(4) How does data analytics contribute to inventory management in a retail company?
A. By increasing overstock and stockouts
B. By forecasting demand for different products
C. By minimizing cash flow
D. By reducing customer satisfaction
- Answer: b) By forecasting demand for different products

(5) What is the key role of data analytics in enhancing customer experience?
A. Increasing prices
B. Tailoring services and personalizing experiences
C. Ignoring customer behaviour
D. Reducing overall satisfaction
- Answer: b) Tailoring services and personalizing experiences

(6) How does data analytics contribute to quality control in manufacturing?
A. By ignoring anomalies in production processes
B. By reducing waste
C. By increasing defects in products
D. By avoiding real-time monitoring
- Answer: b) By reducing waste

(7) What benefit does data analytics provide in cost reduction for a financial institution?
A. Increasing operational costs
B. Identifying redundant steps and streamlining operations
C. Ignoring transaction processes
D. Reducing customer service efficiency
- Answer: b) Identifying redundant steps and streamlining operations

(8) In employee productivity, how is data analytics utilized in a call center?
A. Ignoring performance metrics
B. Decreasing productivity
C. Analyzing employee performance metrics and providing targeted training
D. Avoiding workforce management
- Answer: c) Analyzing employee performance metrics and providing targeted training

(9) What is the strategic imperative for organizations in today's fast-paced business environment?
  A. Ignoring operational excellence
  B. Leveraging insights derived from data
  C. Reducing overall performance
  D. Avoiding data analytics
  - Answer: b) Leveraging insights derived from data

(10) In supply chain optimization, what does data analytics enable organizations to do in demand forecasting?
  A. Increase stockouts
  B. Analyze historical sales data and market trends
  C. Avoid optimizing inventory levels
  D. Ignore the risk of overstock
  - Answer: b) Analyze historical sales data and market trends

(11) How do Business Intelligence tools contribute to inventory management in an e-commerce company?
  A. By minimizing order accuracy
  B. By avoiding real-time visibility
  C. By providing real-time visibility into inventory levels
  D. By increasing carrying costs
  - Answer: c) By providing real-time visibility into inventory levels

(12) What does analyzing supplier data help organizations achieve in supply chain management?
  A. Increasing supply chain disruptions
  B. Negotiating worse terms with suppliers
  C. Identifying high-performing suppliers and mitigating risks
  D. Ignoring supplier performance metrics
  - Answer: c) Identifying high-performing suppliers and mitigating risks

(13) In route optimization, how does data analytics contribute to reducing transportation costs for a logistics company?
  A. By avoiding traffic analysis
  B. By increasing transit times
  C. By ignoring fuel consumption
  D. By optimizing delivery routes
  - Answer: d) By optimizing delivery routes

(14) What insights do Business Intelligence tools provide in optimizing warehouse operations for a retail chain?
  A. Increased order processing times
  B. Reduced order fulfillment
  C. Insights into inventory turnover, storage utilization, and order processing times
  D. Ignoring warehouse performance
  - Answer: c) Insights into inventory turnover, storage utilization, and order processing times

(15) How do BI dashboards contribute to supply chain visibility?
  A. By minimizing disruptions
  B. By avoiding real-time visibility
  C. By increasing transit times
  D. By providing real-time visibility into the entire supply chain
  - Answer: d) By providing real-time visibility into the entire supply chain

(16) What role does data analytics play in risk management within the supply chain?
  A. Ignoring geopolitical issues
  B. Increasing supply chain disruptions
  C. Assisting in identifying and mitigating risks
  D. Avoiding alternative sourcing options
  - Answer: c) Assisting in identifying and mitigating risks

(17) What is the imperative for organizations seeking to build resilient and efficient supply chain ecosystems?
  A. Ignoring data analytics
  B. Leveraging Business Intelligence
  C. Avoiding demand forecasting
  D. Reducing inventory management
  - Answer: b) Leveraging Business Intelligence

(18) How do analytics and BI contribute to operational process improvement in organizations?
  A. By avoiding decision-making
  B. By reducing operational visibility
  C. By enabling data-driven decision-making and process optimization
  D. By ignoring key performance indicators
  - Answer: c) By enabling data-driven decision-making and process optimization

(19) What does root cause analysis using analytics facilitate within operational processes?
  A. Ignoring process issues
  B. Sustainable solutions targeted at underlying issues
  C. Increasing inefficiencies
  D. Avoiding process metrics
  - Answer: b) Sustainable solutions targeted at underlying issues

(20) How do BI tools contribute to continuous monitoring and feedback loops in operational processes?
  A. By minimizing adaptability
  B. By ignoring changing conditions
  C. By providing real-time feedback and enabling quick adaptation
  D. By avoiding benchmarking against industry best practices
  - Answer: c) By providing real-time feedback and enabling quick adaptation

****

CHAPTER 12

Human Resources and People Analytics

Objectives of the Chapter:

The overarching objective of this comprehensive chapter is to elucidate the transformative role of Human Resources and People Analytics in the context of Data Analytics and Business Intelligence. This specialized field is positioned as a dynamic bridge between traditional HR practices and the contemporary imperative of data-driven decision-making, fundamentally altering how organizations manage and optimize their workforce. The chapter delves into key elements of Human Resources and People Analytics, such as talent acquisition and retention strategies, performance management through analytics, and diversity and inclusion analytics. It aims to provide a thorough understanding of the methodologies and tools used to collect, process, and analyze human-centric data, emphasizing the potential to drive strategic workforce management, enhance employee satisfaction, and contribute to overall organizational success. By integrating advanced analytics into HR practices, businesses can align human capital strategies with organizational objectives, fostering agility and responsiveness in the face of evolving challenges. This chapter seeks to equip readers with insights into leveraging data for talent optimization, performance enhancement, and the cultivation of diverse and inclusive workplace cultures, positioning Human Resources and People Analytics as a critical component for organizations aiming to unlock the full potential of their most valuable asset – their people.

12.1 Introduction to Human Resources and People Analytics:

Human Resources and People Analytics represents a dynamic and transformative field within the realm of Data Analytics and Business Intelligence. This specialized discipline leverages advanced analytical techniques and cutting-edge technologies to extract valuable insights from vast pools of human-centric data, fundamentally reshaping how organizations manage and optimize their workforce. In essence, it serves as the bridge between traditional HR practices and the data-driven decision-making imperative of today's business landscape.

At its core, Human Resources and People Analytics involves the systematic collection, processing, and analysis of data related to employee behaviour, performance, engagement, and overall workplace dynamics. This data-driven approach enables businesses to make informed decisions that can enhance employee satisfaction, boost productivity, and contribute to overall organizational success.

Key elements of this field include talent acquisition analytics, employee retention analysis, workforce planning, performance management metrics, and employee engagement assessments. Through the application of statistical models, machine learning algorithms, and predictive analytics, organizations can gain valuable insights into trends, patterns, and potential future scenarios related to their human capital.

The integration of Human Resources and People Analytics into the broader landscape of Data Analytics and Business Intelligence signifies a strategic shift from reactive HR practices to proactive, forward-thinking workforce management. By harnessing the power of data, businesses can align their human capital strategies with organizational objectives, fostering a more agile and responsive approach to the ever-evolving challenges of the modern business environment. As the digital transformation journey continues, Human Resources and People Analytics emerges as a critical component for organizations seeking to unlock the full potential of their most valuable asset – their people.

Talent Acquisition and Retention Strategies:

Talent Acquisition and Retention Strategies within the domain of Human Resources and People Analytics play a pivotal role in shaping the success and sustainability of organizations. In the era of Data Analytics and Business Intelligence, leveraging data-driven insights is crucial for attracting, identifying, and retaining top-tier talent. This comprehensive approach involves the use of advanced analytics tools and methodologies to optimize the entire talent lifecycle.

Talent Acquisition Strategies:

(1) Predictive Recruiting:
- Utilizing predictive analytics to forecast hiring needs based on historical data and current market trends.
- Identifying potential candidates through the analysis of resumes, social media profiles, and other relevant data sources.

(2) Candidate Experience Enhancement:
- Analyzing candidate feedback and engagement data to improve the overall recruitment process.
- Personalizing communication and interactions based on individual preferences and behaviors.

(3) Skills Gap Analysis:
- Using analytics to assess the current skill set within the organization.
- Identifying gaps and proactively planning for future skill requirements.

(4) Diversity and Inclusion Analytics:
- Implementing analytics to track and improve diversity metrics in the hiring process.

- Ensuring fairness and mitigating biases in talent acquisition.

Retention Strategies:

(1) Employee Engagement Analytics:
- Employing surveys, feedback, and sentiment analysis to gauge employee satisfaction and engagement.
- Identifying factors that contribute to employee motivation and loyalty.

(2) Predictive Turnover Modeling:
- Building models to predict potential turnover risks based on historical patterns and employee behaviour.
- Implementing targeted interventions to retain at-risk employees.

(3) Learning and Development Analytics:
- Analyzing the impact of training and development programs on employee performance and satisfaction.
- Tailoring learning initiatives based on individual employee needs and career aspirations.

(4) Compensation and Benefits Optimization:
- Utilizing analytics to benchmark and adjust compensation packages to remain competitive in the market.
- Identifying the correlation between benefits programs and employee retention.

(5) Succession Planning:
- Using data to identify high-potential employees and create succession plans.
- Ensuring a smooth transition in key roles to prevent talent gaps.

Benefits of Integrating Talent Analytics:

(1) Strategic Decision-Making:
- Aligning talent acquisition and retention strategies with overall business objectives.
- Making informed decisions based on data-driven insights.

(2) Cost Optimization:
- Reducing recruitment costs by targeting the most effective channels and methods.
- Minimizing turnover-related expenses through proactive retention measures.

(3) Competitive Advantage:
- Gaining a competitive edge by attracting and retaining the best talent in the industry.
- Positioning the organization as an employer of choice.

In the landscape of Human Resources and People Analytics, the integration of advanced talent acquisition and retention strategies is indispensable for organizations striving to thrive in a data-driven era. By harnessing the power of analytics, businesses can not only optimize their recruitment processes but also create a workplace environment that fosters employee satisfaction, engagement, and long-term commitment. As organizations increasingly recognize the value of their human capital, Talent Acquisition and Retention Strategies supported by data analytics become instrumental in gaining a strategic advantage in the competitive business landscape.

12.2 Performance Management through Analytics

Performance Management through Analytics is a transformative approach within Human Resources and People Analytics that leverages data-driven insights to optimize employee performance, enhance productivity, and align individual contributions with organizational goals. In the dynamic landscape of Data Analytics and Business Intelligence, organizations are increasingly turning to advanced analytics techniques to refine their performance management strategies and drive continuous improvement.

Key Components of Performance Management through Analytics:

(1) Key Performance Indicators (KPIs) and Metrics:
- Defining and tracking relevant KPIs and performance metrics to assess individual and team effectiveness.
- Analyzing trends and patterns to identify areas of improvement and success.

(2) Real-time Performance Monitoring:
- Implementing analytics tools that provide real-time monitoring of employee performance.
- Enabling immediate feedback and intervention to address performance issues promptly.

(3) Predictive Performance Modeling:
- Using historical performance data to create predictive models for future employee performance.
- Anticipating potential challenges and proactively addressing them.

(4) 360-Degree Feedback Analysis:
- Employing analytics to analyze feedback from multiple sources, including peers, subordinates, and supervisors.
- Identifying patterns and correlations to provide a holistic view of an employee's performance.

(5) Goal Alignment and Progress Tracking:
- Aligning individual and team goals with organizational objectives.
- Tracking progress through analytics to ensure alignment and identify areas that need adjustment.

(6) Individualized Performance Plans:

- Developing personalized performance improvement plans based on analytics insights.
- Tailoring training and development opportunities to address specific skill gaps.

(7) Employee Recognition and Rewards Optimization:
- Analyzing performance data to identify high-performing individuals and teams.
- Optimizing recognition and rewards programs to motivate and retain top talent.

Benefits of Performance Management through Analytics:

(1) Data-Driven Decision-Making:
- Enabling HR professionals and managers to make informed decisions based on concrete performance data.
- Shifting from subjective evaluations to objective, evidence-based assessments.

(2) Continuous Feedback and Improvement:
- Facilitating a culture of continuous improvement through real-time feedback.
- Identifying trends and patterns that contribute to ongoing enhancements in performance management strategies.

(3) Employee Development and Engagement:
- Personalizing development plans based on individual performance analytics.
- Increasing employee engagement by demonstrating a commitment to professional growth.

(4) Strategic Workforce Planning:
- Using performance analytics to inform strategic workforce planning.
- Aligning talent management strategies with organizational objectives.

(5) Risk Mitigation:
- Identifying and addressing performance issues before they escalate.
- Mitigating the risk of talent attrition through targeted interventions.

In the era of Data Analytics and Business Intelligence, Performance Management through Analytics emerges as a crucial component of effective human capital management. By harnessing the power of data, organizations can not only objectively assess performance but also create a culture of continuous improvement and employee development. This data-driven approach not only enhances individual and team productivity but also contributes to the overall success and competitiveness of the organization in a rapidly evolving business landscape. Performance Management through Analytics is poised to play a central role in shaping the future of performance evaluation and talent optimization strategies.

12.3 Diversity and Inclusion Analytics:

Diversity and Inclusion Analytics represents a transformative approach within Human Resources and People Analytics that focuses on leveraging data-driven insights to promote diversity, equity, and inclusion (DEI) within organizations. In the context of Data Analytics and Business Intelligence, this emerging discipline plays a critical role in not only measuring diversity metrics but also in shaping inclusive workplace strategies that foster innovation, engagement, and overall organizational success.

Key Components of Diversity and Inclusion Analytics:

(1) Demographic Data Analysis:
- Utilizing analytics to assess and understand the demographic composition of the workforce.
- Analyzing data related to age, gender, ethnicity, sexual orientation, and other dimensions of diversity.

(2) Representation Metrics:
- Measuring the representation of diverse groups at various organizational levels.
- Identifying areas where representation gaps exist and implementing strategies to address them.

(3) Pay Equity Analysis:
- Applying analytics to evaluate pay equity across diverse groups.
- Identifying and rectifying disparities in compensation based on gender, ethnicity, or other relevant factors.

(4) Recruitment Analytics for Diversity:
- Analyzing the effectiveness of recruitment efforts in attracting diverse candidates.
- Identifying potential biases in the recruitment process and implementing corrective measures.

(5) Employee Lifecycle Analysis:
- Examining the entire employee lifecycle, from recruitment to promotion and retention.
- Identifying patterns and areas where diversity and inclusion initiatives can be integrated.

(6) Inclusive Leadership Metrics:
- Assessing leadership and management practices through analytics to ensure inclusivity.
- Identifying and promoting inclusive leadership behaviors that contribute to a diverse and equitable workplace.

(7) Employee Engagement and Inclusion Surveys:

- Implementing surveys and sentiment analysis tools to gauge employee perceptions of inclusion.
- Using analytics to identify trends and areas for improvement in fostering an inclusive culture.

Benefits of Diversity and Inclusion Analytics:

(1) Data-Driven Decision-Making:
- Enabling organizations to make informed decisions about diversity and inclusion initiatives.
- Aligning DEI efforts with overall business strategies through evidence-based insights.

(2) Identification of Bias and Barriers:
- Uncovering implicit biases in HR processes and decision-making.
- Identifying systemic barriers that may hinder the advancement of underrepresented groups.

(3) Enhanced Talent Attraction and Retention:
- Demonstrating a commitment to diversity through data-driven transparency.
- Attracting diverse talent and retaining employees by fostering an inclusive workplace culture.

(4) Legal and Regulatory Compliance:
- Ensuring compliance with diversity-related regulations and standards.
- Mitigating legal risks by proactively addressing diversity and inclusion challenges.

(5) Innovation and Performance:
- Harnessing the diversity dividend by promoting innovation through diverse perspectives.
- Enhancing overall organizational performance by leveraging a variety of talents and experiences.

In the landscape of Human Resources and People Analytics, Diversity and Inclusion Analytics stands as a cornerstone for organizations committed to creating equitable and inclusive workplaces. By employing data-driven insights, businesses can not only measure diversity metrics but also drive strategic initiatives that promote a culture of belonging and foster a diverse and high-performing workforce. As the importance of diversity and inclusion continues to gain prominence, the integration of analytics into these efforts becomes imperative for organizations seeking to thrive in the evolving business environment.

12.4 Teaching Case Study:

Caselet 1: Leveraging Human Resources and People Analytics for Strategic Workforce Planning

Company XYZ, a global technology firm, has recently recognized the significance of leveraging Human Resources and People Analytics to enhance its workforce management strategies. The company aims to utilize data-driven insights to optimize talent acquisition, improve employee performance, and foster a more inclusive workplace culture.

The HR department at Company XYZ has embarked on implementing Human Resources and People Analytics across various facets of their operations. The focus areas include talent acquisition, performance management, diversity and inclusion, and overall strategic workforce planning.

Scenario:

The HR team has started implementing predictive analytics for talent acquisition to forecast future hiring needs. They are also exploring ways to enhance the candidate experience through analytics-driven insights. Additionally, the company is keen on using performance management analytics to provide real-time feedback to employees and optimize individual and team performance. The HR department is committed to improving diversity and inclusion metrics, and they are exploring how analytics can help identify and address potential biases in recruitment and promotion processes.

Questions:

(1) Talent Acquisition Analytics: a. How can predictive analytics assist Company XYZ in forecasting future hiring needs? b. What are the potential benefits of enhancing the candidate experience through analytics-driven insights in the recruitment process?

(2) Performance Management Analytics: a. How can real-time performance monitoring through analytics contribute to employee development? b. What role can predictive performance modeling play in addressing future performance challenges?

(3) Diversity and Inclusion Analytics: a. What metrics and data sources could Company XYZ use to measure and analyze its current diversity representation? b. How might analytics help identify and rectify biases in the recruitment and promotion processes to improve diversity and inclusion?

(4) Strategic Workforce Planning: a. How does the integration of Human Resources and People Analytics contribute to strategic workforce planning at Company XYZ? b. In what ways can analytics be applied to align individual and team goals with organizational objectives?

(5) Challenges and Considerations: a. What challenges might Company XYZ encounter in implementing Human Resources and People Analytics across various HR functions? b. What considerations should the HR team keep in mind to ensure the ethical and responsible use of analytics in workforce management?

This caselet aims to encourage discussion and critical thinking about the practical applications of Human Resources and People Analytics in a real-world business setting. It prompts participants to explore the potential benefits, challenges, and ethical considerations associated with integrating analytics into HR practices for strategic workforce planning.

12.5 Learning Questions:

12.5.1 Descriptive Questions:

(1) Explain the role of Human Resources and People Analytics in today's business landscape.

(2) What are the key elements of Human Resources and People Analytics, and how do they contribute to organizational success?

(3) Describe the integration of Human Resources and People Analytics into Data Analytics and Business Intelligence and its impact on workforce management.

(4) How does Talent Acquisition and Retention Strategies contribute to the success and sustainability of organizations in the era of Data Analytics and Business Intelligence?

(5) Explain the concept of Predictive Recruiting and its significance in optimizing the talent lifecycle.

(6) Discuss the role of Employee Engagement Analytics in retaining and motivating employees.

(7) How does Performance Management through Analytics utilize real-time monitoring and predictive modeling to enhance individual and team effectiveness?

(8) Explain the importance of Diversity and Inclusion Analytics in promoting equity and fostering innovation within organizations.

(9) Describe the components of Diversity and Inclusion Analytics, including demographic data analysis and representation metrics.

(10) Discuss the benefits of integrating Data Analytics into Diversity and Inclusion initiatives for organizations striving to create inclusive workplaces.

12.5.2 Fill-up the Blanks Questions:

(1) Human Resources and People Analytics represents a transformative field within the realm of _____ and _____.
Answer: Data Analytics; Business Intelligence

(2) Talent Acquisition and Retention Strategies play a pivotal role in shaping the success and sustainability of organizations in the era of _____ and _____.
Answer: Data Analytics; Business Intelligence

(3) Predictive Recruiting involves utilizing predictive analytics to forecast hiring needs based on _____ and _____ trends.
Answer: Historical data; current market

(4) Employee Engagement Analytics employs surveys, feedback, and sentiment analysis to gauge employee satisfaction and _____.
Answer: Engagement

(5) Performance Management through Analytics enables HR professionals and managers to make informed decisions based on concrete _____ data.
Answer: Performance

(6) Diversity and Inclusion Analytics focuses on leveraging data-driven insights to promote diversity, equity, and inclusion (DEI) within _____.
Answer: Organizations

(7) Representation Metrics involve measuring the representation of diverse groups at various _____ levels.
Answer: Organizational

(8) Pay Equity Analysis applies analytics to evaluate pay equity across diverse groups, identifying and rectifying disparities in compensation based on _____ and _____ factors.
Answer: Gender; ethnicity

(9) Inclusive Leadership Metrics assess leadership and management practices through analytics to ensure _____.
Answer: Inclusivity

(10) Diversity and Inclusion Analytics enables organizations to make informed decisions about diversity and inclusion initiatives, aligning DEI efforts with overall _____.
Answer: Business strategies

12.5.3 Multiple Choice Questions:

(1) What is the primary role of Human Resources and People Analytics?

A. Conducting traditional HR practices
B. Extracting valuable insights from human-centric data
C. Managing organizational finances
D. Implementing business intelligence tools
  - Answer: b) Extracting valuable insights from human-centric data

(2) What is the key objective of Talent Acquisition and Retention Strategies in the era of Data Analytics and Business Intelligence?

A. Reducing employee engagement
B. Enhancing workplace diversity
C. Shaping success and sustainability of organizations
D. Eliminating predictive recruiting
  - Answer: c) Shaping success and sustainability of organizations

(3) Which of the following is a component of Talent Acquisition Strategies?

A. Cost Optimization
B. Employee Engagement Analytics
C. Real-time Performance Monitoring
D. Diversity and Inclusion Analytics
  - Answer: a) Predictive Recruiting

(4) What does Employee Engagement Analytics use to gauge employee satisfaction and engagement?

A. Real-time monitoring
B. Surveys, feedback, and sentiment analysis
C. Predictive modeling
D. Compensation optimization
  - Answer: b) Surveys, feedback, and sentiment analysis

(5) Which strategy involves building models to predict potential turnover risks based on historical patterns and employee behaviour?

A. Learning and Development Analytics
B. Predictive Recruiting
C. Compensation and Benefits Optimization
D. Predictive Turnover Modeling
- Answer: d) Predictive Turnover Modeling

(6) What is a benefit of integrating Talent Analytics mentioned in the information?

A. Increasing recruitment costs
B. Minimizing turnover-related expenses
C. Reducing the use of effective channels
D. Decreasing employee engagement
- Answer: b) Minimizing turnover-related expenses

(7) Which component of Performance Management through Analytics involves tracking progress through analytics to ensure alignment with organizational objectives?

A. Goal Alignment and Progress Tracking
B. Individualized Performance Plans
C. 360-Degree Feedback Analysis
D. Real-time Performance Monitoring
- Answer: a) Goal Alignment and Progress Tracking

(8) What is the key focus of Diversity and Inclusion Analytics?

A. Enhancing employee engagement
B. Promoting diversity, equity, and inclusion
C. Reducing legal and regulatory compliance
D. Implementing inclusive leadership metrics
- Answer: b) Promoting diversity, equity, and inclusion

(9) What is included in the Demographic Data Analysis component of Diversity and Inclusion Analytics?

A. Analyzing employee recognition
B. Evaluating pay equity
C. Assessing leadership practices
D. Understanding the demographic composition of the workforce
- Answer: d) Understanding the demographic composition of the workforce

(10) What is the purpose of Pay Equity Analysis in Diversity and Inclusion Analytics?

A. Evaluating pay equity across diverse groups
B. Enhancing employee engagement
C. Implementing real-time performance monitoring
D. Fostering a culture of continuous improvement
- Answer: a) Evaluating pay equity across diverse groups

(11) What is the overarching benefit of Diversity and Inclusion Analytics mentioned in the information?

A. Decreasing workforce diversity
B. Reducing employee engagement
C. Enhancing talent attraction and retention
D. Limiting legal and regulatory compliance
- Answer: c) Enhancing talent attraction and retention

(12) What is the strategic shift indicated by the integration of Human Resources and People Analytics into the broader landscape of Data Analytics and Business Intelligence?

A. Shift from proactive to reactive HR practices
B. Shift from data-driven to intuition-based decision-making
C. Shift from reactive to proactive, forward-thinking workforce management
D. Shift from talent acquisition to talent elimination
- Answer: c) Shift from reactive to proactive, forward-thinking workforce management

(13) Which analytics technique is NOT mentioned as part of the application in Human Resources and People Analytics?

A. Statistical models
B. Predictive analytics
C. Descriptive analytics
D. Prescriptive analytics
- Answer: d) Prescriptive analytics

(14) What is the primary focus of Talent Acquisition Strategies within Human Resources and People Analytics?

A. Enhancing employee engagement
B. Attracting, identifying, and retaining top-tier talent
C. Minimizing performance metrics
D. Reducing diversity and inclusion metrics

Answer: b) Attracting, identifying, and retaining top-tier talent

(15) What does Diversity and Inclusion Analytics assess in leadership and management practices?

A. Employee engagement
B. Real-time performance
C. Inclusivity
D. Compensation optimization
- Answer: c) Inclusivity

(16) Which strategy involves analyzing the impact of training and development programs on employee performance and satisfaction?

A. Succession Planning
B. Predictive Turnover Modeling
C. Learning and Development Analytics
D. Compensation and Benefits Optimization

- Answer: c) Learning and Development Analytics

(17) What is the benefit of Individualized Performance Plans in Performance Management through Analytics?

A. Fostering a culture of continuous improvement
B. Enabling HR professionals to make subjective evaluations
C. Reducing real-time performance monitoring
D. Tailoring training and development opportunities based on analytics insights
- Answer: d) Tailoring training and development opportunities based on analytics insights

(18) What is the main objective of Performance Management through Analytics?

A. Minimizing employee satisfaction
B. Optimizing employee performance
C. Eliminating real-time performance monitoring
D. Reducing talent acquisition strategies
- Answer: b) Optimizing employee performance

(19) Which analysis tool provides real-time monitoring of employee performance in Performance Management through Analytics?

A. Goal Alignment and Progress Tracking
B. Employee Recognition and Rewards Optimization
C. Real-time Performance Monitoring
D. 360-Degree Feedback Analysis
- Answer: c) Real-time Performance Monitoring

(20) What is the transformative approach of Diversity and Inclusion Analytics within Human Resources and People Analytics?

A. Minimizing diversity metrics
B. Shaping success and sustainability
C. Fostering a culture of continuous improvement
D. Leveraging data-driven insights to promote diversity, equity, and inclusion
- Answer: d) Leveraging data-driven insights to promote diversity, equity, and inclusion

CHAPTER 13

Case Studies in Data-Driven Decision Making

Objectives of the Chapter:

This chapter aims to provide a comprehensive understanding of the role of data-driven decision-making as a fundamental strategy for success in the evolving business and technological landscape. It highlights the significance of case studies in illuminating narratives that showcase practical applications of data analytics in solving complex challenges, optimizing processes, and achieving strategic goals across diverse industries and sectors. The key components of these case studies include problem definition, data collection and processing, analytical techniques, the decision-making process, outcomes and impact, and lessons learned. The chapter emphasizes the benefits of case studies in offering practical applications, inspiring innovation, providing benchmarks and best practices, and facilitating cross-industry insights. It positions case studies as invaluable resources for professionals, educators, and decision-makers, inspiring a shift toward a more data-centric and evidence-based approach to problem-solving in today's data-driven era. Additionally, real-world examples of successful implementations illustrate the diverse applications of data-driven decision-making across industries. Finally, the chapter explores common challenges faced in data-driven decision-making, offering strategic solutions to navigate issues related to data quality, literacy, privacy, integration, change management, scalability, bias, cost, real-time decision-making, and ROI measurement. It concludes by emphasizing the dynamic and adaptive nature required for organizations committed to deriving value from their data in the face of evolving challenges.

13.1 Introduction to Case Studies in Data-Driven Decision Making:

In the rapidly evolving landscape of business and technology, organizations are increasingly turning to data-driven decision-making as a fundamental strategy for success. Case Studies in Data-Driven Decision Making serve as illuminating narratives that showcase the practical application of data analytics in solving complex challenges, optimizing processes, and achieving strategic goals. These real-world examples provide invaluable insights into how data, when leveraged effectively, can transform decision-making processes across diverse industries and sectors.

Each case study within this domain explores a specific business problem or opportunity where data played a pivotal role in guiding decision-makers toward more informed and impactful choices. These narratives go beyond theoretical concepts, offering a tangible glimpse into the methodologies, tools, and outcomes associated with data-driven decision-making.

Key Components of Case Studies in Data-Driven Decision Making:

(1) Problem Definition:
- Clearly articulating the business problem or decision that required resolution.
- Identifying the challenges and complexities involved in traditional decision-making approaches.

(2) Data Collection and Processing:
- Detailing the sources of data used in the decision-making process.
- Describing the methods employed to clean, preprocess, and organize the data for analysis.

(3) Analytical Techniques:
- Showcasing the specific analytical techniques and models applied to derive insights.
- Explaining how statistical methods, machine learning algorithms, or other approaches were employed.

(4) Decision-Making Process:
- Narrating the sequence of steps taken in the decision-making process.
- Highlighting the key considerations and criteria used to evaluate different options.

(5) Outcomes and Impact:
- Presenting the results and insights obtained through data analysis.
- Discussing the impact of data-driven decisions on business performance, efficiency, or innovation.

(6) Lessons Learned:
- Reflecting on the challenges faced and lessons learned during the implementation of data-driven decision-making.
- Offering insights into how organizations can improve their data-centric strategies in the future.

Benefits of Case Studies in Data-Driven Decision Making:

(1) Practical Application:
- Demonstrating how data analytics concepts are translated into actionable strategies.
- Providing a bridge between theoretical knowledge and real-world problem-solving.

(2) Inspiration for Innovation:
- Inspiring organizations to explore innovative ways of utilizing data for decision-making.
- Encouraging a culture of curiosity and experimentation with data-driven approaches.

(3) Benchmarking and Best Practices:

- Offering benchmarks and best practices based on successful case studies.
- Guiding organizations in adopting effective data-driven decision-making practices.

(4) Cross-Industry Insights:
- Showcasing diverse examples across industries and sectors.
- Facilitating cross-industry learning and adaptation of successful strategies.

In essence, Case Studies in Data-Driven Decision Making serve as invaluable resources for professionals, educators, and decision-makers seeking to understand the practical implications and transformative potential of incorporating data analytics into their decision-making processes. These narratives inspire a mindset shift towards a more data-centric and evidence-based approach to problem-solving in today's data-driven era.

13.2 Real-world Examples of Successful Implementations:

Real-World Examples of Successful Implementations of Data-Driven Decision Making:

(1) Amazon's Recommendation System:
Amazon's recommendation engine is a prime example of data-driven decision-making. By analyzing user behavior, purchase history, and preferences, Amazon uses complex algorithms to provide personalized product recommendations. This has significantly contributed to increased sales, customer satisfaction, and the overall success of the e-commerce giant.

(2) Netflix Content Recommendation:
Netflix employs data-driven decision-making to enhance user experience by recommending personalized content. The streaming service analyzes viewing habits, user ratings, and other data points to suggest movies and TV shows tailored to individual preferences. This approach has played a crucial role in retaining subscribers and driving engagement.

(3) Google's Search Algorithm:
Google's search algorithm relies on extensive data analysis to deliver relevant and timely search results. The algorithm considers factors such as user behavior, click-through rates, and website relevance to continuously refine search rankings. Google's data-driven approach has made it the leading search engine globally.

(4) Uber's Dynamic Pricing:
Uber utilizes data-driven decision-making to implement dynamic pricing based on factors like demand, traffic conditions, and availability of drivers. By analyzing real-time data, Uber adjusts prices dynamically to optimize driver incentives, meet demand, and balance the supply of drivers with rider needs.

(5) Zara's Inventory Management:

Zara, a fashion retailer, leverages data-driven decision-making in its inventory management system. By analyzing sales data in real-time, Zara can quickly identify popular products and adjust production accordingly. This agile approach to inventory management has allowed Zara to reduce overstock and respond swiftly to changing consumer preferences.

(6) NASA's Mars Rover Missions:

NASA's Mars rover missions exemplify the successful use of data-driven decision-making in space exploration. The rovers collect and analyze data on the Martian environment, geology, and climate to make informed decisions about where to explore, dig, and conduct scientific experiments. This approach has led to groundbreaking discoveries on Mars.

(7) Airbnb's Dynamic Pricing Strategy:

Airbnb utilizes data-driven decision-making to implement dynamic pricing based on factors such as location, seasonality, and demand. The platform analyzes data on property characteristics, user behavior, and market trends to adjust prices in real-time. This strategy maximizes revenue for hosts and enhances the competitiveness of listings.

(8) Walmart's Supply Chain Optimization:

Walmart employs data-driven decision-making to optimize its supply chain. By analyzing historical sales data, inventory levels, and market trends, Walmart can accurately forecast demand, streamline inventory management, and reduce stockouts. This data-driven approach helps Walmart maintain efficient operations and meet customer demand.

(9) Tesla's Autopilot System:

Tesla's Autopilot system relies on extensive data from its fleet of vehicles to improve and optimize autonomous driving capabilities. Real-world data on road conditions, driver behavior, and vehicle performance are continuously analyzed to enhance the safety and reliability of Tesla's self-driving technology.

(10) Healthcare Predictive Analytics at Mayo Clinic:

Mayo Clinic utilizes predictive analytics in healthcare to improve patient outcomes and resource allocation. By analyzing patient data, medical histories, and treatment outcomes, Mayo Clinic can predict disease progression, identify at-risk patients, and personalize treatment plans. This data-driven approach enhances patient care and contributes to medical research.

These real-world examples highlight the diverse applications of data-driven decision-making across industries, demonstrating how organizations leverage data analytics to drive innovation, enhance efficiency, and achieve strategic objectives.

13.3 Challenges Faced and Solutions Employed:

Challenges Faced and Solutions Employed in Data-Driven Decision Making

As organizations increasingly embrace data-driven decision-making within the realms of Data Analytics and Business Intelligence, they encounter a host of challenges that require strategic solutions to unlock the full potential of their data. Navigating these challenges is essential for ensuring that data-driven initiatives contribute effectively to organizational objectives. Below, we explore common challenges and the solutions employed in the dynamic landscape of Data-Driven Decision Making:

(1) Data Quality and Integration:

- Challenge: Inconsistent or poor-quality data from various sources can hinder the accuracy of analyses and decision-making.
- Solution: Implement data governance practices, establish data quality standards, and invest in robust data integration tools. Regularly audit and clean datasets to ensure reliability and consistency.

(2) Lack of Data Literacy:

- Challenge: Many employees may lack the necessary skills to interpret and leverage data effectively, leading to underutilization of available insights.
- Solution: Provide training programs to enhance data literacy across the organization. Foster a culture of continuous learning, and encourage collaboration between data experts and non-experts.

(3) Privacy and Security Concerns:

- Challenge: The use of sensitive data raises concerns about privacy breaches and unauthorized access, especially with evolving data protection regulations.
- Solution: Implement robust data security measures, including encryption, access controls, and compliance with data protection regulations such as GDPR. Develop and communicate clear policies on data privacy and ethical use.

(4) Integration of Analytics into Decision-Making Workflows:

- Challenge: Embedding analytics seamlessly into existing decision-making processes can be challenging, leading to a disconnect between insights and actions.
- Solution: Integrate analytics tools into existing business intelligence platforms and workflow systems. Ensure that decision-makers have easy access to relevant insights at the right point in their decision-making processes.

(5) Change Management and Cultural Shift:

- Challenge: A resistance to change or a lack of a data-driven culture within an organization can impede the successful implementation of data-driven decision-making.
- Solution: Implement change management strategies to foster a culture that values data-driven insights. Communicate the benefits of data-driven

decision-making and encourage leaders to set an example by incorporating data into their decision processes.

(6) Scalability and Infrastructure:
- Challenge: As data volumes grow, organizations may face challenges in scaling their infrastructure to handle the increased computational and storage demands.
- Solution: Invest in scalable cloud-based solutions, adopt big data technologies, and regularly assess and upgrade infrastructure to accommodate growing data needs.

(7) Model Interpretability and Bias:
- Challenge: Machine learning models may lack interpretability, and biases in the data can be unintentionally perpetuated, leading to skewed insights.
- Solution: Prioritize transparent and interpretable models where possible. Regularly audit and address biases in data and models. Implement ethical guidelines and diversity considerations in the development and deployment of algorithms.

(8) Cost Management:
- Challenge: The costs associated with implementing and maintaining data-driven initiatives, including technology investments and talent acquisition, can be substantial.
- Solution: Conduct a cost-benefit analysis to ensure that investments align with business goals. Explore cost-effective solutions, consider outsourcing certain functions, and continually assess the return on investment.

(9) Real-Time Decision-Making:
- Challenge: Traditional decision-making processes may not accommodate the need for real-time insights, especially in fast-paced industries.
- Solution: Invest in real-time analytics tools and platforms. Implement automated alerts and notifications to facilitate timely responses to critical insights. Establish processes for continuous monitoring and adjustment based on real-time data.

(10) Measuring and Demonstrating ROI:
- Challenge: Quantifying the return on investment (ROI) of data-driven initiatives can be challenging, making it difficult to justify ongoing investments.
- Solution: Define clear metrics and key performance indicators (KPIs) aligned with organizational goals. Regularly assess and communicate the impact of data-driven decisions on business outcomes. Use success stories and case studies to demonstrate tangible ROI.

In conclusion, the challenges faced in the realm of Data-Driven Decision Making are diverse and dynamic. Organizations must proactively address these challenges with strategic solutions to ensure the effective utilization of data analytics and business intelligence in shaping their decision-making processes. As technology and business landscapes continue to evolve, staying adaptable and responsive to emerging challenges remains crucial for organizations committed to deriving value from their data.

13.4 Lessons Learned from Case Studies:

Lessons Learned from Case Studies of Data-Driven Decision Making

Case studies of Data-Driven Decision Making provide valuable insights into the successes and challenges faced by organizations in their journey towards leveraging data analytics and business intelligence. Analyzing these cases reveals several lessons learned that can guide other organizations in adopting and optimizing their own data-driven strategies. Table x presents some key lessons gleaned from real-world case studies:

Table 13.1: Lessons learned from real-world case studies:

S. No.	Key Lessons	Description
1	Clear Business Objectives Are Essential	Successful data-driven initiatives begin with well-defined business objectives. Clarity on the desired outcomes ensures that data analytics efforts align with organizational goals.
2	Cultural Transformation is Critical	A shift towards a data-driven culture requires more than just technological adoption. Successful organizations prioritize cultural transformation, fostering a mindset where data is embraced, valued, and integrated into everyday decision-making.
3	Invest in Data Quality and Governance	Poor data quality can undermine the effectiveness of data-driven decision-making. Organizations must invest in data governance practices to ensure data accuracy, consistency, and reliability.
4	Data Literacy Empowers Decision-Makers	Enhancing data literacy across the organization empowers decision-makers at all levels to understand, interpret, and effectively use data. Training programs and support for non-technical staff are essential components of a successful data-driven strategy.
5	Agility and Iteration Drive Success	Agile methodologies and iterative approaches are crucial in the dynamic field of data analytics. Organizations that embrace flexibility, adaptability, and continuous improvement are better positioned to respond to changing business needs.
6	Ethical Considerations Are Non-Negotiable	Ethical considerations must be at the forefront of data-driven decision-making. Organizations should prioritize transparency, fairness, and accountability, addressing potential biases and ensuring compliance with privacy regulations.
7	Collaboration Between Data Experts and	Effective collaboration between data experts and business stakeholders is essential. A cross-functional team approach ensures that data analytics efforts are aligned with business

	Business Stakeholders	objectives and that insights are actionable.
8	Balancing Automation with Human Judgment	While automation is a key component of data-driven decision-making, organizations should strike a balance between automated processes and human judgment. Human expertise is crucial for contextual understanding and nuanced decision-making.
9	Continuous Monitoring and Evaluation	Successful organizations continually monitor and evaluate their data-driven initiatives. Regular assessments, feedback loops, and performance metrics enable organizations to adapt and refine their strategies based on real-world outcomes.
10	Effective Communication of Insights	Communicating insights effectively is as important as generating them. Successful organizations prioritize clear and concise communication, ensuring that decision-makers understand and trust the insights derived from data analytics.
11	Alignment of Data Strategy with Organizational Strategy	Data strategy must align seamlessly with overall organizational strategy. Successful organizations integrate data-driven decision-making into their strategic planning processes, ensuring a cohesive and unified approach.
12	Scalability and Future-Proofing	Organizations that consider scalability and future-proofing in their data architecture and analytics solutions are better positioned for sustained success. Scalable infrastructure and technologies that can adapt to evolving business needs are crucial.
13	User-Centric Design of Analytics Tools	The design of analytics tools should be user-centric, ensuring that decision-makers can easily access and interpret insights. Intuitive interfaces and user-friendly dashboards enhance adoption and effectiveness.
14	Flexibility in Choosing Technology Stack	The choice of technology stack should align with organizational needs and capabilities. Flexibility in selecting tools and platforms allows organizations to adapt to changing technology landscapes and leverage the best solutions for their specific requirements.
15	Value Over Volume	Prioritize the value of data over its volume. Successful organizations focus on collecting and analyzing relevant data that directly contributes to meaningful insights and actionable decisions, avoiding unnecessary data clutter.

In conclusion, the lessons learned from case studies of Data-Driven Decision Making emphasize the importance of a holistic approach that encompasses cultural, organizational, and technological aspects. Successful organizations recognize that data-driven decision-making is not a one-time initiative but an ongoing journey that requires continuous learning, adaptation, and a commitment to driving business value through data analytics and business intelligence.

13.5 Teaching Case Study:

Caselet Title: Transforming Operations through Data-Driven Decision Making

Company ABC, a global logistics and supply chain management firm, is seeking to enhance its operational efficiency and customer satisfaction through the adoption of Data-Driven Decision Making (DDDM). Faced with increasing competition and rising customer expectations, the company has recognized the potential of leveraging data analytics and business intelligence to gain actionable insights and optimize its decision-making processes.

Scenario:

Company ABC manages a vast network of warehouses, transportation routes, and distribution centers. The company collects a diverse set of data, including inventory levels, transportation schedules, delivery times, customer feedback, and market trends. The leadership team believes that harnessing this data can lead to improvements in route optimization, inventory management, and overall supply chain efficiency.

The company has invested in implementing data analytics tools and business intelligence platforms to analyze historical data, monitor real-time operations, and derive predictive insights. The goal is to make informed decisions that minimize costs, reduce delivery times, and enhance the overall customer experience.

Questions for Analysis:

(1) Data Sources and Collection: a. What are the key data sources available to Company ABC for improving its logistics and supply chain operations? b. How can the company ensure the quality and relevance of the data collected from various sources?

(2) Operational Challenges: a. Identify potential operational challenges faced by Company ABC in its logistics and supply chain management. b. Discuss how data-driven decision-making can address or mitigate these challenges.

(3) Implementation of Data Analytics Tools: a. How should Company ABC go about implementing data analytics tools and business intelligence platforms effectively? b. What considerations should be taken into account during the integration of these tools into existing operations?

(4) Key Performance Indicators (KPIs): a. Define relevant Key Performance Indicators (KPIs) that Company ABC should monitor to measure the success of its data-driven initiatives. b. How can these KPIs be used to assess improvements in operational efficiency and customer satisfaction?

(5) Predictive Analytics for Supply Chain Optimization: a. Discuss the potential applications of predictive analytics in optimizing Company ABC's supply chain. b. How might predictive analytics contribute to better decision-making in areas such as inventory management and demand forecasting?

(6) Balancing Automation and Human Decision-Making: a. How can Company ABC strike a balance between automated decision-making processes and the need for human judgment in its operations? b. Identify scenarios where human expertise is essential in the decision-making process.

(7) Challenges in Cultural Transformation: a. What challenges might Company ABC face in fostering a data-driven culture among its employees? b. Suggest strategies to overcome resistance to cultural transformation and promote the widespread adoption of data-driven decision-making.

(8) Customer-Centric Decision-Making: a. How can data-driven decision-making contribute to a more customer-centric approach in Company ABC's operations? b. Provide examples of how customer feedback and data analytics can be integrated to improve the overall customer experience.

(9) Continuous Improvement and Learning: a. Discuss the importance of continuous improvement and learning in the context of data-driven decision-making. b. Propose

mechanisms through which Company ABC can adapt its strategies based on insights gained from data analytics.

(10) Ethical Considerations: a. Identify potential ethical considerations related to the use of data in logistics and supply chain management. b. How can Company ABC ensure ethical practices in its data-driven decision-making processes?

This caselet is designed to prompt thoughtful analysis and discussion about the practical implementation of Data-Driven Decision Making in a real-world business scenario. It encourages participants to consider various aspects, including data sources, operational challenges, tool implementation, KPIs, predictive analytics, cultural transformation, customer-centricity, continuous improvement, and ethical considerations.

13.6 Learning Questions:

13.6.1 Descriptive Questions:

(1) Describe the role of Case Studies in Data-Driven Decision Making in the context of business and technology evolution.

(2) Explain the significance of the "Problem Definition" component in Case Studies in Data-Driven Decision Making.

(3) Provide insights into the methodologies and tools discussed in the "Data Collection and Processing" component of Case Studies in Data-Driven Decision Making.

(4) Illustrate the impact of analytical techniques in the context of Case Studies in Data-Driven Decision Making.

(5) Detail the sequence of steps and considerations highlighted in the "Decision-Making Process" component of Case Studies in Data-Driven Decision Making.

(6) Discuss the importance of presenting "Outcomes and Impact" in Case Studies and its implications for business performance and innovation.

(7) Elaborate on the lessons organizations can learn from the "Lessons Learned" component in Case Studies in Data-Driven Decision Making.

(8) Examine the benefits of Case Studies in Data-Driven Decision Making, particularly in terms of their practical application and role as a bridge between theoretical knowledge and real-world problem-solving.

(9) Explore how Case Studies serve as inspiration for innovation, encouraging organizations to explore innovative ways of utilizing data for decision-making.

(10) Analyze the value of Case Studies in providing cross-industry insights and facilitating learning and adaptation of successful strategies in diverse industries and sectors.

(11) Provide a detailed overview of Amazon's Recommendation System as a real-world example of successful data-driven decision-making.

(12) Examine the challenges associated with data quality and integration in the realm of Data-Driven Decision Making and the strategic solutions employed.

(13) Discuss the impact of a lack of data literacy within organizations on the effective utilization of data-driven insights and the solutions to address this challenge.

(14) Explore the privacy and security concerns related to the use of sensitive data in data-driven decision-making and the solutions implemented to mitigate these concerns.

(15) Illustrate the challenges organizations face in integrating analytics into decision-making workflows and the strategic solutions employed to address these challenges.

(16) Examine the role of change management and cultural shift in the successful implementation of data-driven decision-making and the strategies to foster a data-driven culture within organizations.

(17) Analyze the scalability and infrastructure challenges organizations may encounter as data volumes grow and the solutions employed to address these challenges.

(18) Discuss the challenges associated with model interpretability and bias in machine learning models and the strategies implemented to prioritize transparency and address biases.

(19) Examine the cost management challenges organizations face in implementing and maintaining data-driven initiatives and the strategic solutions employed to manage costs effectively.

13.6.2 Fill-up the Blanks Questions:

(1) Case Studies in Data-Driven Decision Making serve as illuminating narratives that showcase the practical application of _____ in solving complex challenges, optimizing processes, and achieving strategic goals.
Answer: data analytics

(2) Each case study explores a specific business problem or opportunity where data played a pivotal role in guiding decision-makers toward more informed and impactful choices, going beyond _____.
Answer: theoretical concepts

(3) Key Components of Case Studies in Data-Driven Decision Making include clearly articulating the business problem or decision in the _____ phase.
Answer: Problem Definition

(4) In Data-Driven Decision Making, detailing the sources of data used in the decision-making process is a crucial aspect of the _____ component.
Answer: Data Collection and Processing

(5) Analytical Techniques in Case Studies involve showcasing specific _____ applied to derive insights.
Answer: analytical techniques and models

(6) The Decision-Making Process component of Case Studies involves narrating the sequence of steps taken and highlighting the key considerations used to evaluate different _____.
Answer: options

(7) Outcomes and Impact in Case Studies include presenting the results and insights obtained through _____.
Answer: data analysis

(8) Lessons Learned in Case Studies involve reflecting on the challenges faced and offering insights into how organizations can improve their _____ in the future.
Answer: data-centric strategies

(9) Benefits of Case Studies include demonstrating how data analytics concepts are translated into actionable _____.
Answer: strategies

(10) Case Studies in Data-Driven Decision Making serve as invaluable resources for professionals, educators, and decision-makers seeking to understand the practical implications and transformative potential of incorporating _____ into their decision-making processes.
Answer: data analytics

13.6.3 Multiple Choice Questions:

(1) What is emphasized as a fundamental strategy for success in the rapidly evolving landscape of business and technology?
A) Traditional decision-making
B) Data-driven decision-making
C) Theoretical concepts
D) Innovation practices
Answer: B) Data-driven decision-making

(2) What is the primary purpose of Case Studies in Data-Driven Decision Making?
A) Exploring theoretical concepts
B) Demonstrating data analytics concepts
C) Providing a historical overview
D) Discrediting traditional decision-making
Answer: B) Demonstrating data analytics concepts

(3) In the Key Components of Case Studies, what is the focus of the "Problem Definition" phase?
A) Analyzing data sources
B) Describing analytical techniques
C) Clearly articulating business problems
D) Discussing outcomes and impact
Answer: C) Clearly articulating business problems

(4) What does the "Data Collection and Processing" component of Case Studies involve?
A) Describing analytical techniques
B) Narrating the decision-making process
C) Detailing sources and processing data
D) Reflecting on lessons learned
Answer: C) Detailing sources and processing data

(5) Which aspect is covered in the "Analytical Techniques" component of Case Studies?
A) Highlighting key considerations
B) Discussing outcomes and impact
C) Showcasing specific models and techniques
D) Offering insights for improvement
Answer: C) Showcasing specific models and techniques

(6) What is the main focus of the "Outcomes and Impact" component in Case Studies?
A) Describing data sources
B) Highlighting key considerations
C) Presenting results and insights
D) Offering insights for improvement
Answer: C) Presenting results and insights

(7) What does the "Lessons Learned" component of Case Studies involve?
A) Narrating the decision-making process
B) Reflecting on challenges and offering insights
C) Demonstrating data analytics concepts
D) Clearly articulating business problems
Answer: B) Reflecting on challenges and offering insights

(8) Which benefit is associated with Case Studies in Data-Driven Decision Making?
A) Discrediting data analytics concepts
B) Demonstrating theoretical knowledge
C) Providing a bridge between theory and practice
D) Fostering a culture of resistance
Answer: C) Providing a bridge between theory and practice

(9) What is the purpose of "Inspiration for Innovation" in the Benefits of Case Studies?
A) Discouraging curiosity and experimentation
B) Encouraging theoretical knowledge
C) Inspiring innovative use of data
D) Discrediting data-driven approaches
Answer: C) Inspiring innovative use of data

(10) What does "Cross-Industry Insights" in the Benefits of Case Studies aim to achieve?
A) Limiting examples to a specific industry
B) Facilitating cross-industry learning and adaptation
C) Promoting theoretical concepts
D) Discrediting successful strategies
Answer: B) Facilitating cross-industry learning and adaptation

(11) Which organization uses data-driven decision-making for dynamic pricing based on factors like demand, traffic conditions, and driver availability?
A) Zara
B) Uber
C) Amazon
D) Google
Answer: B) Uber

(12) In Zara's Inventory Management, what allows the company to respond swiftly to changing consumer preferences?
A) Machine learning algorithms
B) Real-time sales data analysis
C) Dynamic pricing strategy
D) Traditional decision-making
Answer: B) Real-time sales data analysis

(13) What does NASA's Mars Rover Missions exemplify in the realm of data-driven decision-making?
A) Dynamic pricing strategy
B) Real-time analytics
C) Successful space exploration
D) Application of machine learning
Answer: C) Successful space exploration

(14) Which platform utilizes data-driven decision-making for dynamic pricing based on location, seasonality, and demand?
A) Netflix
B) Airbnb
C) Walmart
D) Tesla
Answer: B) Airbnb

(15) What does Walmart optimize using data-driven decision-making?
A) Autonomous driving capabilities
B) Supply chain
C) Content recommendation
D) Inventory management
Answer: B) Supply chain

(16) Which company relies on extensive data from its fleet of vehicles for the improvement of autonomous driving capabilities?
A) Google
B) Uber
C) Amazon
D) Tesla
Answer: D) Tesla

(17) How does Mayo Clinic use predictive analytics in healthcare?
A) Inventory management
B) Dynamic pricing
C) Autonomous driving
D) Personalized treatment plans
Answer: D) Personalized treatment plans

(18) What is a common challenge addressed in the "Privacy and Security Concerns" section?
A) Lack of data literacy
B) Model interpretability
C) Poor-quality data

D) Unauthorized access
Answer: D) Unauthorized access

(19) Which challenge involves a resistance to change or a lack of a data-driven culture within an organization?
A) Lack of data literacy
B) Change management and cultural shift
C) Real-time decision-making
D) Measuring and demonstrating ROI
Answer: B) Change management and cultural shift

(20) What is the suggested solution for the challenge of "Real-Time Decision-Making"?
A) Implementing real-time analytics tools
B) Prioritizing transparent models
C) Establishing data quality standards
D) Conducting cost-benefit analysis
Answer: A) Implementing real-time analytics tools

****

Future Trends in Data Science and Business Intelligence

Objectives of the Chapter:

This chapter aims to explore the dynamic and evolving landscape of Data Science and Business Intelligence, driven by technological advancements, changing business landscapes, and the increasing volume of data. The objectives are to provide a comprehensive understanding of the key future trends shaping these fields. The identified trends include augmented analytics, automated machine learning (AutoML), natural language processing (NLP) integration, edge analytics, explainable AI (XAI), blockchain in business intelligence, continuous intelligence, DataOps and ModelOps, ethics and responsible AI, and the impact of quantum computing. The chapter delves into the description and impact of each trend, highlighting their significance in transforming how data is analyzed, interpreted, and applied to drive business outcomes. It emphasizes the importance of staying abreast of these trends for organizations to remain competitive and leverage data as a strategic asset in an increasingly data-driven world. Additionally, the chapter includes sections on emerging technologies in BI and Data Science, predictions and speculations for the future, and guidance on adapting to evolving trends, providing a comprehensive overview of the evolving landscape of Data Science and Business Intelligence.

14.1 Introduction to Future Trends:

The field of Data Science and Business Intelligence is dynamic and ever-evolving, driven by technological advancements, changing business landscapes, and the increasing volume of data generated daily. As organizations continue to recognize the strategic value of data, several trends are shaping the future of Data Science and Business Intelligence, revolutionizing how insights are derived, interpreted, and applied to drive business outcomes.

(1) Augmented Analytics:
- Description: Augmented Analytics integrates artificial intelligence (AI) and machine learning (ML) algorithms into traditional analytics tools, enhancing the ability of business users to derive insights without requiring specialized data science skills.
- Impact: Streamlining the analytics process and enabling more users to harness the power of data for informed decision-making.

(2) Automated Machine Learning (AutoML):
- Description: AutoML automates the end-to-end process of applying machine learning to real-world problems, making ML more accessible to

non-experts and reducing the time and resources required for model development.

- Impact: Accelerating the adoption of machine learning across industries and democratizing data-driven decision-making.

(3) Natural Language Processing (NLP) Integration:

- Description: Integrating NLP capabilities into Business Intelligence tools allows users to interact with data using natural language queries and receive insights in a more conversational manner.
- Impact: Improving accessibility and fostering broader user engagement by enabling more intuitive and user-friendly interactions with data.

(4) Edge Analytics:

- Description: Edge Analytics involves analyzing data close to its source, often at the edge of the network or on IoT devices. This trend enables real-time decision-making without the need to transmit data to a centralized server.
- Impact: Enhancing the efficiency of IoT applications, reducing latency, and enabling quicker responses to events in real-time.

(5) Explainable AI (XAI):

- Description: XAI focuses on developing AI models that provide transparent and understandable explanations for their decisions, addressing the "black box" nature of complex algorithms.
- Impact: Building trust in AI systems, meeting regulatory requirements, and facilitating better decision-making by making AI outputs more interpretable.

(6) Blockchain in Business Intelligence:

- Description: Blockchain technology is being integrated into Business Intelligence processes to enhance data security, traceability, and transparency.
- Impact: Addressing concerns related to data integrity and fostering trust in analytics outputs, especially in industries where data accuracy is critical.

(7) Continuous Intelligence:

- Description: Continuous Intelligence involves real-time analytics and decision-making capabilities, providing insights as events occur to enable immediate responses.
- Impact: Enabling organizations to act on insights in real-time, improving operational efficiency, and supporting dynamic business environments.

(8) DataOps and ModelOps:

- Description: DataOps and ModelOps extend DevOps principles to data and machine learning processes, emphasizing collaboration, automation, and continuous delivery.

- Impact: Enhancing the efficiency of data and model development pipelines, reducing time-to-insight, and improving collaboration between data scientists and IT teams.

(9) Ethics and Responsible AI:
- Description: With increased scrutiny on the ethical implications of AI and data-driven decisions, organizations are prioritizing ethical considerations in their data science practices.
- Impact: Mitigating biases, ensuring fairness, and adhering to ethical standards, which is crucial for building public trust and meeting regulatory requirements.

(10) Quantum Computing and Advanced Analytics:
- Description: The advent of quantum computing is poised to revolutionize advanced analytics by solving complex problems at unprecedented speeds, unlocking new possibilities for data analysis.
- Impact: Transforming industries with the ability to handle vast datasets and perform computations beyond the capabilities of classical computing systems.

In conclusion, the future of Data Science and Business Intelligence is marked by a convergence of cutting-edge technologies, increased accessibility, and a heightened emphasis on ethics and transparency. These trends collectively shape a landscape where organizations can harness the power of data more efficiently, derive meaningful insights, and drive innovation in an increasingly data-driven world. As organizations prepare for the future, staying abreast of these trends will be crucial for staying competitive and leveraging data as a strategic asset.

14.2 Emerging Technologies in BI and Data Science

Emerging Technologies in Business Intelligence (BI) and Data Science are continually shaping the landscape, offering new opportunities and capabilities for organizations to derive valuable insights and make data-driven decisions. Let's explore and evaluate some of the notable emerging technologies in BI and Data Science:

(1) Natural Language Processing (NLP):
- Description: NLP enables machines to understand, interpret, and respond to human language. In BI, NLP allows users to interact with data using natural language queries.
- Analysis: NLP enhances accessibility, allowing users with varying technical backgrounds to derive insights without the need for complex queries. It fosters a more intuitive and user-friendly BI experience.
- Evaluation: The integration of NLP addresses the challenge of data literacy and promotes wider adoption of BI across organizational levels.

(2) Automated Machine Learning (AutoML):

- Description: AutoML automates the end-to-end process of applying machine learning to real-world problems, making machine learning more accessible to non-experts.
- Analysis: AutoML accelerates the development and deployment of machine learning models, reducing the barrier to entry for organizations without extensive data science expertise. It streamlines the model development process.
- Evaluation: This technology democratizes machine learning, enabling organizations to leverage predictive analytics without significant investments in specialized talent.

(3) Explainable AI (XAI):
- Description: XAI focuses on developing AI models that provide transparent and understandable explanations for their decisions, addressing the "black box" nature of complex algorithms.
- Analysis: XAI is crucial for building trust in AI systems, especially in applications where decision-making impacts individuals. It aids in compliance with regulatory requirements and enhances accountability.
- Evaluation: Organizations are increasingly recognizing the importance of ethical AI practices, making XAI a vital component in ensuring responsible and fair use of AI.

(4) Augmented Analytics:
- Description: Augmented Analytics integrates artificial intelligence and machine learning into traditional analytics tools, providing automated insights and recommendations.
- Analysis: Augmented Analytics enhances the capabilities of business users to derive insights without deep statistical expertise. It automates the process of finding patterns, trends, and anomalies in data.
- Evaluation: The automation of analytics tasks improves efficiency and allows users to focus on strategic decision-making rather than manual data analysis.

(5) Blockchain in BI:
- Description: Blockchain technology is being integrated into BI processes to enhance data security, traceability, and transparency.
- Analysis: Blockchain ensures the integrity of data by providing an immutable ledger. This is particularly valuable in scenarios where data accuracy and trust are paramount, such as in financial transactions.
- Evaluation: While the integration of blockchain adds an extra layer of security, its adoption is subject to the specific needs and regulatory considerations of each organization.

(6) Edge Analytics:

- Description: Edge Analytics involves analyzing data close to its source, often at the edge of the network or on IoT devices, enabling real-time decision-making.
- Analysis: Edge Analytics reduces latency by processing data locally, enabling organizations to respond to events in real-time. It is particularly beneficial in scenarios where immediate action is required.
- Evaluation: The adoption of Edge Analytics is contingent on the nature of an organization's data and the need for real-time insights in specific use cases.

(7) Continuous Intelligence:

- Description: Continuous Intelligence involves real-time analytics and decision-making capabilities, providing insights as events occur.
- Analysis: Continuous Intelligence enables organizations to act on insights in real-time, supporting dynamic business environments and facilitating quick responses to changing conditions.
- Evaluation: The effectiveness of Continuous Intelligence depends on the industry and operational context, with real-time requirements being more critical in certain scenarios.

(8) Graph Analytics:

- Description: Graph Analytics explores relationships between entities in data, revealing complex connections and patterns.
- Analysis: Graph Analytics is valuable for uncovering hidden relationships and patterns in interconnected data, making it suitable for scenarios like fraud detection, social network analysis, and recommendation systems.
- Evaluation: The adoption of Graph Analytics depends on the nature of an organization's data and the specific use cases that benefit from analyzing relationships.

(9) Quantum Computing and Advanced Analytics:

- Description: Quantum Computing is a revolutionary technology that leverages the principles of quantum mechanics to perform complex computations at unprecedented speeds.
- Analysis: Quantum Computing has the potential to transform advanced analytics by solving problems that are currently beyond the capabilities of classical computing.
- Evaluation: Quantum Computing is still in the early stages of development, and its practical applications in BI and Data Science are expected to evolve over time.

(10) DataOps and ModelOps:

- Description: DataOps and ModelOps extend DevOps principles to data and machine learning processes, emphasizing collaboration, automation, and continuous delivery.

- Analysis: DataOps and ModelOps enhance the efficiency of data and model

Emerging Technologies in Business Intelligence (BI) and Data Science:
The world of data is constantly evolving, and with it, the tools and techniques used to extract insights and make informed decisions. In both Business Intelligence (BI) and Data Science, several emerging technologies are reshaping the landscape and promising significant advancements. Here's a detailed look at some of the most prominent:

(1) Artificial Intelligence (AI) and Machine Learning (ML):
- Description: AI and ML algorithms are being integrated into BI and data science workflows to automate tasks, uncover hidden patterns, and generate predictive insights. This includes anomaly detection, forecasting, and even personalized data recommendations.
- Analysis: AI in BI can significantly streamline data preparation, analysis, and reporting, freeing up valuable time for human analysts to focus on strategic interpretation and decision-making. ML enables advanced predictive analytics, allowing organizations to anticipate future trends and optimize their operations.
- Evaluation: While AI and ML offer tremendous potential, they also raise concerns around bias, interpretability, and explainability. Careful consideration of data quality, algorithmic fairness, and transparent communication of results are crucial for responsible and effective implementation.

(2) Augmented Analytics:
- Description: This refers to BI tools that incorporate AI and NLP capabilities to empower non-technical users with self-service analytics. Users can ask questions in plain language, receive insights through interactive visualizations, and explore data without needing deep technical expertise.
- Analysis: Augmented analytics democratizes data analysis, fostering a data-driven culture within organizations. It allows wider participation in decision-making processes and unlocks valuable insights hidden from those who rely solely on traditional dashboards and reports.
- Evaluation: Although empowering, augmented analytics requires careful attention to data security and access control. Additionally, the accuracy and interpretability of the AI-generated insights need to be transparently communicated to avoid misinterpretations or misuse.

(3) Edge Computing and Decentralized Data Processing:
- Description: This involves processing and analyzing data closer to its source, on devices and local servers, rather than relying on centralized

cloud platforms. This reduces latency, improves real-time decision-making, and potentially addresses privacy concerns in certain situations.

- Analysis: Edge computing is particularly helpful for analyzing time-sensitive data from IoT sensors, mobile devices, and industrial machinery. It enables faster feedback loops and autonomous decision-making at the edge of the network.
- Evaluation: Security and data governance become even more critical in decentralized environments. Scalability and interoperability challenges also need to be addressed to ensure seamless data integration and analysis across different edge devices and platforms.

(4) Explainable AI (XAI) and Trustworthy AI:

- Description: This emerging field focuses on making AI models and their predictions more transparent and understandable. XAI techniques help explain how AI algorithms arrive at their conclusions, building trust in their results and enabling better decision-making.
- Analysis: XAI is crucial for mitigating the risks of bias, discrimination, and unintended consequences associated with AI-powered BI and data science applications. Building trust in AI through explainability will be essential for widespread adoption and effective utilization.
- Evaluation: XAI is still in its early stages, and developing effective and universally applicable techniques remains a challenge. However, research in this area is rapidly advancing, promising to unlock the full potential of AI in responsible and trustworthy data analysis.

These are just a few examples of the emerging technologies transforming BI and data science. Each one presents opportunities and challenges, and it's crucial to evaluate them carefully based on specific organizational needs and data contexts. By embracing these advancements while addressing their potential drawbacks, organizations can leverage the power of data to achieve unprecedented levels of efficiency, competitiveness, and decision-making accuracy.

14.3 Predictions and Speculations for the Future:

Predictions and Speculations for the Future of Data Science and Business Intelligence:

(1) Integration of AI and BI:
Prediction: The integration of artificial intelligence (AI) will become more seamless within Business Intelligence (BI) platforms, allowing for enhanced automation, predictive analytics, and intelligent decision support.

(2) AI-Powered Natural Language Processing (NLP):

Prediction: AI-powered NLP capabilities will evolve, enabling more sophisticated and context-aware interactions with data. Users will have conversational experiences, making data analysis more intuitive.

(3) Automated Data Discovery:

Prediction: Automated data discovery tools will gain prominence, allowing organizations to automatically identify patterns, anomalies, and trends within vast datasets without explicit queries.

(4) Augmented Analytics Adoption:

Prediction: Augmented Analytics will witness increased adoption, with more organizations leveraging machine learning algorithms to augment human intelligence in the data analysis process.

(5) Enhanced Explainability in AI Models:

Prediction: There will be a concerted effort to improve the explainability of AI models, addressing concerns about the opacity of complex algorithms. Explainable AI (XAI) will become a standard practice.

(6) Edge Analytics Maturity:

Prediction: Edge Analytics will mature as more organizations recognize the value of processing data closer to the source. This will be particularly crucial in industries requiring real-time decision-making, such as IoT and manufacturing.

(7) Blockchain for Data Trust and Security:

Prediction: Blockchain technology will play a larger role in ensuring data trust and security. It will be used to maintain transparent and tamper-proof records, enhancing the integrity of data used in analytics.

(8) Advanced Visualization Techniques:

Prediction: Advanced visualization techniques, including immersive and augmented reality visualizations, will become more prevalent, providing richer and more interactive ways to explore and communicate data insights.

(9) Extended Use of Predictive and Prescriptive Analytics:

Prediction: Predictive and prescriptive analytics will see extended use across industries, allowing organizations not only to forecast future trends but also to proactively prescribe actions to optimize outcomes.

(10) Data Privacy Innovations:

Prediction: Innovations in data privacy solutions will emerge to address growing concerns. Techniques such as privacy-preserving analytics and federated learning will gain traction to ensure compliance with stringent privacy regulations.

(11) Human-AI Collaboration:

Prediction: Human-AI collaboration will become more prevalent, with AI systems assisting and augmenting human decision-making processes. This collaborative approach will lead to more effective and ethically sound outcomes.

(12) Advanced Cybersecurity Analytics:

Prediction: Advanced analytics will be increasingly applied to cybersecurity, with AI-powered tools detecting and responding to cyber threats in real-time, bolstering organizations' defense mechanisms.

(13) Evolving Role of Data Scientists:

Prediction: The role of data scientists will evolve to encompass more strategic and business-focused responsibilities. Data scientists will play a pivotal role in translating data insights into actionable strategies.

(14) Continuous Intelligence Adoption:

Prediction: Continuous Intelligence will be widely adopted across industries, enabling organizations to make data-driven decisions in real-time and respond swiftly to changing business conditions.

(15) Quantum Computing Impact:

Speculation: While in its infancy, the impact of quantum computing on Data Science and BI could be transformative, addressing complex problems at speeds that were previously inconceivable.

(16) Personalized and Adaptive Analytics:

Speculation: Analytics platforms will become more personalized and adaptive, tailoring insights and recommendations based on individual user preferences and behavior, enhancing user experience.

(17) Responsible AI Frameworks:

Speculation: Comprehensive responsible AI frameworks and standards will emerge, guiding organizations in ethical and transparent AI practices, including fairness, accountability, and mitigating biases.

(18) Augmented Reality (AR) for Data Exploration:

Speculation: AR technologies will be leveraged for immersive data exploration, allowing users to interact with data in three-dimensional spaces, providing a new dimension to data visualization.

As the field of Data Science and Business Intelligence continues to evolve, these predictions and speculations offer glimpses into the potential directions and innovations that may shape the future. Adapting to these trends will be crucial for organizations seeking to harness the full potential of data in driving innovation and making informed decisions.

14.4 Adapting to Evolving Trends:

Adapting to Evolving Trends in Data Science and Business Intelligence
In the fast-paced realm of Data Science and Business Intelligence (BI), staying ahead requires continuous adaptation to emerging trends and technologies. Organizations seeking to derive maximum value from their data must proactively respond to the ever-changing landscape of data analytics. Adapting to evolving trends involves strategic considerations, technological investments, and fostering a culture of innovation. Here's a descriptive note on how

organizations can navigate and embrace the dynamic shifts in Data Science and BI:

(1) Strategic Alignment: Adapting to evolving trends begins with strategic alignment. Organizations should regularly reassess their business goals, operational challenges, and market dynamics. Understanding how data analytics aligns with strategic objectives enables the identification of relevant trends that can drive meaningful impact.

(2) Agility and Flexibility: Agility is a cornerstone of adapting to evolving trends. Organizations need to cultivate a culture of flexibility, allowing for quick responses to emerging technologies and methodologies. Agile frameworks facilitate iterative development, enabling teams to incorporate new tools and practices seamlessly.

(3) Continuous Learning and Skill Development: The rapid evolution of Data Science and BI demands continuous learning. Organizations should invest in upskilling their workforce, ensuring that data professionals are equipped with the latest tools, programming languages, and methodologies. Continuous education helps teams adapt to new trends and leverage advanced capabilities.

(4) Innovation Ecosystem: Building an innovation ecosystem involves fostering an environment where experimentation is encouraged. Organizations should provide resources for R&D, proof-of-concept projects, and innovation labs. This encourages the exploration of cutting-edge technologies and ensures that the organization remains at the forefront of industry trends.

(5) Data Governance and Ethics: As the volume and complexity of data increase, so does the importance of robust data governance. Adhering to ethical data practices and ensuring data quality are paramount. Organizations should establish clear data governance frameworks, addressing issues such as privacy, security, and compliance with regulations.

(6) Technological Investments: Adapting to evolving trends often requires strategic technological investments. This may involve upgrading existing BI tools, incorporating advanced analytics platforms, or migrating to cloud-based solutions. Investing in scalable and flexible technologies ensures that the organization can accommodate future developments.

(7) Collaboration Across Functions: Data Science and BI are inherently interdisciplinary fields. Effective adaptation to trends requires collaboration between data professionals, business analysts, and domain experts. Cross-functional teams facilitate a holistic understanding of business needs, leading to more effective implementation of data-driven strategies.

(8) Real-Time Analytics and Decision-Making: Evolving trends emphasize the importance of real-time analytics for timely decision-making. Organizations should assess the feasibility of adopting real-time data processing and analytics tools to enable quick responses to dynamic market conditions and emerging opportunities.

(9) User-Centric Design: Adapting to trends involves considering the needs and preferences of end-users. Implementing user-centric design principles in BI dashboards and analytics tools enhances user experience and ensures that insights are accessible and actionable for a broader audience.

(10) Cultivating a Data-Driven Culture: The most successful adaptations to trends occur in organizations with a pervasive data-driven culture. This involves instilling a mindset where data is integral to decision-making at all levels. Leadership plays a crucial role in fostering this culture, setting an example through their reliance on data for strategic choices.

In conclusion, adapting to evolving trends in Data Science and Business Intelligence is not a one-time effort but an ongoing journey. Organizations that prioritize strategic alignment, agility, continuous learning, and a data-driven culture are better positioned to navigate the dynamic landscape of data analytics successfully. By embracing change and proactively responding to emerging trends, organizations can leverage data as a strategic asset, driving innovation and maintaining a competitive edge in their respective industries.

14.5 Teaching Case Study

Caselet: Seizing Future Opportunities in Data Science and Business Intelligence

Company XYZ, a mid-sized tech company, has recognized the pivotal role that Data Science and Business Intelligence (BI) play in gaining a competitive edge and fostering innovation. The leadership team at XYZ is deliberating on future opportunities in the field to ensure that the organization remains at the forefront of data-driven decision-making. This caselet explores the potential avenues for growth and transformation in the dynamic landscape of Data Science and BI.

Scenario:

Company XYZ operates in a highly competitive industry where technological advancements and data-driven insights can make a significant impact on business outcomes. The leadership team acknowledges that staying ahead of the curve in Data Science and BI is critical for sustained success. The company has a talented team of data scientists, analysts, and BI specialists but is keen on exploring future opportunities to maximize the value derived from data.

Questions for Analysis:

(1) Current State Assessment: a. What is the current state of data science and business intelligence capabilities at Company XYZ? b. Identify any existing strengths, weaknesses, opportunities, and threats in the company's current approach to data analytics.

(2) Industry Trends and Emerging Technologies: a. Explore the latest trends and emerging technologies in Data Science and BI. How might these trends impact Company XYZ's industry? b. Identify specific technologies or methodologies that have the potential to revolutionize data analytics for the company.

(3) Competitive Landscape: a. Analyze the data analytics strategies of key competitors. Are there any best practices or innovative approaches that Company XYZ can learn from? b. How can Company XYZ differentiate itself in the market through advanced Data Science and BI practices?

(4) Future Opportunities for Growth: a. Based on industry trends and the competitive landscape, identify potential future opportunities for growth in Data Science and BI for Company XYZ. b. Consider opportunities in areas such as predictive analytics, artificial intelligence, real-time data processing, or personalized analytics.

(5) Customer-Centric Approaches: a. How can Company XYZ adopt customer-centric approaches in its data analytics strategies? Consider the potential benefits of providing personalized insights or improving the overall customer experience through data-driven initiatives. b. Explore ways in which customer feedback and preferences can be incorporated into data analytics processes.

(6) Data Monetization Strategies: a. Investigate potential data monetization strategies for Company XYZ. How can the company leverage its data assets to create new revenue streams? b. Consider partnerships, data-sharing initiatives, or the development of data-driven products and services.

(7) Talent Acquisition and Development: a. Assess the current talent pool at Company XYZ in the context of future opportunities. Are there specific skills or expertise gaps that need to be addressed? b. Discuss strategies for talent acquisition, development, and retention to ensure a skilled and adaptable workforce.

(8) Risk and Compliance Considerations: a. Identify potential risks associated with adopting new technologies or methodologies in Data Science and BI. b. Discuss compliance considerations, including data privacy regulations, and how the company can navigate these challenges.

(9) Implementation Roadmap: a. Develop a high-level implementation roadmap for seizing the identified future opportunities in Data Science and BI. b. Consider phased approaches, key milestones, and resource requirements for successful implementation.

(10) Metrics for Success: a. Define key performance indicators (KPIs) that can measure the success of Company XYZ's initiatives in Data Science and BI. b. Discuss how the organization will assess the impact of its data-driven strategies on business outcomes.

This caselet challenges participants to critically analyze the current state of data analytics at Company XYZ, explore future opportunities, and develop a strategic roadmap for leveraging Data Science and Business Intelligence to drive growth and innovation. It emphasizes the importance of staying abreast of industry trends, adopting customer-centric approaches, and proactively addressing talent and compliance considerations in the ever-evolving landscape of data analytics.

Answers for the Questions in the Caselet:

(1) Current State Assessment: a. The current state of data science and business intelligence at Company XYZ is characterized by a talented team of data scientists, analysts, and BI specialists. The company has established analytics capabilities but may face challenges in

fully leveraging its data for strategic decision-making. b. Strengths: Skilled workforce, existing analytics infrastructure. Weaknesses: Limited integration of data across departments, potential gaps in data quality. Opportunities: Untapped data sources, potential for cross-functional collaboration. Threats: Rapid technological advancements, increasing competition.

(2) Industry Trends and Emerging Technologies: a. Industry trends indicate a shift towards AI-driven analytics, real-time processing, and advanced predictive modeling. Emerging technologies include natural language processing (NLP), augmented analytics, and blockchain for data security. b. Technologies like AI and NLP can enhance data analysis capabilities. Augmented analytics can automate insights, while blockchain can address data integrity concerns.

(3) Competitive Landscape: a. Key competitors are implementing AI-driven analytics, personalized customer experiences, and innovative data monetization strategies. Best practices include leveraging AI for predictive analytics and adopting a customer-centric approach. b. Differentiation for Company XYZ could involve pioneering new data-driven products/services, implementing advanced analytics for unique insights, or adopting innovative customer engagement models.

(4) Future Opportunities for Growth: a. Future growth opportunities lie in predictive analytics for anticipating market trends, leveraging artificial intelligence for automation and efficiency, real-time data processing for quicker decision-making, and personalized analytics to enhance customer experiences. b. Predictive analytics can help in forecasting demand, AI can automate routine tasks, real-time processing can provide agility, and personalized analytics can improve customer satisfaction and loyalty.

(5) Customer-Centric Approaches: a. Adopting customer-centric approaches involves leveraging data to understand customer behavior, preferences, and needs. Providing personalized insights, recommendations, and tailoring products/services based on customer data can significantly enhance the overall customer experience. b. Incorporating customer feedback into data analytics processes can be achieved through sentiment analysis, social media monitoring, and actively seeking customer input in product development.

(6) Data Monetization Strategies: a. Data monetization strategies for Company XYZ may include exploring partnerships for data sharing, developing proprietary data-driven products/services, and identifying opportunities to license or sell valuable datasets. b. Collaborative ventures, creating unique data-driven offerings, and exploring new markets for data products can contribute to successful data monetization.

(7) Talent Acquisition and Development: a. Assessing the current talent pool reveals strengths in technical skills but potential gaps in domain expertise. To address this, strategies should focus on hiring domain specialists, providing continuous training, and creating a culture that fosters both technical and business acumen. b. Talent acquisition strategies involve recruiting specialists in emerging fields, cross-functional training programs, and implementing retention initiatives such as career development opportunities.

(8) Risk and Compliance Considerations: a. Potential risks include data breaches, regulatory non-compliance, and ethical concerns associated with AI. Compliance considerations involve adherence to data privacy regulations such as GDPR, ensuring ethical AI practices, and

maintaining data security. b. Implementing robust cybersecurity measures, regularly updating privacy policies, and establishing an ethics committee can mitigate risks and ensure compliance.

(9) Implementation Roadmap: a. A high-level implementation roadmap involves:

- Phase 1: Conduct a comprehensive data audit and address data quality issues.
- Phase 2: Implement AI-driven analytics for predictive modeling.
- Phase 3: Explore real-time data processing capabilities.
- Phase 4: Develop personalized analytics features for customer engagement. b. Key milestones include successful data integration, AI implementation, and the launch of personalized analytics features. Resource requirements involve technology investments, training programs, and hiring domain experts.

(10) Metrics for Success: a. Key Performance Indicators (KPIs) may include:

- Increased accuracy in predictive analytics models.
- Reduction in data processing time for real-time insights.
- Improvement in customer satisfaction scores. b. Assessing the impact on business outcomes involves regular reviews of KPIs, tracking revenue growth from data-driven initiatives, and analyzing the overall market position compared to competitors.

This analysis and strategic roadmap set the foundation for Company XYZ to leverage Data Science and Business Intelligence for future growth and innovation, ensuring a proactive response to the evolving landscape of data analytics.

14.6 Learning Questions:

14.6.1 Descriptive Questions:

(1) What is Augmented Analytics, and how does it impact the analytics process for business users?

(2) Explain the concept of Automated Machine Learning (AutoML) and its significance in making machine learning accessible.

(3) How does the integration of Natural Language Processing (NLP) into Business Intelligence tools improve user engagement with data?

(4) What is Edge Analytics, and how does it contribute to real-time decision-making in IoT applications?

(5) Describe the importance of Explainable AI (XAI) in addressing the "black box" nature of complex algorithms and its impact on decision-making.

(6) How does Blockchain technology enhance data security and transparency in Business Intelligence processes?

(7) What is Continuous Intelligence, and how does it enable organizations to make real-time data-driven decisions?

(8) Explain the concepts of DataOps and ModelOps and their role in enhancing the efficiency of data and machine learning processes.

(9) Why is Ethics and Responsible AI gaining prominence in data science practices, and what impact does it have on trust and compliance?

(10) How does Quantum Computing have the potential to revolutionize advanced analytics, and what challenges may arise in its practical applications?

14.6.2 Fill-up the Blanks Questions:

(1) The field of Data Science and Business Intelligence is dynamic and ever-evolving, driven by _____, changing business landscapes, and the increasing volume of data generated daily.
Answer: technological advancements

(2) Augmented Analytics integrates _____ into traditional analytics tools, enhancing the ability of business users to derive insights without requiring specialized data science skills.
Answer: artificial intelligence (AI) and machine learning (ML) algorithms

(3) AutoML automates the end-to-end process of applying _____ to real-world problems, making ML more accessible to non-experts and reducing the time and resources required for model development.
Answer: machine learning

(4) Integrating NLP capabilities into Business Intelligence tools allows users to interact with data using _____ queries and receive insights in a more conversational manner.
Answer: natural language

(5) Edge Analytics involves analyzing data close to its source, often at the edge of the network or on IoT devices, enabling _____ decision-making without the need to transmit data to a centralized server.
Answer: real-time

(6) XAI focuses on developing AI models that provide transparent and understandable explanations for their decisions, addressing the "_____" nature of complex algorithms.
Answer: black box

(7) Blockchain technology is being integrated into Business Intelligence processes to enhance data security, traceability, and _____.
Answer: transparency

(8) Continuous Intelligence involves _____ capabilities, providing insights as events occur to enable immediate responses.
Answer: real-time analytics and decision-making

(9) DataOps and ModelOps extend _____ principles to data and machine learning processes, emphasizing collaboration, automation, and continuous delivery.

Answer: DevOps

(10) With increased scrutiny on the ethical implications of AI and data-driven decisions, organizations are prioritizing _____ in their data science practices.
Answer: ethical considerations

(11) The advent of quantum computing is poised to revolutionize advanced analytics by solving complex problems at _____ speeds.
Answer: unprecedented

(12) The future of Data Science and Business Intelligence is marked by a convergence of cutting-edge technologies, increased accessibility, and a heightened emphasis on _____ and transparency.
Answer: ethics

(13) In Emerging Technologies in Business Intelligence (BI) and Data Science, NLP enables machines to understand, interpret, and respond to _____.
Answer: human language

(14) Automated Machine Learning (AutoML) automates the end-to-end process of applying _____ to real-world problems.
Answer: machine learning

(15) XAI focuses on making AI models and their predictions more _____, addressing the "black box" nature of complex algorithms.
Answer: transparent and understandable

(16) Augmented Analytics integrates artificial intelligence and machine learning into traditional analytics tools, providing _____ insights and recommendations.
Answer: automated

(17) Edge Analytics involves analyzing data close to its source, often at the edge of the network or on IoT devices, enabling _____ decision-making.
Answer: real-time

(18) Graph Analytics explores relationships between entities in data, revealing complex connections and _____.
Answer: patterns

(19) Quantum Computing leverages the principles of _____ to perform complex computations at unprecedented speeds.
Answer: quantum mechanics

(20) Adapting to evolving trends in Data Science and Business Intelligence requires strategic alignment, _____, and fostering a culture of innovation.
Answer: agility

14.6.3 Multiple Choice Questions:

(1) What is Augmented Analytics?

A. A technique for enhancing photos in analytics tools.
B. Integrating AI and ML into analytics tools for business users.
C. Augmented reality applied to data visualization.
D. A method for automating manual data entry.

- Answer: B

(2) What is the impact of Automated Machine Learning (AutoML)?
   A. Reducing the need for analytics tools.
   B. Increasing the complexity of model development.
   C. Democratizing data-driven decision-making.
   D. Slowing down the adoption of machine learning.
   - Answer: C

(3) How does Natural Language Processing (NLP) benefit Business Intelligence?
   A. By automating manufacturing processes.
   B. By enabling users to interact with data using natural language.
   C. By providing real-time analytics.
   D. By enhancing data security.
   - Answer: B

(4) What does Edge Analytics involve?
   A. Analyzing data far from its source.
   B. Processing data at the core of a centralized server.
   C. Analyzing data close to its source, often at the edge of the network or on IoT devices.
   D. Focusing on data encryption techniques.
   - Answer: C

(5) Explainable AI (XAI) is focused on:
   A. Developing AI models with unclear decision-making processes.
   B. Making AI models transparent and providing understandable explanations for their decisions.
   C. Enhancing data security through AI.
   D. Integrating AI with blockchain technology.
   - Answer: B

(6) How is Blockchain integrated into Business Intelligence?
   A. Enhancing data security, traceability, and transparency.
   B. Automating data analysis processes.
   C. Enabling natural language processing in analytics.
   D. Improving data governance.
   - Answer: A

(7) What is Continuous Intelligence?
   A. Intelligence that is consistently unreliable.
   B. Providing insights only once a day.
   C. Real-time analytics and decision-making capabilities.
   D. A process with interruptions in data flow.
   - Answer: C

(8) How do DataOps and ModelOps extend DevOps principles?
   A. By discouraging collaboration and automation.
   B. By emphasizing collaboration, automation, and continuous delivery in data and machine learning processes.
   C. By focusing solely on model development.
   D. By decreasing the efficiency of data pipelines.
Answer: B

(9) What is the primary focus of Ethics and Responsible AI in Data Science practices?
   A. Maximizing profits through data analysis.
   B. Speeding up data processing.
   C. Mitigating biases, ensuring fairness, and adhering to ethical standards.
   D. Ignoring regulatory requirements.
   • Answer: C

(10) How is Quantum Computing expected to impact advanced analytics?
   A. Slowing down analytics processes.
   B. Transforming industries by handling vast datasets at unprecedented speeds.
   C. Making analytics less accessible.
   D. Decreasing the volume of data generated daily.
   • Answer: B

(11) In Emerging Technologies in BI and Data Science, what does Natural Language Processing (NLP) enhance?
   A. Data security.
   B. Accessibility, allowing users to derive insights without complex queries.
   C. Real-time decision-making.
   D. Automation of data discovery.
   • Answer: B

(12) How does Edge Analytics reduce latency?
   A. By analyzing data far from its source.
   B. By processing data centrally on cloud servers.
   C. By analyzing data close to its source, enabling quicker responses in real-time.
   D. By encrypting data at the edge of the network.
   • Answer: C

(13) What is the goal of Explainable AI (XAI)?
   A. Creating complex and opaque AI models.
   B. Developing AI models with unclear decision-making processes.
   C. Providing transparent and understandable explanations for AI decisions.
   D. Enhancing data security.
   • Answer: C

(14) What is the primary function of Graph Analytics?
   A. Enhancing data security.
   B. Uncovering hidden relationships and patterns in interconnected data.
   C. Real-time analytics.
   D. Automating machine learning processes.

- Answer: B

(15). What is the status of Quantum Computing in BI and Data Science, according to the text?

    A. Mature and widely adopted.

    B. In its infancy with evolving practical applications.

    C. A technology that slows down data processing.

    D. Suitable for handling small datasets.

- Answer: B

(16) According to predictions, what will be crucial for organizations in the future?

    A. Ignoring the integration of AI and BI.

    B. Lack of explainability in AI models.

    C. Human-AI collaboration for more effective outcomes.

    D. Avoiding real-time analytics.

- Answer: C

(17) What does Adapting to Evolving Trends involve?

    A. Remaining static and resistant to change.

    B. Continuous adaptation to emerging trends and technologies.

    C. Implementing outdated technologies.

    D. Ignoring the need for strategic alignment.

- Answer: B

(18) Why is User-Centric Design important in BI?

    A. It increases data security.

    B. It fosters a data-driven culture.

    C. It enhances user experience and ensures actionable insights.

    D. It automates data analysis processes.

- Answer: C

(19) How can organizations achieve real-time decision-making?

    A. By ignoring technological investments.

    B. By relying solely on historical data.

    C. By cultivating a data-driven culture.

    D. By adopting real-time data processing and analytics tools.

- Answer: D

(20) In the context of the text, what is the role of data scientists in the future?

    A. Limited to technical tasks only.

    B. Translating data insights into actionable strategies and playing a pivotal role in business-focused responsibilities.

    C. Focusing on data literacy only.

    D. Decreasing collaboration with other functions.

- Answer: B

****

CHAPTER 15

Implementing Data Science Strategies in Corporations:

Objectives of the Chapter:

This chapter aims to provide a comprehensive understanding of the strategic importance and key components of data science. The objectives include recognizing data as a strategic asset, understanding the multidisciplinary nature of data science, and acknowledging its transformative potential in enhancing decision-making processes. The strategic importance of data science is emphasized, highlighting its role in informed decision-making, operational efficiency, innovation, and gaining a competitive advantage. The key components of data science strategies are outlined, encompassing data collection, advanced analytics, cross-functional collaboration, data governance, agile processes, and scalable infrastructure. The benefits of implementing data science strategies, such as improved decision-making, operational efficiency, innovation, competitive advantage, and enhanced customer experience, are also elucidated. The roadmap for implementing data strategies in Data Science and Business Intelligence is presented as a structured guide involving defining business objectives, conducting data assessments, establishing governance frameworks, building cross-functional teams, investing in infrastructure, developing analytics capabilities, fostering a data-driven culture, ensuring data security, and continuously monitoring and optimizing strategies. Additionally, the chapter addresses common challenges in implementing data science, providing strategies to overcome resistance to change. Finally, it discusses measuring ROI and success metrics, offering a diverse set of methods, including financial metrics, customer-centric metrics, risk management metrics, and time-based metrics, among others, to evaluate the impact and effectiveness of data science initiatives. The comprehensive approach presented in the chapter aims to guide organizations in leveraging data science for strategic decision-making, fostering a data-driven culture, and overcoming implementation challenges.

15.1 Introduction to Implementing Data Science Strategies in Corporations:

In the rapidly evolving landscape of business and technology, data has emerged as a strategic asset that holds immense potential for corporations. Implementing effective data science strategies has become a crucial initiative for organizations seeking to harness the power of data to drive innovation, enhance decision-making processes, and gain a competitive edge in the market.

The Significance of Data Science:

Data Science, as a multidisciplinary field, encompasses a range of techniques, algorithms, and methodologies aimed at extracting meaningful insights from vast and complex datasets. Corporations are increasingly recognizing the transformative potential of data science in uncovering hidden patterns, predicting future trends, and informing strategic decisions.

Strategic Importance:

Implementing data science strategies is not merely a technical endeavor; it is a strategic imperative for corporations looking to navigate the complexities of the modern business environment. Data-driven insights enable organizations to make informed decisions, optimize operations, and identify opportunities for innovation and growth.

Key Components of Data Science Strategies:

(1) Data Collection and Integration:

Establishing robust mechanisms for collecting and integrating diverse datasets from various sources, ensuring data quality, and creating a unified and comprehensive view of the organization's information.

(2) Advanced Analytics and Modeling:

Leveraging advanced analytics techniques, including machine learning and predictive modeling, to extract valuable patterns, trends, and predictions from large datasets. This enables corporations to move beyond descriptive analytics towards more proactive and prescriptive insights.

(3) Cross-Functional Collaboration:

Fostering collaboration between data science teams, IT professionals, business analysts, and domain experts. Successful data science implementation requires a multidisciplinary approach that combines technical expertise with a deep understanding of business goals and challenges.

(4) Data Governance and Ethics:

Establishing robust data governance frameworks to ensure the integrity, security, and responsible use of data. Adhering to ethical considerations in data science practices is essential to build trust and comply with regulatory requirements.

(5) Agile and Iterative Processes:

Embracing agile and iterative methodologies in data science projects to adapt to evolving business needs. Flexibility and responsiveness are critical as corporations navigate dynamic markets and changing customer demands.

(6) Scalable Infrastructure:

Investing in scalable and efficient infrastructure to handle the growing volume of data. Cloud computing and big data technologies play a pivotal role in providing the computational power and storage capacity required for large-scale data science initiatives.

Benefits of Implementing Data Science Strategies:

(1) Informed Decision-Making:

Data science empowers corporations to make data-driven decisions based on evidence and insights, reducing reliance on intuition and improving the accuracy of strategic choices.

(2) Operational Efficiency:

Optimization of operational processes through data-driven insights leads to increased efficiency, reduced costs, and improved resource allocation.

(3) Innovation and Product Development:

Identification of new opportunities for innovation, product development, and market expansion through a deeper understanding of customer behaviors, preferences, and emerging trends.

(4) Competitive Advantage:

Gaining a competitive advantage by leveraging data science to stay ahead of industry trends, respond to market dynamics in real-time, and deliver superior products or services.

(5) Customer Experience Enhancement:

Improving the overall customer experience by personalizing offerings, anticipating customer needs, and delivering tailored solutions based on data-driven insights.

In conclusion, implementing data science strategies is not merely a technological upgrade; it is a strategic imperative for corporations aiming to thrive in the data-driven era. As organizations embrace the power of data science, they position themselves to navigate complexities, drive innovation, and achieve sustained success in an increasingly competitive and dynamic business environment.

15.2 Roadmap for Implementing Data Strategies:

Roadmap for Implementing Data Strategies in Data Science and Business Intelligence:

Implementing effective data strategies for Data Science and Business Intelligence (BI) involves a comprehensive and structured approach. The following roadmap provides a detailed guide for organizations seeking to leverage data for informed decision-making:

1. Define Business Objectives and Goals:

Objective: Clearly articulate the business objectives that data strategies aim to support.

Activities:

(i) Engage with key stakeholders to understand business priorities.

(ii) Align data strategies with organizational goals, such as revenue growth, cost optimization, or customer satisfaction.

2. Conduct Data Assessment:

Objective: Evaluate the current state of data assets, infrastructure, and analytics capabilities.

Activities:

(i) Perform a comprehensive data audit to identify existing data sources.

(ii) Assess data quality, completeness, and relevance.

(iii) Evaluate the scalability and efficiency of the current data infrastructure.

3. Establish Data Governance Framework:

Objective: Define rules, policies, and processes to ensure the integrity, security, and responsible use of data.

Activities:

(i) Develop a data governance framework outlining roles and responsibilities.

(ii) Implement data quality standards and protocols.

(iii) Address compliance requirements and privacy considerations.

4. Build Cross-Functional Teams:

Objective: Foster collaboration between data scientists, BI analysts, IT professionals, and business domain experts.

Activities:

(i) Form cross-functional teams to encourage diverse perspectives.

(ii) Facilitate regular communication and knowledge-sharing sessions.

5. Invest in Data Infrastructure:

Objective: Ensure a scalable and efficient infrastructure to handle data processing and storage needs.

Activities:

(i) Evaluate cloud-based solutions for scalability.

(ii) Implement big data technologies for handling large datasets.

(iii) Ensure data accessibility and ease of integration.

6. Develop Data Analytics and BI Capabilities:

Objective: Enhance analytical capabilities to extract meaningful insights from data.

Activities:

(i) Invest in BI tools and platforms for visualization.

(ii) Provide training for data scientists and analysts.

(iii) Explore advanced analytics techniques, such as machine learning and predictive modeling.

7. Implement Agile and Iterative Processes:

Objective: Adopt agile methodologies for flexibility and responsiveness to changing business needs.

Activities:

(i) Implement iterative development cycles for data projects.

(ii) Conduct regular reviews and adjustments based on feedback.

8. Foster a Data-Driven Culture:

Objective: Instill a mindset where data is integral to decision-making at all levels of the organization.

Activities:

(i) Communicate the value of data-driven decisions.

(ii) Encourage data literacy programs and training for all employees.

9. Implement Data Security Measures:

Objective: Ensure data security and compliance with regulatory requirements.

Activities:

(i) Implement encryption and access controls.

(ii) Regularly update security protocols to address emerging threats.

(iii) Conduct regular compliance audits.

10. Develop Personalized Analytics Features:

Objective: Enhance customer experiences by providing personalized insights and recommendations.

Activities:

(i) Leverage customer data to understand preferences.

(ii) Develop and deploy personalized analytics features.

11. Monitor and Evaluate Performance:

Objective: Continuously monitor and assess the performance and impact of data strategies.

Activities:

(i) Define Key Performance Indicators (KPIs) aligned with business objectives.

(ii) Establish regular review cycles for performance assessments.

12. Iterate and Optimize:

Objective: Continuously iterate on data strategies based on insights and evolving business requirements.

Activities:

(i) Gather feedback from stakeholders.

(ii) Implement optimizations and updates based on lessons learned.

13. Enable Continuous Learning:

Objective: Facilitate ongoing learning and development in data science and BI.

Activities:

(i) Provide training programs and resources.

(ii) Encourage participation in industry conferences and workshops.

14. Communicate Success and Learnings:

Objective: Share successes, challenges, and learnings with the broader organization.

Activities:

(i) Create communication channels for sharing success stories.

(ii) Conduct post-implementation reviews to identify areas for improvement.

This roadmap provides a structured approach for organizations to implement effective data strategies for Data Science and Business Intelligence, fostering a data-driven culture and enabling informed decision-making across all levels of the organization.

15.3 Overcoming Resistance to Change:

Overcoming resistance to change is a common challenge in implementing data science strategies in corporations. Here are some strategies and descriptions to address this resistance effectively:

(1) Communication and Transparency:

Description: Lack of clear communication about the reasons behind the data science initiatives can lead to skepticism and resistance. Transparent communication is essential to build understanding and trust.

Strategy: Regularly communicate the purpose, benefits, and expected outcomes of the data science initiatives. Provide updates on progress and address concerns openly.

(2) Education and Training:

Description: Resistance often stems from a lack of understanding or fear of the unknown. Employees may be apprehensive about using new technologies or methodologies.

Strategy: Offer comprehensive training programs to enhance data literacy. Provide workshops and resources to help employees understand the value of data science in their roles.

(3) Involvement and Collaboration:

Description: Employees are more likely to resist change if they feel excluded from the decision-making process. Lack of involvement can lead to a perception of imposed changes.

Strategy: Involve employees in the planning and decision-making stages of data science initiatives. Establish cross-functional teams that include representatives from different departments.

(4) Highlight Quick Wins:

Description: Demonstrating early successes can counter resistance by showcasing the tangible benefits of data science initiatives.

Strategy: Start with small, manageable projects that can deliver quick wins. Highlight these successes to build confidence and momentum for broader implementation.

(5) Address Cultural Barriers:

Description: Corporate culture can resist changes that challenge established norms and ways of working.

Strategy: Assess the existing organizational culture and align data science initiatives with cultural values. Encourage a culture of innovation, learning, and adaptability.

(6) Create Change Champions:

Description: Resistance can be mitigated by identifying and empowering individuals who champion data science within the organization.

Strategy: Identify key influencers and proponents of data science initiatives. Empower them to advocate for change, address concerns, and serve as mentors to their peers.

(7) Recognize and Celebrate Contributions:

Description: Employees may resist change if they feel their contributions are not acknowledged or valued.

Strategy: Recognize and celebrate the efforts of individuals and teams involved in the data science initiatives. This fosters a positive environment and encourages continued engagement.

(8) Provide Support and Resources:

Description: Lack of resources or inadequate support can lead to frustration and resistance.

Strategy: Ensure that employees have the necessary tools, resources, and support to adapt to new data science practices. Offer ongoing assistance through training and mentorship.

(9) Manage Fear of Job Insecurity:

Description: Employees may resist data science initiatives if they fear job displacement or changes to their roles.

Strategy: Clearly communicate that the goal is to enhance existing roles and create new opportunities. Provide assurance about the value of human expertise in conjunction with data science capabilities.

(10) Iterative Implementation:

Description: Implementing changes gradually can be more effective than a sudden and complete overhaul.

Strategy: Adopt an iterative approach, allowing employees to adjust gradually. Gather feedback at each stage, make necessary adjustments, and involve employees in the evolution of data science initiatives.

(11) Continuous Feedback Loop:

Description: Lack of feedback mechanisms can lead to ongoing resistance due to unaddressed concerns.

Strategy: Establish a continuous feedback loop where employees can share their thoughts, concerns, and suggestions. Act on feedback promptly to demonstrate responsiveness.

By employing these strategies, corporations can proactively address resistance to change and create a more supportive environment for the successful implementation of data science strategies. The key is to foster a culture of collaboration, open communication, and continuous learning throughout the transformation process.

15.4 Measuring ROI and Success Metrics:

Measuring the return on investment (ROI) and success metrics is crucial for assessing the impact and effectiveness of data science strategies in corporations. Here are various methods and metrics to evaluate the success of data science initiatives:

(1) Financial Metrics:

ROI (Return on Investment): Calculate the ROI by comparing the financial benefits gained from data science initiatives against the costs incurred. This can include increased revenue, cost savings, or improved operational efficiency.

(2) Revenue Impact:

(i) Increase in Sales: Measure the direct impact on sales revenue attributed to data-driven insights and strategies.

(ii) Customer Lifetime Value (CLV): Evaluate if data science initiatives contribute to higher CLV by improving customer retention, cross-selling, and upselling.

(3) Cost Savings and Efficiency:

(i) Operational Efficiency: Assess the impact of data science on streamlining operations, reducing waste, and improving overall efficiency.

(ii) Cost Reduction: Measure cost savings achieved through optimized processes, resource allocation, and automation.

(4) Customer-Centric Metrics:

(i) Customer Satisfaction: Gauge improvements in customer satisfaction scores resulting from personalized experiences and better-targeted services.

(ii) Net Promoter Score (NPS): Track changes in NPS to evaluate the impact of data-driven strategies on customer loyalty and advocacy.

(5) Product and Service Innovation:

(i) New Product Launches: Measure the success of new products or features influenced by data science insights.

(ii) Time-to-Market: Assess the speed at which new products or services are brought to market with the help of data science.

(6) Risk Management Metrics:

(i) Fraud Detection and Prevention: Measure the effectiveness of data science in identifying and preventing fraudulent activities.

(ii) Risk Mitigation: Evaluate the impact of data-driven risk models on minimizing potential risks in business operations.

(7) Employee Productivity and Satisfaction:

(i) Employee Productivity: Assess improvements in employee productivity resulting from streamlined processes and data-driven decision-making.

(ii) Employee Satisfaction: Measure the impact of data science initiatives on employee satisfaction through surveys and feedback.

(8) Data Quality and Accuracy:

(i) Data Accuracy: Assess the accuracy and reliability of data used in decision-making processes.

(ii) Data Quality Metrics: Utilize metrics such as completeness, consistency, and timeliness to ensure high-quality data.

(9) Time-Based Metrics:

(i) Time-to-Insight: Evaluate the speed at which actionable insights are generated from data.

(ii) Time-to-Decision: Measure the time taken to make decisions based on data-driven insights.

(10) Adoption and Utilization Metrics:

(i) Tool Adoption Rates: Track the adoption rates of new data science tools and technologies.

(ii) User Engagement: Measure user engagement with BI dashboards, reports, and analytics tools.

(11) Benchmarking Against Industry Standards:

(i) Industry Comparisons: Benchmark the corporation's data science performance against industry standards or competitors.

(ii) Best Practices Adoption: Assess the adoption of industry best practices in data science methodologies.

(12) Predictive Accuracy Metrics:

(i) Model Accuracy: Evaluate the accuracy of predictive models by comparing predictions to actual outcomes.

(ii) Precision and Recall: Measure the precision and recall of classification models to assess their effectiveness.

(13) Social and Environmental Impact:

(i) Sustainability Metrics: Evaluate the social and environmental impact of data science strategies, such as reductions in resource consumption or carbon footprint.

(ii) Corporate Social Responsibility (CSR): Assess contributions to CSR goals through data-driven initiatives.

(14) Customer Retention and Churn Reduction:

(i) Churn Rate: Measure the reduction in customer churn attributed to data-driven retention strategies.

(ii) Customer Retention Rate: Evaluate the success of initiatives in retaining existing customers over time.

(15) Continuous Improvement Metrics:

(i) Feedback Incorporation: Measure the frequency and effectiveness of incorporating feedback into data science processes.

(ii) Iterative Improvement: Assess the success of iterative improvements based on insights gained from ongoing monitoring and feedback.

It's essential for corporations to select a combination of these metrics based on their specific goals, industry, and the nature of their data science initiatives. Regularly evaluating these metrics provides valuable insights for continuous improvement and demonstrates the impact of data science on overall business performance.

15.5 Teaching Case Study:

Title: Transformative Analytics: Implementing Data Science Strategies at Tech Innovations Inc.

Introduction: Tech Innovations Inc., a leading technology company, recognized the strategic importance of leveraging data for innovation and growth. In a bid to transform into a data-driven organization, the leadership decided to embark on a comprehensive journey to implement data science strategies. This caselet explores the challenges, strategies, and outcomes of implementing data science at Tech Innovations Inc.

Background: Tech Innovations Inc. operates in a dynamic industry where technological advancements and customer preferences change rapidly. The leadership team acknowledged that tapping into the power of data was essential for staying ahead of the curve, making informed decisions, and maintaining a competitive edge. The company had a wealth of data but lacked a cohesive strategy to extract meaningful insights and turn them into actionable outcomes.

Challenges Faced:

(1) Data Silos: The company had data scattered across various departments and systems, leading to inefficiencies and a lack of a unified view.

(2) Limited Analytical Capabilities: While the company had a skilled IT team, there was a need to enhance analytical capabilities, especially in the context of advanced analytics and machine learning.

(3) Cultural Shift: Introducing data science required a cultural shift, with employees accustomed to traditional decision-making processes.

Objectives:

(1) Establish a centralized data repository.
(2) Develop advanced analytics capabilities.
(3) Foster a data-driven culture across departments.
(4) Drive innovation through data science.

Strategies Implemented:

(1) Data Integration and Centralization:

(i) Engaged in a comprehensive audit to identify existing data sources and integration points.

(ii) Implemented a centralized data repository using cloud-based solutions.

(iii) Established protocols for data quality and consistency.

(2) Talent Development:

(i) Conducted training programs to upskill existing employees in data science and analytics.

(ii) Recruited data scientists and analysts with expertise in advanced analytics and machine learning.

(iii) Formed cross-functional teams to encourage collaboration between IT, business, and data science professionals.

(3) Cultural Transformation:

(i) Launched an internal communication campaign to emphasize the importance of data-driven decision-making.

(ii) Encouraged a culture of curiosity and experimentation by celebrating small wins and lessons learned.

(iii) Established regular forums for knowledge-sharing and cross-departmental collaboration.

(4) Pilot Projects:

(i) Initiated small-scale pilot projects to demonstrate the value of data science.

(ii) Focused on projects with tangible and quick-to-realize outcomes to build confidence.

(iii) Gathered feedback from employees involved in pilot projects to address concerns and refine strategies.

Outcomes and Success Metrics:

(1) Improved Decision-Making:

Implemented predictive analytics models that improved forecasting accuracy by 20%, leading to more informed decision-making.

(2) Operational Efficiency:

Reduced processing time for data queries by 30%, enhancing overall operational efficiency.

(3) Revenue Growth:

Identified cross-selling opportunities, contributing to a 15% increase in overall revenue.

(4) Employee Engagement:

Employee surveys indicated a 20% increase in satisfaction with the organization's data-driven approach.

(5) Innovation:

Successfully launched a new product based on insights derived from data science, gaining a competitive advantage in the market.

Challenges and Lessons Learned:

(1) Change Management:

The initial resistance was higher than anticipated, emphasizing the need for a robust change management plan.

(2) Data Governance:

Ongoing efforts were required to ensure data quality and adherence to data governance protocols.

(3) Continuous Learning:

Establishing a culture of continuous learning proved vital as technology and industry trends evolved.

Conclusion:

Tech Innovations Inc. successfully implemented data science strategies, achieving transformative outcomes in decision-making, efficiency, and innovation. The case study highlights the importance of a holistic approach that combines technological advancements with cultural and organizational changes. The journey demonstrated that, when strategically executed, data science can be a powerful catalyst for corporate growth and competitiveness.

15.6 Learning Questions

15.6.1 Descriptive Questions:

(1) How has data evolved into a strategic asset, and why is it considered crucial for corporations in the current business and technological landscape?

(2) What multidisciplinary aspects does Data Science encompass, and how do these contribute to extracting meaningful insights from vast and complex datasets?

(3) Why is implementing data science strategies not just a technical endeavor, but a strategic imperative for corporations navigating the complexities of the modern business environment?

(4) What are the key components of effective data science strategies, particularly focusing on data collection and integration, advanced analytics, cross-functional collaboration, data governance, agile processes, and scalable infrastructure?

(5) In what ways do data-driven insights empower organizations to make informed decisions, optimize operations, and identify opportunities for innovation and growth?

(6) How does the roadmap for implementing data strategies guide organizations in leveraging data for informed decision-making, and what are the key steps involved in this comprehensive approach?

(7) What are the common challenges in implementing data science, and how can strategies such as communication, transparency, education, and training help overcome resistance to change?

(8) What metrics and methods are recommended for measuring the return on investment (ROI) and success of data science initiatives, especially considering financial impacts, customer-centric outcomes, efficiency improvements, and risk management?

(9) How does fostering a data-driven culture contribute to the successful implementation of data science strategies, and what activities are recommended to instill this mindset across all levels of the organization?

(10) Why is it crucial for corporations to continuously monitor and assess the performance of data strategies, and what activities are involved in iterative optimization and fostering continuous learning in data science and business intelligence?

(1) _____ is a strategic asset that holds immense potential for corporations in the rapidly evolving landscape of business and technology.
Answer: Data

(2) Implementing effective data science strategies is a _____ initiative for organizations aiming to harness the power of data for innovation, decision-making, and gaining a competitive edge.
Answer: Crucial

(3) Data Science, as a _____ field, encompasses a range of techniques, algorithms, and methodologies aimed at extracting meaningful insights from vast and complex datasets.
Answer: Multidisciplinary

(4) Establishing robust mechanisms for collecting and integrating diverse datasets, ensuring data quality, and creating a unified view of the organization's information are key components of _____.
Answer: Data Collection and Integration

(5) Leveraging machine learning and predictive modeling to extract valuable patterns, trends, and predictions from large datasets is a part of _____.
Answer: Advanced Analytics and Modeling

(6) Fostering collaboration between data science teams, IT professionals, business analysts, and domain experts is a crucial aspect of _____.
Answer: Cross-Functional Collaboration

(7) Ensuring the integrity, security, and responsible use of data through robust frameworks is a key focus of _____.
Answer: Data Governance and Ethics

(8) Embracing agile and iterative methodologies in data science projects to adapt to evolving business needs is highlighted in _____.
Answer: Agile and Iterative Processes

(9) Investing in scalable and efficient infrastructure, including cloud computing and big data technologies, is emphasized in _____.
Answer: Scalable Infrastructure

(10) Gaining a competitive advantage, optimizing operational processes, and enhancing the overall customer experience are among the _____ of implementing data science strategies.
Answer: Benefits

15.6.3 Multiple Choice Questions:

(1) What is the primary focus of implementing effective data science strategies in corporations?
    A. Technological upgrades
    B. Innovation and growth
    C. Strategic imperative

D. Competitive disadvantage
- Answer: C) Strategic imperative

(2) What does Data Science aim to achieve as a multidisciplinary field?
   A. Streamlining operations
   B. Predicting market dynamics
   C. Extracting insights from complex datasets
   D. Cost reduction
   - Answer: C) Extracting insights from complex datasets

(3) Why is cross-functional collaboration crucial in successful data science implementation?
   A. To minimize data collection efforts
   B. To reduce the need for advanced analytics
   C. To foster collaboration between IT professionals
   D. To combine technical expertise with business understanding
   - Answer: D) To combine technical expertise with business understanding

(4) What is the main objective of establishing data governance frameworks in corporations?
   A. Promoting data breaches
   B. Ensuring responsible use of data
   C. Avoiding collaboration
   D. Encouraging unethical practices
   - Answer: B) Ensuring responsible use of data

(5) Which component of data science strategies involves adapting to evolving business needs and dynamic markets?
   A. Data Collection and Integration
   B. Agile and Iterative Processes
   C. Scalable Infrastructure
   D. Data Governance and Ethics
   - Answer: B) Agile and Iterative Processes

(6) What plays a pivotal role in providing computational power and storage capacity for large-scale data science initiatives?
   A. Traditional databases
   B. Cloud computing and big data technologies
   C. Manual data processing
   D. Small-scale infrastructure
   - Answer: B) Cloud computing and big data technologies

(7) Which benefit is associated with the implementation of data science strategies?
   A. Operational inefficiency
   B. Increased reliance on intuition
   C. Reduced costs
   D. Decreased accuracy of strategic choices
   - Answer: C) Reduced costs

(8) How does data science contribute to improving the overall customer experience?
   A. Standardizing offerings

B. Reducing personalization

C. Anticipating customer needs

D. Ignoring data-driven insights

- Answer: C) Anticipating customer needs

(9) What does the roadmap for implementing data strategies aim to achieve in the first step?

A. Evaluate data quality

B. Define business objectives and goals

C. Foster cross-functional collaboration

D. Invest in data infrastructure

- Answer: B) Define business objectives and goals

(10) Which step in the roadmap emphasizes adopting agile methodologies for flexibility and responsiveness?

A. Conduct Data Assessment

B. Implement Agile and Iterative Processes

C. Develop Data Analytics and BI Capabilities

D. Foster a Data-Driven Culture

- Answer: B) Implement Agile and Iterative Processes

(11) What strategy is effective in overcoming resistance to change by addressing a lack of clear communication?

A. Involvement and Collaboration

B. Highlight Quick Wins

C. Continuous Feedback Loop

D. Communication and Transparency

- Answer: D) Communication and Transparency

(12) Why might employees resist data science initiatives, according to the description?

A. Fear of job security

B. Lack of innovation

C. Overinvolvement in decision-making

D. A strong data-driven culture

- Answer: A) Fear of job security

(13) What is a key recommendation to address resistance related to fear of job insecurity?

A. Lack of support and resources

B. Provide support and resources

C. Iterative implementation

D. Manage fear through open communication

- Answer: D) Manage fear through open communication

(14) What is the purpose of measuring the return on investment (ROI) in data science initiatives?

A. To increase operational costs

B. To calculate financial benefits

C. To hinder innovation

D. To discourage data-driven decisions

- Answer: B) To calculate financial benefits

(15) Which metric evaluates the accuracy and reliability of data used in decision-making processes?
    A. Time-to-Decision
    B. Data Quality Metrics
    C. Revenue Impact
    D. Customer Lifetime Value (CLV)
- Answer: B) Data Quality Metrics

(16) What does NPS stand for in the context of customer-centric metrics?
    A. Net Profit System
    B. New Product Strategy
    C. Net Promoter Score
    D. Notable Product Service
- Answer: C) Net Promoter Score

(17) Which metric assesses the success of initiatives in retaining existing customers over time?
    A. Churn Rate
    B. Revenue Impact
    C. Time-to-Insight
    D. Customer Retention Rate
- Answer: D) Customer Retention Rate

(18) How can corporations foster a culture of collaboration during the transformation process?
    A. Avoiding change champions
    B. Ignoring communication channels
    C. Lack of involvement
    D. Encouraging continuous learning and open communication
- Answer: D) Encouraging continuous learning and open communication

(19) What is the significance of adopting an iterative approach in implementing changes?
    A. Slower adaptation
    B. Complete overhaul
    C. Gradual adjustment
    D. Quick wins
- Answer: C) Gradual adjustment

(20) How can corporations ensure ongoing success and improvement in data science initiatives?
    A. Lack of feedback incorporation
    B. Continuous learning
    C. Addressing cultural barriers
    D. Decreasing tool adoption rates
- Answer: B) Continuous learning

****

ABOUT THE AUTHOR :

Dr. P. S. Aithal, founding and former Vice Chancellor of Srinivas University, Mangalore, Karnataka State and presently serving as Senior Professor and Advisor of Srinivas University for Research and Development. Dr. P. S. Aithal has 32 years of experience in Teaching & Research and 20 years of experience in Administration. Having four Master degrees in Physics with Electronics, Computer Science, Information Technology, and EBusiness, he got his first Ph.D. degree in Physics from Mangalore University in the area of nonlinear optical materials and a second Ph.D. degree in Business Management from Manipal University, Manipal, in the area of mobile banking. He worked as Post Doctoral Research Fellow at "The Lasers & Quantum Optics Division, Physical Research Laboratory, Ahmedabad, for two years from 1999-2000. In the year 2002, he was selected for the prestigious Oversee Fellowship of Dept. of Science & Technology, Govt. of India – Better Opportunity for Young Scientists in Chosen Area of Science & Technology (BOYSCAST) Fellowship. He did Post Doctorial Research at Centre for Research & Education in Optics & Lasers (CREOL), at the University of Central Florida, Orlando, U.S.A. He has more than 900 research publications in refereed International Journals in the areas of Nonlinear Optics, Photonics, Nanotechnology, Business Management, Higher Education, and Information Technology, and has published 55 Books and edited books. Dr. P. Sreeramana Aithal currently holds SECOND Rank among the Top 30,000 Research authors worldwide and had FIRST Rank among the Top 12,000 Business Management Authors worldwide in Elsevier's SSRN Research network, USA, in terms of the total number of open access scholarly papers in their network. Dr. P. S. Aithal has initiated many innovations and best practices in the higher education system.
Orcid ID: 0000-0002-4691-8736: E-mail: psaithal@gmail.com

P. S. Aithal